I Fly

TRUE

STORIES

OF

OVERCOMING

ADVERSITY

Annette Densham
Bisi Osundeko
Bonnie Jo Guidry
Brett D. Scott
Camilla Constance
Charleen Siteine
Charlene Kay Fouts
Dr Sherine Price
Gabrielle Conescu
Ivan Brewer

Jo Jacobs
Juliette Mullen
Kenneth Nathan
Lisa Boorer
Marsha Schults
Marta Madeira-Mulungo
Mary Wong
Peta Cashion
Roslyn Donaldson
Taryn Claire Le Nu

Compiled, edited, and published by  CHANGE EMPIRE BOOKS

WRITE YOUR BOOK. BUILD YOUR EMPIRE

Published by Change Empire Books
www.changeempire.com

Edited & designed by Change Empire Books

LETTER FROM THE PUBLISHER

Grief, loss, and pain permeate the lives of us all. Some have endured more than others. As a Book Coach and Publisher, my highest purpose is to get beautiful books out into the world, and to inspire, educate, and change the lives of readers. When I thought about collating and publishing a collection of stories by real people (ie. people who, for the most part, weren't already authors) I asked my community who wanted to be involved and was overwhelmed by the response. In a matter of 24 hours I was swamped with applications to be part of this book. People who had not only survived trauma, tragedy, and adversity, but who had thrived on the other side.

Out of this long list of applications, I chose 20 incredible people to take part in a book which would touch, move, and inspire readers of all ages, nationalities, backgrounds, and genders.

Along with my magnificent colleague, Veronica McDermott, we coached, trained, supported, and encouraged these extraordinary people to share their stories with the world. For many of them, it's the first time they have shared these stories with anybody except their closest family and friends. For some, not even then.

What inspired them all was the hope that somebody out there facing the same thing would no longer feel alone. Would no longer feel so isolated, afraid, and in the dark. Would know that even in their desperation and darkness, there was hope and light.

The stories you will read are true stories, by real people. In some cases, names, places, and details have been changed to protect others. In some stories, events have been merged or changed for the sake of brevity. Some authors had been through so much trauma and tragedy, we had to workshop with them to find only one story to share.

Through coaching and multiple rounds of editing, we have sought to preserve the author's voice and regional spelling choices. Some of the grammar or phrasing isn't perfect. We don't want it to be. We want it to be real. We have authors from Australia, the United States, the United Kingdom, and Africa. They are all beautifully, uniquely, different.

When we first collated the stories into one document and I read them through, I cried. In fact, I bawled. I cried because of the sheer and overwhelming injustice in the world – how can anyone survive what some of these people have been through? Then I cried for the bravery of these remarkable authors, and how proud I am of this book.

I hope that reading this book is a moving experience for you. There are sad and difficult stories to read. Every person in this book has been through adversity – some of it is difficult beyond words. But each person has moved through these challenges and out the other side to be a bright, shining star of love and light in their lives today. They have created businesses, support groups, and charities to support others in similar situations.

If reading this book triggers anything in you, I urge you to please seek professional help. Don't do this alone. Most of the authors have included their contact details at the end of the book so that you may reach out to them, but none of them are therapists or mental health professionals, so please reach out to your support network if you are in need.

This book contains adult concepts and is not suitable for children or young people.

Every single one of these authors inspires me. I hope they do the same for you. Please reach out to us using our contact details in the back of the book and tell us how you feel about this book. And please, buy official copies, and leave reviews on your book retailer's website, as all these authors will directly benefit. Please share it on your social networks and with your friends so that these stories can reach more who may need them.

If you are going through difficulty, all of us are collectively sending you our support, love, and strength. We hope that you can move through your adversity, and that you too, may fly.

Cathryn Mora

Founder, Head Coach and Publishing Director
Change Empire Books

I: @change.empire.book.coaching
L: linkedin.com/in/cathryn-mora/
E: hello@changeempire.com

CONTENTS

Authors

CHAPTER 1

And still I rise

Roslyn Donaldson

Get up. Get up. Get up. You have to get up. You have to hold on. You have to stay calm and not make him any angrier than he already is.

I keep repeating it in my head as his leather belt swipes me again, bringing with it a sting I will feel for days.

I cringe in pain as the belt buckle cuts into my back, hitting the skin and opening the same wound where he hit me only a few nights ago.

I want to die there and then on the floor, but if I don't take the beating and get up, he will start on my mother. I feel a strong need to protect her, even at seven years old.

If I'm not able to take the beating, he will save his anger and seek her out to unleash it on. But she's too thin and weak. I am young – I can withstand his rage.

It's better for him to hit me.

Mum had taken her fair share of beatings from his rough hands. Her frail, thin body is bruised enough from his drunken rages.

Her thin flesh is on bone, she hardly eats for herself to ensure us children have food.

When we open the cupboard door, to find only one tin or packet of food, she insists that we share, and she will go without.

Her tall, slender body has given him seven children. And he has given her nothing but pain.

I can take some of the pain for her. I don't want him to hurt her again.

She says, "Don't let him corner you. If he hits you and you go down, you have to get up," or sometimes, "You have to get away from him, out of his reach. He's too strong for you, he's too strong for us..."

Partway through the beating, a thought pops into my mind. *It's my eighth birthday tomorrow.*

But it doesn't matter. There won't be any presents. There never is. There are no birthdays, Christmas, the Easter Bunny or Tooth Fairy in our house. We don't have enough money to buy food, let alone presents. Christmas is just another day and birthdays are not longed for like other children.

He has enough money for booze though. And pills. So many pills. I watch him hide his pill bottles. He seems to be storing them up, pushing the pill bottles to the back of the cupboard.

It doesn't make much sense, and I find it strange that no one else in my family seems to notice. I guess we are all just surviving.

The impact of his work boot snaps me back into the moment and he kicks me in the stomach again. I feel like I am going to be sick, but nothing comes out as I haven't eaten anything all day. My stomach is growling with starvation. It's so empty, the pain is unbearable.

I am overcome with fear and unable to control what is happening to my body as he continues to kick me, again and again.

There has to be a better life for me. Don't I have a right to be happy, too? Don't I have the right to be safe like my friends, with parents that feed them and clothe them and love them?

Why can't I have Sunday dinners, like my best friend Cheryle's parents made her with peas, roast potatoes, gravy and roast chicken? I can taste it now. OMG, I had never smelt a baked dinner before I went to her house.

The delicious smell of the roast chicken makes me smile as I remember it, then the taste of salty tears run into my mouth and I remember where I am.

I am lying on the cold, hard floor, and he shouts at me to clean up my mess. He's finished with me now.

Who is this man who feels he has the right to do this to me? Just because he's my father, it doesn't give him the right. Shouldn't he protect and love me?

Even in my sleep there is no reprieve.

I wet the bed every night... and every night I go to bed and pray, "Please, dear God, please don't let it be wet tonight."

He comes into our bedrooms and checks our beds to see if the sheets are wet.

But every night I wake up and my bed is wet. He drags me out of the bed by the hair and tells me how disgusting I am.

Then he tells me to go back and sleep in the wet bed.

I get back in bed and curl up on the cold, wet sheets, trying to go back to sleep.

He is a monster.

But everyone in town loves him. He is a first-grade soccer and cricket player, a champion darts player. He is seen as masculine and strong, and he is everyone's hero, but he is none of these to us.

Sunny Robbo is his best mate. He owns the picture show in town and all the taxi cabs. He sends Dad home in a cab every night after the pub.

The cab always pulls up out the front, and I yell to Mum, "He's home!" We need to get my baby brother out of his cot and into the pram, and escape out the back door, otherwise he will beat us. Even a baby can't escape his wrath.

Mum grabs my brother in her arms, and I get the pram. We escape down the side of the house, holding our breath in case he sees us as he's coming in the front door.

Mum and I wander around the streets. We know all their names like best friends.

We know it's safe to return in the morning, when the sun rises. When he's sober.

It's late, cold, dark, and scary as we walk around the streets. Mum and I talk about the next time we can go to my Nanna and Grandpa's house for a visit. We will catch the train with my baby brother, who's only six months old.

It's always wonderful at Nanna's. I wish we could live there.

But it just gets worse.

There's something else happening in this house... something more evil than the beatings. I'm not sure what it is, but I've seen it in the face of my big sister, and I'm glad it hasn't found its way to me yet. I feel it and I know it's coming closer to me, but I keep praying to God to keep me safe.

I'll continue to take the beatings. I can take those but I'm not sure if I can take his other abuse. I'll stay out of his way and continue to take his beatings. God help me. God help us all.

I have to get out of here one day before I die or before he dies.

I don't really want to think about that, but I can't help it. I think about it all the time.

How can I do it and free us all from this hell?

...but that would make me a bad person and I'm not a bad person.

One day I'll be free from him. One day I'll make a better life for myself.

But how can I stop him from hurting us and especially Mummy...? I'm afraid he'll kill her one day. He's already taken away her chance of having a normal life, a normal family, and a normal husband. She's sentenced with him, just like we are.

I want to kill him.

I want to die.

I want to be released from all this pain.

How can I kill him?

What can I use?

*

The long black hearse came around the corner and pulled into our driveway.

It drove slowly down the driveway with the sun hitting the rear vision mirror on the left side of the car. It was blinding as it came to take him away.

The sun was also shining on me that day as I was finally free of him.

My dad had finally taken all those pills, the ones I saw him hiding in the back of the cupboard. He'd finally had enough of his life too.

The night it happened, he had stayed home and not gone to the pub, which he never did. He said it was because he had to get up early for an important meeting in the city.

He just sat there watching TV with us, and I was thinking, "That's strange."

The next morning, my older brother couldn't wake him, so he came into the bedroom room, where Mum, my little brother and I slept, and woke us up.

He said, "I can't wake up Dad, and he's got to go to the City today for that important meeting."

I went out into the lounge room where he was lying, and touched him. He was cold.

I turned him over. His face had turned a blue colour as he had been dead for quite a few hours.

He was gone.

It turned out that after we had gone to bed, he got all the pill bottles he had been saving and took every one. He wanted it to be over.

I can't believe he's dead and I didn't have to do it.

I felt the weight lift from my body. I was smiling and crying at the same time. As hard as it was going to be from here, I was not afraid anymore.

I felt stronger than I'd ever felt because I could finally be free and finally be me.

I was 12 years old, and it was the first night I didn't wet the bed. I never did again from that day on.

*

It had been hard as a little girl, going to school in plastic shoes. We couldn't afford black school shoes or a uniform.

When I was in primary school, the kids' parents said they weren't allowed to play with me as I was dirty and I smelt and I lived in 'that' house.

I would sit in the playground on my own; my friend Cheryle was the only one who would come over and sit with me.

She had a bike and I would run beside her while she rode home. We only lived one street away from each other and she would play with me on weekends too.

Her parents owned the local cake shop and we would stop by on our way, as we were riding home and her Mum would give us a cake to eat.

I loved my best and only friend.

She was all I needed. I didn't care about the rest of the kids. I had her and she liked me.

But after my father died, my life changed.

Finally, we had someone to take care of us financially. Legacy was a charity which provided services to families suffering from the death of a parent after their defence force service. They stepped in and supported us.

My younger brother was five years old at the time our dad died.

Mum was now a war widow and from that moment, I wasn't that scared little girl anymore.

For the first time in my life I had school shoes and a school uniform. Legacy set up an account for my Mother at our local store and we were able to go and buy everything I needed for school.

I was 12 years old and finally felt normal like everyone else.

I also got a brand new dress. Not a hand-me-down, but a brand new one from a shop, just for me. I never had a new dress before and as I walked out of that store, I felt like a million dollars.

I felt like somebody for the first time in my life. I skipped all the way home.

It felt wonderful to buy something brand new from a fancy shop. I experienced retail shopping and I loved it; I wanted to become part of it. I wanted to help others feel the way I felt in that moment – special.

I got a job in the local grocery store working Friday nights and weekends, to help support my Mum and younger brother.

The Widow's Pension didn't exist in those days, so although Legacy paid for lots of necessities, we still had to support ourselves.

Mum couldn't go to work as she was too traumatised. The lady next door had a word for it – agoraphobia. I wasn't sure what that meant but Mum couldn't leave the house.

She used to send me to that same grocery store to ask for credit, so when I applied for a job, the owner knew me, and he hired me.

I loved working there, especially on Housie night. The customers would come in to buy their pens, lollies, and chocolates. Sometimes they would buy a few extra chocolates for me and I'd take them home. They tasted so amazing, so sweet and creamy… they would melt in our mouths. They tasted nearly as good as the Sunday roast dinners I had at my girlfriend Cheryle's house.

The store owner put me on full time when I turned fourteen, so I left school and worked there every day. We needed the money at home so Mum could pay the debts my father had left behind. I ran the shop for him for two years.

One day, Cheryle came in and said a department store was opening and putting on staff as Cadets. It was a 45-minute train trip from our home, and she said, "We can catch the train together."

They were going to train us to become department managers.

We would be someone.

We both applied and we both got the jobs. Cheryle was put in the office to learn all about administration, since she had completed her school certificate.

Since I didn't have my school certificate, I was put in the Cosmetics Department. It didn't make any sense as I didn't even wear lipstick. Dad wouldn't let any of us girls wear it.

Once he saw my eldest sister wearing it. She was walking home, and he was sitting outside the pub with his mates and he saw her. When he got home, he gave her the biggest hiding and told her, "Only certain girls wear lipstick."

So, I never did.

When I told the Department Manager I didn't wear lipstick, she said, "You have to wear it at work, because you have to sell it." She was a very stern woman, so I did. Soon I got to like it, and besides, he wasn't here anymore.

I gave Mum all my pay, except for the cost of my weekly train ticket, and kept $2 a week for myself.

I was still able to save, and I had the phone put on, which was connected in my room. I had seen it on TV and always wanted a phone in my own bedroom. Mum wasn't interested in a phone anyway. She said she didn't have any friends to call.

I paid off a pink studded bedroom suite and it felt so good sleeping in it. I felt like a Princess.

I was becoming someone. I felt safe, I felt happy.

"You look immaculate," people at work would say. I learnt it from shopping at the opp shop. I could pull together a skirt, top, scarf, shoes, and jewellery for next to nothing.

I would lay in my new bed and think about what else I could achieve. I wanted to do things and have things. I identified in my mind what they were and how I could achieve them.

I started cutting out pictures from magazines and put them up on my wall next to my bed. I ended up making a vision board which covered my bedroom wall.

The pictures were all the things I'd ever dreamt about. I'd focus on one thing at a time, looking at the picture, imagining them as being real and how I would feel.

It always seemed to work. I was able to achieve my goals with the help of creative visualisation... although I didn't know that's what I was doing at the time.

One of my main goals was to get a job as an account executive with a cosmetic company. Every month my account executive from Helena Rubinstein Cosmetics would come into the department store to check on my sales and tell me all about the latest skin care and beauty products.

She wore a dark blue tailored suit, high heels, carried a briefcase, and had business cards. She was stunningly put together and had the job I aspired to.

I'd come a long way from that little girl who had flea bites all over her, smelt of urine, nits in her hair, ringworms, no shoes, and was constantly filthy, as we only had a cheap water heater and bathed just once a week.

My Dad had to cut the wood to heat up the water and we would all have a bath, taking it in turns based on age. I was the second youngest so was the sixth child bathed in the water.

I applied for every role I could find, but they kept telling me, "You haven't got any experience."

Then it happened. I got an interview with a cosmetic company who were looking for a pharmacy Territory Manager.

I took a deep breath and headed to their Head Office.

When I walked in, it took my breath away.

The walls were covered with pictures of beautiful women dressed in designer clothing and wearing the makeup from their line. There were bottles of sweet-smelling fragrance and lipsticks lined up in every colour. I had to pinch myself.

I smiled as I thought of the possibility of getting hired… and I took a deep breath.

Carmen Brown came out of her office to greet me. She was a very tall, immaculate, and sophisticated woman; Carmen was the State Manager and Account Executive who managed all the accounts for David Jones and Myer Dept stores in NSW.

She studied me up and down, as if she was looking at a new cosmetic line for approval. She invited me into her office for the interview. It was fabulously decorated and the chair I sat on was like a silk cushion.

I watched her facial expressions as I answered all her questions, one after the other, until she put down her pen and smiled for the first time.

I felt the lump in my throat slide down and I could breathe again.

After the interview I knew she liked me as she said, "I'm going to introduce you to our National Sales Manager, Alan Hemmingway, and if he likes you, you'll have the role."

Alan did like me. I'll never forget what he said after the interview. "You don't have any experience, but with a smile like that you'll open any door. You're hired."

This cosmetic company didn't test on animals, which I really loved. In my childhood years, my dog Nicky had licked my cuts and healed my bruises with his unconditional love, and I had loved animals ever since.

I worked hard, I travelled, I created business performance plans, set goals, and then after a couple of years the NSW Account Executive left and Alan offered me her role.

I was no longer that scared, beaten, smelly little girl. I still had her inside me, and she was part of my past, but now that little girl had the courage to believe in herself, set the goals, see the vision, go after her dreams and know that they are possible.

I had the job, the tailored suit, the briefcase, the business card; I had my dream. All dreams are different, and success isn't the same for everyone, but I achieved what I had visualised and I had reached my destination.

I achieved my dream and it felt great.

I was one of the most successful executives as the buyers and all the cosmetic consultants in every store loved me. I treated them with kindness and respect. I treated everyone as I wanted to be treated, and the beautiful energy always came back to me.

*

When I was a little girl, hiding at the back of my dog kennel so my dad couldn't find me, I would write poems. I still write them today to express my feelings.

Take me in your arms and hug away the pain
My heart is so broken out there in the rain
Crying, crying to release all the heartache
Building my resilience so that I didn't break
In front of the Monster I called Dad
Knowing if I showed him my pain he would be glad
He wanted to break me as he did my sisters and
brothers
But I had to show him I wasn't like the others
Even as a little girl, I knew he was wrong
Telling us we were nothing and we didn't belong
Telling us we would never amount to anything
Gave me the courage to stand up and sing.

I love the song *I Am Woman* by Helen Reddy and often sing or hum along when I hear it. The lyrics are powerful and still make me cry today. Songs can give us the courage and the words we need.

I became a successful Account Executive with a cosmetic company, working in a very glamorous world, looking fabulous and feeling good about myself, not in a fake way, but in a genuine way. Being my authentic self – me.

And I am enough.

I finally like myself and accept myself for who I am.

I'm not perfect. I have still gone through stages of struggling every day. I still made mistakes. I am honest and real.

I like myself for who I am and finally, I can look in the mirror, see myself, and not cry.

I can smile.

CHAPTER 2

Breaking the silence
Mary Wong

"Why'd ya leave?' he asks. I make room on the sticky discomfort of the vinyl couch as Bruce lowers himself to sit beside me.

"Coz I don't fit in."

"Like how?"

"I just don't. Nobody gets me – they never have. I have no friends."

He looks at me incredulously. "So, what do you call those three upstairs?"

"They're not really my friends. We all just hang around together and pretend to like each other so we aren't so lonely."

"Is that why I don't see you here so often?"

"Nah. I'm not supposed to leave the school yard. My Mum'd kill me if she knew I was here."

"So, why are you here?"

"This girl in my class said she'd punch my teeth in if she saw me at lunch time. She would too – she did it to Jenny last week. She picks on all of us misfits."

"Oh! Not fun."

We sit quietly for a moment, before he turns and leans slightly towards me.

"You know what I think? I think you're a really clever, pretty girl, who has a lot to offer the world."

He thinks I'm pretty?

"You think?" My voice catches as he begins to trace the bead of sweat running down my arm with his finger.

"I think people try to pull you down to make themselves feel better. You'll light up the world one day. I'm sure of it!"

I don't know what to say. Silence.

Say something, Mary!

More awkward silence.

God, what should I say?

Nobody says nice things like that to me.

He's gorgeous. Why is he here talking with me?

I stare out into the back yard, trying to hide my thoughts. My heart and soul crave the attention, the validation. He's so dreamy – in the way only men of the 70's could be. Tall. Curly, sandy-coloured hair to his shoulders. Lean body, thin face, wire-rimmed Lennon-esque spectacles. The cousin of my friend Jane, he boards with her family.

Jane's been my 'friend' since I started at the school. That is, she allows me into her world – me and the two boys who treat us like sisters, never trying to do anything they shouldn't. We bump along together, more out of loneliness and fear, than out of shared tastes or values.

They are all upstairs, with her parents, eating lunch, as is their daily ritual.

Say something, Mary!

"I can't believe Jane's parents talk like that!" I blurt.

"Like what?"

"You know... about...well, um, sex and stuff." My face is the colour of a ripe tomato.

"It's 1979, everyone talks about sex!" He laughs.

"Not me," I mumble. *Oh my God! I don't want to talk about this!*

More awkward silence.

Why do people have to talk about sex so much? Sex isn't something you should take lightly. Sex is about love, not something you just do. Sex is for the one who loves and marries you.

I've been brought up to know that a girl should look for marriage and love, settle down, and raise a tribe of kids – like my parents did. My Mum always talks about how we girls will one day walk up the aisle in a white gown, veil flowing to meet our prince. We'll be virgins – beautiful, pure, worthy. We'll wear our veil with pride, knowing it's our right, not like those girls Mum always scoffs at.

"Dunno why she's wearing a veil. She's no virgin," she'd say at their wedding. Sex is taboo. We aren't to speak of it and other than our brothers, we aren't to spend time with boys. Boys are bad. Boys only want one thing.

This boy. NO, this MAN. He's different. He's really talking with me, taking the time to get to know who I am. He's not like the boys at school – only interested in one thing... not like Greg, that's for sure!

Greg, the first boy who had ever kissed me at the end of eighth grade, when I was 12. The recently emigrated American boy in my class, who everyone thought was gorgeous. The boy who, incredibly experienced in relationships, had amazed me by wanting to kiss me!

My thoughts wandered back to that first kiss, behind the local church after school.

"Heyyy," he'd drawled in that alluring accent of his. "Come sit with me. I wanna talk with you."

"Me?" I'd squeaked.

He'd laughed. "Yeah, babe. You. I wanna talk with you."

Who was I to argue? We met weekly for a couple of months after school behind the local church, ironically.

He'd kissed me that first day, softly, sweetly. As his hand wandered up the back of my skirt and inside the leg of my underwear.

"No! It's wrong. We mustn't," I'd cried, as I pulled away from his hand.

Why? Why did he do that? He ruined it! My first kiss wasn't supposed to be like that!

He'd laughed. "Oh baby, don't be like that. I know you'll like it. All the girls I've been with like it."

"It's dirty."

"It's not dirty – it's just a bit of fun. Come on – you'll love it."

And so I let him. But I didn't like it. Not that day, nor the next time, nor any of the times when we met.

"You're weird," he said. "There must be something wrong with you. All the other girls got wet, when I touched them like this."

He rubbed harder sometimes, softer other times, but to no avail. Apparently, my body wouldn't work right. Not only was I dirty, but I was a failure.

What is wrong with me? Why can't I do what other girls do? I don't even know what he means by wet – am I supposed to pee or something?

Prepubescent, I didn't know anything about my body – nobody spoke of bodies or how they worked at home.

All I knew was I shouldn't be alone with a boy because he would want sex, even though I didn't really know what that was.

We hid our relationship. "Babe, this is special," he'd said. "I don't want the kids at school to ruin it with gossip."

I went along with that because I wanted desperately to fit in, and if I was with him, I might. I ached for it to work, even though I knew it was against the rules for me to be with him.

Maybe my body will start to work right if I keep letting him touch me.

I really liked him, despite him touching me where I didn't want him to. I was sure that if I stopped allowing it, he'd stop seeing me.

I feel weird, dirty.

But I couldn't speak up. I couldn't say it. I didn't know how.

No one would ever believe me if I told them – as if the class dreamboat would want a misfit like me!

In the end, I slipped a note in his school bag, telling him how I felt – that I wanted to keep seeing him but didn't want him to keep touching me 'down there'. He never met me again in our secret spot and proved me and Mum right. Boys only wanted one thing.

So, when Bruce starts talking with me, I figure he just wants one thing.

"I came downstairs to check on you, because I thought you looked uncomfortable," his voice breaks the awkwardness of the long silence.

I look at him, disconcerted. "I... I didn't like them making fun of your name." His surname was kind of different.

He laughs wryly. "I'm used to it – had it all my life".

"That doesn't make it right," I say.

I know how it is to be bullied. Bullying has been my constant companion since I made friends with the unkempt girl in the first grade. They all said she had germs, don't go near her. But I did – I believed in kindness. She moved away, and my new nickname 'Johnson's germs' and the exclusion which accompanied it for most of primary school was the legacy of my first friendship.

"Keep away from her! Don't touch her, you'll get Johnson germs!" they taunted.

Being excluded and feeling lonely was the reason I stayed friends with a girl who only spoke to me when out of sight of the schoolyard because she didn't want to be branded as germy, and excluded too.

The same girl whose brother stole my shoes one day after I stopped outside their home for a drink of water. He hid them behind the piano, then held loaded guns to my head and forced me to go into the house, telling me he would kill me if I didn't find them.

In the aftermath I was branded a liar.

And I learned to keep quiet, to not share my truth, because my voice had no value.

"Sounds like you've been there," he says, and I tell him about the germs.

"People are arseholes," he says.

I agree, they can be.

"Don't let the turkeys get you down," he says, with a cute, crooked smile.

I laugh. That saying has never made sense to me. I seem to feel emotional pain more easily than most. When there is angst around me, I am in turmoil. And angst seems to surround me most days.

How am I supposed to not let it get me down? My emo thing is the thing that makes me most weird.

Shh, Mary, don't tell him. He'll be gone like a shot!

I like the attention he is giving me, so I keep quiet.

"You are a lovely girl," he says. "Better get back to school before you get in trouble. The bell will be going soon."

I run off, elated. He touched me, but only on the arm. Of far greater importance, he SEES me!

Maybe this one is different and doesn't want just one thing. Maybe this one is a safe one.

I wish I could talk with someone about this. Share my joy, my excitement about how this dreamy man had treated me and my anxiety about whether it was safe. But there is nobody. I cannot speak up.

Nobody would believe me.

I go back, day after day. And we sit on the couch and talk.

Jane's parents tell me I shouldn't spend so much time with him – at 28, he is twice my age. But they are wrong about him. I know they are.

He hasn't tried anything. I can trust him.

They make sure we are not alone together, getting Jane or the boys to be with us when we are downstairs. We laugh, we play games, we have fun.

Jane invites me to her birthday party, and I beg my parents to let me go.

I haven't been invited to a birthday party since the second grade, when I was six. The kid's parents thought they should do the right thing and invite me regardless of their child's objections. I remember spending most of that party in the kitchen with the kid's mother, because none of the kids wanted to be near me. Germs, of course.

Jane says she wants me to come. For the first time in my life, I feel like I have friends.

Bruce doesn't come to the party. I am devastated.

"Where's Bruce?" I casually ask Jane's mum.

She says he had to work.

They play spin the bottle and one of the boys has to kiss me. We run away around the side of the house and don't do anything – neither of us wants to. I wish it was Bruce.

The next time I go to their house, the parents are out. Bruce is there, and the others stay upstairs.

We are alone. We talk about the party. I tell him about the bottle, and the non-kiss.

He laughs. "That boy must be out of his mind, not to kiss you!"

My breath catches. Our bodies are close today, closer than usual.

"Don't blame him," I say. "I didn't want to either."

He rests his arm along the back of the chair behind me and his voice drops. "Don't you like to kiss?" he asks. His voice getting softer, his hand drops from the chair to my shoulder, drawing me nearer to him. My breath catches.

"I haven't done it that much," I admit, embarrassed by my lack of experience.

"Really?" he pauses. "Are you a virgin, Mary?" he asks, gently mocking me.

My voice is gone, and I nod, eyes downcast. I don't like the teasing about my name and am embarrassed by the question. I feel somehow inadequate. All my friends make out that they are doing it, but my experience is limited to Greg touching me behind the church.

"Ahhh... You're such a temptation," he says.

Breathing so closely I can almost taste his last cigarette, I am a deer in a headlight. Staring at him, wide eyed, as his lips brush mine, his hand stroking the back of my neck.

We hear the others coming down the stairs and he pulls away. "Beautiful girl, you need to go back to school," he says, his voice husky.

My heart is singing as I walk back to school. Jane notices something is different about me and asks what happened. "Nothing," I say. "We were just talking."

"It doesn't look like it," she says.

It takes a couple of weeks before we are alone together again. He pulls me close. "I can't get you out of my mind," he says.

He kisses me, thrusting his tongue into my mouth. My eyes pop. It feels weird.

"I want you so bad," he breathes into my mouth, as he opens my top button with one hand and slips his hand into my bra. I pull back.

"It's OK," he says, taking his hand away. "I won't force anything on you that you don't want."

So we kiss, as his hands wander around my back and neck, and as he presses his body against me, I feel a hardness in his pants against my tummy.

"Thank you," I whisper.

"For kissing you?"

"No, silly. For understanding. For waiting."

He pauses, looking deeply into my eyes as his hand cradles the back of my head.

"Beautiful girl, I will wait as long as it takes for you."

I believe him. I feel safe with him. I think I am in love and start to dream he will wait 'til I grow up and marry me.

A week later, things change.

He takes my hand and puts it in his pants. It feels somehow soft and hard at the same time. I am repulsed and pull back.

"Stop being such a baby," he growls, pushing my head down as he opens his fly. "Kiss me."

I try to stand up, so I can kiss him.

He laughs derisively. "Down there!" he commands. "Kiss me there!"

I am horrified. *Do girls actually do that?*

"Come on," he says. "Everyone does it and as long as you are teasing me, I need some relief."

Oh, God. Of course. How could I be so mean?

I allow him to push my head down, holding me in place there. It smells funny, looks gross and feels wrong being so close to his pants.

I can't breathe properly.

He breathes deeply, "Beautiful girl, you're so special, so beautiful. I can't get enough of you."

He says all the right things as he touches me, holding my ponytail in his hand in a way that won't let me take my head away. He thrusts his body towards me and runs his other hand along the crack of my bottom, under it, then between my legs.

I gasp, trying not to retch.

"Oh baby," he says, "you are growing up, so beautifully. You are amazing, you feel so good."

Suddenly, he lets go of my hair and wraps his thing in tissues. Then he closes his fly, and holds me close. I'm confused, violated, sore where he rubbed me with his finger, and my hair hurts.

It's new territory.

My mind wanders to the science class, the teacher droning on with the diagrams of male and female anatomy while we students sit red-faced, giggling. He talks about intercourse. About inserting penises into vaginas.

I know that didn't happen, so figure I am still a virgin.

But I don't know what it was that we just did.

"Are you okay?" he asks.

I'm not.

I feel dirty, disgusted, repulsed.

It's not supposed to be this way! I thought you loved me. I wasn't ready for that.

What happened?

How did it all go so wrong? You said you would wait for me. Why? Why did you go and mess it all up?

But I can't say it.

I nod slightly, confused, dazed.

"It's all your doing," he says. "You tease me with your arse and your boobs. Your eyes say they want me – you ask for it every time you look at me. There's a limit to how much a man can take, you know."

Oh my God... He's right. He's never tried to push me before. It's all my fault.

"I'm sorry," I whisper.

"You'll get into a lot of trouble if you tell anyone," he says. "This has to be our secret."

I nod my agreement. I am used to keeping quiet, that won't be difficult. I feel like a slut and don't want anyone to know. Besides, if my parents found out, I'd be in huge trouble, just for being here.

It happens two more times before Jane walks in on us. She tells her parents and there's a big scene. They tell him he can't live with them anymore and he moves interstate.

I am heartbroken. I have lost my friend, my confidante. I don't understand why he couldn't stay, after all it was all my fault. I teased him until he couldn't help himself.

Jane's parents tell me I mustn't tell anyone, so I don't say anything about it for over 30 years, until, in my mid 40's I share with my counsellor about him. About how I caused him to be sent away, and how I always felt so guilty about leading him on until he couldn't help himself.

In her soft voice, she says, "Mary, any reasonable 28-year-old would never have allowed that to happen. They would have run the other way. He knew what he was doing. It's how they operate – these men who prey on children."

"What do you mean?" I ask, surprised.

"It's called grooming. They look for the loners, the ones who aren't likely to speak up; the ones that are hurting, lost, lonely, or broken already. Those are the easy targets."

"I was definitely that. But he was so nice... so kind to me. I really cared for him."

"Yep, it's all part of the profile – they take their time to build deep trust until you are at a point where they can manipulate you into believing whatever happens is all your doing."

So, I'm not a slut?

My thoughts raced.

What would have happened if I had spoken up? I could have stopped it before it happened! So, in a way, it was my fault... I should have said something.

"I sense you are processing. Do you want to share?"

"I feel responsible still, because if I had spoken up, it could have been stopped before it started."

"It's easy to beat ourselves up as adults for the things we did or didn't do as a child. Knowing what you know now, you feel you could have spoken up. Because now, you are an adult, and you are used to being able to make your own decisions and act upon them. Back then, you were a child at the mercy of adults around you who made the decisions for you."

"I chose to keep going."

"Yes. You did. But the thing that kept you going was manipulation. He showed you kindness and caring – something you were craving, but he did that to get you to a place where you would do anything to please him. When someone who is lost and lonely is given connection and caring, they take it, even though it may be dangerous for them – as it was for you in this case."

She's right. All I wanted was a friend. Wow. It could have been so different. How much more would have been different if only I'd spoken up?

My mind wandered to the reason I had sought the psychological assistance in the first place.

After my second child was born, I developed severe postnatal depression. Again, I didn't speak up. Instead, I carried with me a sense of increasing failure, as I constantly battled on, believing that I should strive to be perfect. I had to sort it alone, believing that I was a burden to anyone else if I asked for help.

So I fought on, hiding my sense of failure, which was compounded by not being able to do that thing that I considered the basic function of a woman – to conceive a child, then deliver that baby into the world naturally. The combination of exhaustion, a baby that would not breast-feed (another failure, in my mind), and the cocktail of IVF hormones and post-caesarean pain that ravaged my body led me to a very dark place – a place where I was no longer safe.

Overpowered by pain, guilt and a sense of failure, my thoughts became irrational. I decided there was only one way to fix this – and that was to leave the planet.

But who will take care of my babies if I'm not here? I'll have to take them with me.

Good God, NO! What are you thinking?

Oh God, I am really in trouble here.

The realisation of where my thoughts were going made me reach out for help.

The therapist recognised that underpinning the postnatal depression was other trauma. Trauma which needed to be cleared. I underwent treatment for quite some time. Therapy was just the start. I had to learn to communicate, to trust, to connect with people.

After the therapy finally ended, I discovered a whole new way of being. I took every opportunity to study – I learnt counselling, business management, leadership, coaching, and mentoring. I studied how the brain works, thinking patterns, emotional and conversational intelligence.

As part of my journey, I made myself face a fear of speaking up by learning to speak in public. This is one of the things most humans are terrified of. I joined an organisation that supports people to become comfortable speaking to a group, and gradually my confidence grew.

I became an internationally accredited speaker trainer. I trained in leadership, coaching, and mentoring, always applying my learnings to myself.

Now, I combine the benefits of my lived experience with what I learnt when training in my business as an executive coach, specialising in connection and communication.

I regularly work with people who struggle to speak up, to share their message, to speak their truth – just as I once did. It's my personal victory to be able to not only speak up for myself, but to empower others to do the same. I'm a great believer in paying forward to support others travelling a similar path.

I know the consequences of not speaking up – silence can become betrayal. The incident with Bruce was just one of many times when, if I had shared with someone what was happening earlier, they might have helped me recognise and process what was going on behind the scenes, with very different outcomes.

Not speaking up catalyses issues on every level; physically, emotionally, spiritually; even financially.

It's not just a personal issue; it is an issue for all of humanity.

As humans, we are hardwired to connect, to share our experiences and to grow and benefit from being part of the collective. None of us is meant to be completely self-sufficient. Speaking up when there is an issue, a new idea, or knowledge to share, is crucial to our well-being and the well-being of the planet as a whole.

And as for perfection? I regularly get things wrong. What I have learnt, is to recognise imperfection as a gift. Instead of judging myself a failure for being imperfect, I now know I can take the lessons with me as I connect and work with others, sharing the wisdom I have gained.

I truly believe that through connecting, communicating and co-creating, humanity will overpower the darkness of silence.

It's my way of bringing more light into the world.

CHAPTER 3

I changed my mind: A story of overcoming OCD

Bonnie Jo Guidry

Sharp pain preceded the crimson shower which spews from my neck. Scissors. Lodged in my flesh. My instinct is to vigorously jerk them out.

"Oh my God!" Brandi rolls me over, putting pressure on the wound.

"911. What's your emergency?"

"There's been an accident! There's blood everywhere! Send help now!"

The ambulance never came.

In fact, there is no blood. No wound. No fall. I never tripped on the Christmas wrapping materials. This horrific scene took place only for a few seconds. In my head.

I close my eyes, inhale to fill my lungs and belly to full capacity, releasing slowly. I know that if I can't gain control over my thoughts soon, my demented brain would have me at my own funeral, playing the scene out in baroque detail.

"Can you pass the tape, please?" Brandi gets louder. "Helloooo. Can you pass the tape?"

"Oh sure," I respond as I toss her the tape. "I think this is the last gift I'll wrap. I've got to get dressed for the party."

"You always seem to be in another world. You and your deep thoughts."

If you only knew about my thoughts.

Brandi smiles. "I'm looking forward to an evening out."

My black, sequined cocktail dress, shimmering with hints of silvers and blues, hangs from the top of my bedroom door. Perfectly paired strappy heels placed just beneath my dress. Centered. Not too far to the left or right.

Steam begins to rise from the running shower. The ritual of getting dressed was about to commence, with precise order. Because doing anything out of order causes feelings of unrest.

Cautiously, with irrational foreboding, I pull the shower curtain back just enough to see behind it. The soaked, masked man with smirking face and knife in hand was, yet again, not there.

Deep breath. I can do this.

Warm water running on my head and down my neck and back offers a brief moment of solace, calming my brain, relaxing my body.

So far, so good... My make-up is on point. I am ready to dry and style my hair. Make-up always comes before hair. Its beauty gives me the ability to sometimes accept less than perfect hair. The anticipated problem, though, was that my gorgeous dress and shoes demand flawless make-up and hair.

Brandi was always dressed before me. It is no surprise to hear her footsteps coming down the hallway. Intercepting her approach, I blurt out, "I'm good. Almost ready. Be out in a bit."

My chest tightens. The rate of my breathing increases significantly. What I see in the mirror does not resemble perfect hair. Not only was it imperfect, but it looks dirty to me.

Did I put too much product in it? Why does my hair look dirty?

Closing the bathroom door serves to buffer the sound of running water. Kneeling beside the tub, I lean forward to wash my hair. Again. Wash, dry, style. Wash, dry, style. Wash, dry style. Wash... This vicious cycle circles around three more times before Brandi bursts in.

"What the hell are you doing?! The party starts in thirty minutes! We are at least that far away! You told me you were almost ready!"

Her anger provokes more anxiety. My silent tears turn to distressed bawling. Hyperventilating. With breathless resolve, I whimper, "Just go without me, please!"

"Hell, no! I'm not going without you! And I'm not lying to our friends anymore! YOU can tell them why we missed their Christmas party! I can't believe this shit!"

Slam! Brandi yanks the door shut, shaking the walls.

Hair dripping. Convulsively sobbing. I sit undone on the bathroom floor. Mascara streaks my cheeks. Pulling my knees to my chest, I feel helpless. Warm tears run down my face, washing over my bare breast. In vulnerable surrender, I rock as I weep. *What is wrong with me?! Why can't I stop this?!*

Self-loathing thoughts swirl. I'm a freak. Why can't I just be normal? I wish I'd just die. I'm exhausted with this crazy life.

I envision myself in a mental ward. Rocking in a corner, straight jacket tightened around my body. Having worked myself into a state of exhaustion, I roll onto my side in a fetal position. The hard, cold floor beneath my nearly naked body. In a state of fog, no energy to get up. I mentally reach to flip that switch, the imaginary numbing switch that turns off the source to all emotions. This is my superpower – the skill which has protected me for so many years.

Slipping into my pajamas, I begin the bedtime ritual. Wash my face, brush my teeth. Brush my teeth again. I welcome an early night.

I just want to sleep and start fresh in the morning.

Unable to stop thinking about the Christmas party, I lie awake. *What am I going to tell our friends?* I most certainly couldn't tell them, "Sorry I missed your party. I know you think I'm pretty intelligent and emotionally stable, but I have weird thoughts and behaviors. I couldn't stop washing my hair to make it to your party."

Click click. Click click. Click click. The deadbolt was locked for sure. I secretly wish Brandi would come to check on me, but I know she is angry and disappointed. She doesn't get it. I couldn't have expected her to.

I don't understand what's happening to me. How can I expect anyone else to?

This is where the shame, the guilt, the lies come in. If only I could have communicated my pain, my prison, then maybe she would have made the trip down the hall to offer a hug and some reassurance that everything would be okay.

Silent tears, drifting in and out of slumber, racing thoughts during the awake moments, three trips to the bathroom to make sure my bladder really is empty.

Finally, I sleep.

My therapist agrees to see me at short notice.

I only started therapy because my professor asked the entire class to do so. He said the courses would trigger unresolved issues and that we needed to see what it feels like to be on the other side of the chair.

Two years in. Still so much work to be done.

Just thinking about studying for a master's degree in counseling while fighting my own demons provokes doubt.

"Are you having any thoughts of harming yourself?" Krystal raises her eyebrows.

"Oh no, absolutely not." *Make eye contact. Then she'll believe me.* "Killing myself is not an option. I have too many people in my life who love me. I love them the same. I could never inflict that kind of pain on them."

Krystal smiles. "Well, that's reassuring."

"There are days when I wish I would die. But I would never hurt myself. I want to get better. I want to overcome this."

I begin rocking. Pulled my knees to my chest. Wrap my arms around my legs. I fear another panic attack. Like the session I got claustrophobic and yanked my jacket off. Then belt. Then shoes.

Krystal reaches out and puts her hand on my knee. I relax a bit.

"Great that you wouldn't wanna hurt your loved ones, but do you think you could make a list of other reasons your life is worth living?"

"Sure."

"That's your homework. For now, though, I'd like to look at why you felt you needed to see me today."

I give her a brief on the OCD loop I got stuck in on Saturday night.

With a look of empathy, "Tell me how that made you feel."

"Sad. Angry with myself. We missed an important event. I was ashamed. I felt like some strange force had a grip on me. I couldn't break lose. Like I had no control. I knew what I was doing was completely irrational, but I couldn't stop it."

"What do you believe triggered the anxiety that tossed you into the loop of compulsive behaviors?"

The entire episode seemed to have come out of nowhere. After a moment of reflection, I am able to identify some known triggers. Stress with work. The holidays approaching. I hadn't been getting enough rest.

Krystal nods, flipping back in her notepad. "Think about our last session. A lot of crap surfaced as you recalled your childhood. You opened up some old, deep wounds. Time is needed for processing. Sometimes it gets worse before it gets better."

"Yeh, I was exhausted after that meeting. I've had a heaviness in my spirit."

Krystal nods. "Kinda like grief?"

"I guess you can say that."

"That's normal. You're grieving the loss of your childhood. The loss of your dad to alcoholism. The loss of your mom to working multiple jobs. The loss of all the nurturing that every little kid needs during those formative years."

A lightbulb goes off. I know this stuff. We're learning this. Why is it difficult to apply it to my own life?

How the hell am I going to counsel other people if I can't get myself right?

With a gentle lean forward Krystal reassured me, "You're gonna be alright. Healing is a process. But you have awareness. You are determined and resilient."

"Okay, but I'm not taking medicine. I'll work through this. I'll beat it without drugs."

"Fair enough. I'll respect that. I'd like to see you one more time this week, considering this recent episode. I think it would be beneficial to the therapeutic process."

"I'd agree."

Krystal stands up. "Just one more thing…" she stops before reaching for the doorknob. "I want you to work on something before our next meeting."

"Yeh?"

"I want you to become more aware of your thoughts toward yourself. Allow yourself the love and grace you extend to others."

I nod and smile. "You know I always do my homework."

The two-headed OCD monster quiets down for a few weeks. This is not to say life is rainbows and butterflies. The obsessive thoughts and compulsive behaviors still haunt me. Every. Single. Day. But for a brief respite, I am able to function, appearing normal to the outside world.

My closest friends and family members never knew I was fighting this secret battle. Late to work or class could be justified with a tiny white lie. And the "I'm not feeling well" fib, paired with a sincere apology, would take care of a missed family or social event.

For the most part, I am functioning and not wishing I were dead.

Day by day.

Click click, click click, click click. Wash, wash, wash. Count, count, count. Check, check, check. Clean, clean, clean. Make a list, make another list, and maybe one more list.

But I get my ass up, make it to school, go to work, and pretend to be emotionally well.

*

"Hello?" Mary answers the phone with typical enthusiasm.

"I can't do this anymore!" The sobbing begins. I can't breathe. My chest tightens. Every breath gets shallower. This is going to be difficult to explain, but I have to let my intern supervisor know that I am struggling to get through the semester.

"Bonnie, take a deep breath."

I try but can't gain control.

"What is going on? You seemed fine in this morning's meeting."

"I know, I know. That's what I do. I'm good at seeming fine. But if you could have seen what was going on in my head..."

"Whoa, slow down. I'm not following you."

"Of course you're not! How could you? This is freaking insane! I feel like I'm going to lose my damn mind! I am not going to make it to the school this morning to get my intern hours in. You need to know something about me. I can't keep this from you anymore!"

"I can assure you we will work through this. Slow down. Tell me what's upsetting you."

"You thought I was fine this morning, but I had chaos in my head. I kept thinking that my house was burning down." I take a sharp breath and continue. "Couldn't get the image out of my head. Not only did I go back home to check, but while I was there, I washed my hair. And washed my hair again. And again."

"Hmmmmmmmmm." I could almost hear her brain ticking over, digesting what I've said. As a professional counselor, I know Mary isn't new to this stuff.

"Mary, a few years ago I was diagnosed with Generalized Anxiety Disorder and Obsessive-Compulsive Disorder. I've been trying to overcome it without medicine, but it's getting worse. I mean, it comes and goes. But when it hits me hard, it's debilitating. Sometimes I feel like I've lost control of my life. I'm not sure I want to live anymore. It's just too much."

Crying hysterically, my words tumble out on top of each other, fast, releasing the pressure I've been bottling up for so long.

"Mary, I haven't even started writing my final paper. I can't stop researching. I research, print, highlight. Research, print, highlight. Research, print, highlight. The pile of printed research is about two feet deep, and I haven't typed the first word. It's like my brain is stuck. I may not graduate. And how could I possibly counsel others? God! I just can't..."

"Bonnie, this is what I want you to do right now."

I wait silently, longing for direction.

Mary continues, "Call the school. Tell them you're not feeling well."

"But I don't want to lie! I'm tired of lying!"

"Honey, it's not a lie. Do you feel well right now?"

"No, not at all."

"Call the school. Remember, I am your boss this semester."

"Okay, I can do this."

"Great. Meet me at PJ's coffee shop in thirty minutes. We will sort this out."

Sigh. "Okay."

Mary arrived ahead of me and got a table. She embraces me. I must have been holding my breath, because I feel the release when I exhale. Ah, now I can smell the fresh brewed coffee, one of my favorite aromas.

Mary motions for me to sit at the corner table. "You like a latte with raw sugar, right?"

I nod and smile, surprised she remembers.

We both slowly sip in silence for several seconds before Mary initiates conversation.

"I have to share something with you." Putting her hand on top of mine, "You are not crazy. I get you 100%. My son has severe OCD. And it is by no accident that I was chosen to be your supervising LPC for your internship."

Peace comes over me, a feeling I rarely experience. Just knowing there was one person who understands, at least to some degree, brings comfort. The tears now are indicative of a tiny glimpse of joy breaking through the emotional torment.

"I understand your pain," Mary continues. "When you called me, you sounded as though you were ready to give up. But I don't believe that for a second. I see you, Bonnie Guidry. I see your heart."

She gets me.

"You're right. I don't want to give up. I just feel defeated at times. But I want to get better. I know I have so much to offer others."

"Yes, you do!"

Finishing our coffee, Mary looks at her watch. "I've got a meeting starting in just a few minutes downtown. Now that we've established, you're going to be more than okay, are you registered for next month's LCA conference in Lafayette?"

"I sure am."

"Awesome! It's going to be a good one."

"I'm looking forward to it."

*

A month later, on a glorious, crisp morning, I rush into the entrance of the luxury hotel where the Louisiana Counseling Association conference is being held. It is good to see Mary as soon as I walk in.

"Save me a seat for that presentation." She looks up from the registration table with a wink.

"You betcha."

I can't wait to thank Mary for meeting with Brandi and I a few weeks earlier. Her insight made a huge impact on how Brandi was able to handle me and the OCD loops.

The Overcoming OCD session is led by a woman I know from grad school. "Good morning!" Terry approaches the podium with confidence. She has a slide up with side-by-side pictures of two brain scan images. Pointing to the one on the left, "This is a normal functioning orbital cortex." Pointing to the image on the right, "This is an orbital cortex controlled by Obsessive-Compulsive Disorder."

The images are considerably different with significant increased energy use in the orbital cortex of the person with OCD. For the first time in my life I feel like the craziness could be explained. *It really is a brain issue.*

The room is silent. Terry allows time for her audience to process the information she has just presented.

"Most of you in this room signed up for this session for one of the following reasons: You have a client who has been diagnosed with OCD. You have a loved one with OCD. Or you personally have been battling this beast. My goal here today is to help you understand the disorder. But more importantly to share a story of hope. No individual has to suffer in silence with the bizarre symptoms of this biochemical brain disease."

Terry picks up a paperback book. "This book changed my life. It saved my life, in fact. Beyond the cover lies information that can set prisoners free from the chains of obsessive thoughts and compulsive behaviors. Keep in mind, however, knowledge is useless unless applied. The principles here must be acted upon with persistent consistency. And that, my friends, will bring about miracles in the brains of those who want freedom badly enough to do the work."

Click. The next slide is a picture of the book. I begin hastily writing in my notes. 'Brain Lock by Jeffrey Schwartz.' I look around. Several people are writing. As I scan the room, I catch a glimpse of a familiar face. My therapist, Krystal, is two rows up.

Terry continues by telling her story, one all too familiar. The only difference is that she has found freedom. I am still held captive. By the shackles of despondency. Tortured by the demons in my head. Her story does bring hope, though. She discusses the cognitive behavior therapy that changed the brain chemistry in patients with OCD. I am like a sponge, soaking in every word, every image on the slides.

Could this be real? Can behavior therapy change my brain chemistry without medication? Desperate. I need out of this secret, dark dungeon of misery. I close my eyes and visualize the freedom I long for.

The hour seems to fly by, fervently taking notes the entire session. Counselors begin exiting. Krystal and I meet as the crowd merges by the door.

Krystal leans in with a whisper. "You gonna order that book?"

"Yep. As soon as I get back to the hotel."

No other words are needed. We both know we are in the right place at the right time.

It is time for me to heal myself.

*

It is a beautiful spring morning. Hummingbirds flutter about the feeders. Serenity ushered in by the fresh smell of flowers in bloom and the sound of the water spilling from the spa.

In the fifteen years that has passed since the LCA conference, my life has changed in so many ways. I've learned to beat this disease by calling out the symptoms, working around intrusive thoughts, and counting them as worthless distractions. I practice awareness and substitute intrusive thoughts and urges with intentional, constructive thoughts and behaviors. In doing so, I am rewiring my brain for success. I still have OCD tendencies, but in not bowing to this dogged enemy, I win. I have victory over my mind and my life.

The people around me have been supportive. Some have stayed close by on my journey.

Brandi and I are poolside, still in our pajamas, enjoying coffee.

"You ever regret going into business with me? Considering the years and money you invested in a degree you're not using?" she asks, her hands cupping the steaming mug.

"Heck, no! I was born to be an entrepreneur. And furthermore, I do use my degree. Every day."

"Ain't that the truth! With family, friends and employees, you're always playing therapist."

Chuckling. "I love helping others. I'm honored when they come to me for guidance."

Going through grad school impacted my life in so many ways. Getting my master's degree made me a better person. It was part of my journey to healing. It taught me how to communicate and understand human behavior. This was necessary for me to be able to express my gifts of compassion and empathy. I was created to love and serve others in this way.

"But I've heard people make comments about you wasting time and money on a degree you're not using. Doesn't that piss you off?"

"Nope. It's none of my business what other people think about me. I'm doing what I should be doing right now. Think about what has happened in my life just this past year." As I say this, I realize how much I've changed.

"Yeh, good point. Being your own boss was crucial. And I don't think you could have handled all of that earlier in life. You know, when you were not okay?"

I had just gone through the most difficult year of my entire life. While building a new home, my sister's health began to decline. My mom, my hero, was diagnosed with leukemia and passed away. I had never previously met emotional pain of such depth. Five months later, my sister was put on the transplant list for a liver.

Within one week, historic rain fell, flooding the homes of thousands, including my sister's.

Good news came the next morning with a call from the hospital. They had a liver.

Water levels had risen overnight to chest-deep on my street. A neighbor took us out by boat. We managed to get to one of our work trucks and reach the hospital before all major highways were closed.

Surgery was a success. Recovery was long and grueling, not without complications.

I spent most of that year in hospital rooms caring for loved ones. The level of stress I endured that year physically, mentally and emotionally was the ultimate test of my strength and healing. OCD thoughts and behaviors are triggered by stress. But, using the techniques I had learned, I was able to successfully ride out the wrath of this storm.

I've since embarked on self-education of neuroscience. I'm learning of the wondrous workings of the brain. What a fascinating mechanism of plasticity.

All those years ago, I changed my brain chemistry with self-directed cognitive behavior therapy, but I really didn't understand how it worked. Now I'm learning the incredible science behind it.

I still have OCD thoughts, but I stand firm against them.

Today, I laugh in the face of OCD. I might cringe when the waitress talks over my food or when I touch a barbell with someone else's sweat on it. But that two-headed dragon no longer controls my life.

I cringe, but I push through. Because I am in control of my thoughts, emotions and behaviors.

I have total control.

The dragon backs down every time.

Never again will I slip into the sludge of self-pity or meander in the mire of mediocrity.

Should I not reach back to the hands of those still in darkness, my battle would have been fought in vain.

It's not about me.

It's about them.

The ones who suffer in silence.

I have the key to their prison door, the spring for their thirst.

I'm currently working through a pretty intense six-month personal discovery course, diving into the deepest parts of my mind and soul. I'm excited about stepping out in faith to love and serve others on a grander scale. Walking in authenticity, living my intended purpose, whole and healed.

I look into the future. I imagine seeing my name in print as a best-selling author, but it doesn't bring as much joy as knowing that my words have the power to change lives. Speaking on stage only matters if my audience can be impacted for good.

The pain I lived through has purpose. My victory an instrument for the healing of others.

CHAPTER 4

Healing my inner child
Peta Cashion

He wasn't always like this.

A good looking, tall, dark, and handsome man with a charismatic charm, with magnetic energy that would draw you onto his stage. He was well liked and appeared to know anyone passing by. His friendliness made it appear that way.

His character was mesmerizing, drawing me in; every time believing the spoken words which came from his amplifying voice and captivated my attention.

With a day job as a plant operator, he had a mastery of 'just knowing' how mechanical things worked. He could pull things apart and put them back together again almost with his eyes closed.

His skilful understanding how machinery worked made him uniquely talented.

When I visited on school holidays, we would go cruising in his shiny gold Holden Kingswood. I would be perched up on the front bench seat, sitting next to him, careful not to bump the oxygen bottle strapped to the back of his seat.

I felt happy and content in his company, loved and connected. The small increments of trust between us were built in sliding door moments.

He used to say, "You know how much I love you, right?"

"Yes," I would say. "I love you, too."

"I will only ever love one woman you know, and that's your mother. No one could ever replace her. She will always be my one and only true love."

I believed every word he had to say, I held onto every word of his declared love for us both.

*

My Father never did marry again after their divorce was final.

Not long after that he was diagnosed with emphysema, a long-term progressive disease. His health dramatically deteriorated. Due to his illness he was unable to drink alcohol or smoke. Prescribed medication took its place as he struggled with the over-inflation of his lung capacity, shortness of breath, and the dependency on having an oxygen mask to stay alive.

He gave me a teddy bear when I visited for school holidays. 'Heart-to-Heart Bear' had a plastic red-shaped heart the size of your palm tucked inside a pocket down its side.

When you hugged it tight the sound of the heart beat identical to that of a living heartbeat.

"I want you to think of my heart beating," he said. "We will always be together no matter how far away we are. Our hearts beat together."

Having been able to share an emotional connection with my father, I felt seen, heard and valued. I felt accepted.

I felt so much pain every time I had to leave him and my brothers. I missed them so much and was torn and heartbroken. It was so difficult growing up without them.

When returning home after each stay, boarding the aeroplane, I would look out the window at the last glimpse of him standing there, waving to me.

Will this be the last time I see him standing there?

I loved my father, but he was complicated. He had this strong, amiable, loving side, but he wasn't always such a charming character.

When he had been drinking, everything changed.

Filled with alcohol, his fits of rage and anger would erupt. The next day he'd apologise. He'd say how sorry he was; that he didn't know why he did what he did, then… it would happen again and again.

Eventually, mum packed us up to move from Hobart to Melbourne, in efforts to live away from the drunken outbursts.

My Mother was attractive, energetic, and caring. She enjoyed helping people and basically lived to serve and care for others. It wasn't unusual for her to invite strangers over to our house and join us for Christmas lunch; mostly those that didn't have family or a place to go and celebrate.

She was empathic, kind, and forgiving. She saw the best in others even if they weren't at their best. She struggled with her own self love and creating healthy boundaries. And often put others' needs before herself.

She was too forgiving, really.

Mum worked day/night shifts as a nurse at a psychiatric hospital, dealing with patients with a wide variety of psychological illnesses.

At night when she worked, we would be left home alone to take care of ourselves.

My oldest brother would stay awake for hours in his bed listening to every strange sound, and slept with a knife under his bed because he felt an enormous responsibility to protect us.

 We seemed to just adapt to what was happening around us. We didn't know anything different as this was just how we lived.

We were hiding from my father… but he tracked us down, and convinced Mum to bring us to Tasmania to visit.

After spending the night on the Spirit of Tasmania ferry, we docked at the port of Launceston.

Mum and dad greeted each other distantly. Exchanging in small talk awkwardly.

My mother asked us, "Who do you want to ride with?"

My brothers said, "We are going to ride with Dad."

I replied, "You, Mummy." A young child clinging to her mother, I gripped her skirt; this little six-year-old girl was hanging on for dear life and never letting go.

Unaware of what was happening, this become the parting of our family as I knew it. This was the defining moment of separation. We would no longer live together.

My father and brothers went in one car, and my mother and I hopped in the Datsun.

We parted ways and drove off with an overbearing feeling of gut-wrenching sadness mixed with grief. They were off to live with my dad and his aunt. I was with Mum.

Mum found a place to stay for a few nights in a small white caravan, out in the middle of nowhere. A remote and secluded place, it was so quiet, you could hear the sounds of ringing in your ears.

At night in the pitch-black darkness the stars in the sky shone so brightly it felt like you could almost reach up to touch them. There was not another house to be seen for miles. Next to the caravan was a dilapidated barn that looked so scary at night, I daren't go near it.

The giant willow trees nearby appeared like monsters with long arms hanging down its side. My childish imagination ran wild as to what could be lurking around there.

It felt warm and cosy inside the caravan, but being alone with my mother did feel quite strange as I was really missing my brothers.

Mum tried to distract me. We snuggled up in bed listening to music on the radio. It made us feel happy.

Music brought us to a place of heartfelt nostalgia, alleviating any worries, and bringing joy to the present moment. That's all we could cling onto.

Eventually, we would sleep.

*

The headlights from a car were shining so bright they were blinding.

The caravan door was ripped clean off its hinges, and the noise engulfed us with even more fear.

Our bodies became frozen stiff in fear, embracing and gripping hold of one another; every nerve in my body on alert.

The scurry and force of a tall dark man holding a large, sharp bladed butcher's knife, came charging toward us. We stayed frozen and bound to each other, holding on for dear life.

As he approached, he grabbed and pulled mum's hair with his clenched fist, forcefully dragging her away from me, twisting her silk nightie tightly and ripping it, tossing her around like a rag doll, while he was screaming at her.

"I'm going to kill you!" he threatened, whilst he held the knife and pressed it against the skin of her neck, pulling her face up towards his as he stood over her.

Time stopped for a split second. She didn't move an inch as he raised his right hand.

He held the knife up high. The threat of danger sent painful tingles all through my body. My heart beat even faster, rapid breathing rushed the blood to my head. My ears were pounding with pressure, and my body was physically preparing to activate the 'fight or flight' response.

My tiny body's sympathetic nervous system sent out the impulse hormone to fight off the danger, and I pushed my way in front of her to protect her.

I looked up, straight into the monster's eyes.

It was my father.

A surge of adrenaline bursting from my adrenal glands brought a courageous instinct which took over the fear of threat, my vulnerability formed a shield of armour around my tiny body, my chest puffed out to appear bigger and imposing.

The fact it was my father made me even more determined to fight him off.

"You're not going to hurt my mummy!"

I heard myself scream, "If you're going to kill her, you have to kill me first!"

I was a terrified six-year-old girl, who showed no fear confronting the force of his threatening attack, without a second thought to save my mother from possibly being stabbed to death.

At that moment he retreated. He let go of his clenched fist and threw the knife down on the table as he staggered out the doorway.

Not long after, the police arrived and took him away.

The next day brought about a change. We left the caravan and went to stay with a friend of my mother's.

I didn't see my father for a long time.

Mum and I stayed in a few different places to seek comfort and safety. I went to preschool soon after this happened, and they called my mother expressing concerns for my health as I was always sleeping. Looking back now, I understand why.

*

A well-presented man soon appeared in our lives, resembling a knight in shining armour, to sweep mum off her feet and rescue her from the devastatingly abusive life she once had.

He was charming, generous, believable, knowledgeable, and almost 'God-like.

Like the saying, "If it's too good to be true, it probably is."

He rescued us, promising a better life by moving to Sydney.

That was until the cracks started to appear and his mask began to fall. He proved to be more like a devil in disguise. Although, it only seemed to be this way in our presence, as he was completely different again in the eyes of others.

He was a real-life Jekyll and Hyde.

His contrasting behaviour seriously had us doubting our own thoughts. I truly believe this created devastating confusion in my mother's mind. Only later I realised how this had such a tormenting effect on her. It affected her so much at times that it literally sent her into despair and a loss of her own sanity.

He was fooling everyone with his false self, and if he was exposed, he would become even more threatening, controlling, and aggressive.

He wasn't just aggressive fuelled with alcohol. He was a ticking time bomb on any given day and would explode with words like metal shards that would cut into your heart and make you bleed, leaving you vulnerable and wounded.

Bashing her black and blue in fits of rage, his anger and strength was no match for either of us. I witnessed him punch her in the face with a closed fist like a brick to her head. He knocked her unconscious and her body went limp as she fell backwards into a chair. It all happened so fast I didn't even see it coming. I was in total shock.

I really feared him. He was a monster. I thought he killed her. I thought she was dead.

No matter how many times I saw this or felt threatened it soon became a familiar experience as a result of his behaviour.

I understood it was not acceptable, I just didn't know what I could do to make it stop. With holding shame and guilt, I never spoke a word.

I was told, "Children are to be seen but not heard," and I truly believed that. I carried fear for both of us.

Sadly, I adapted to living a false self also. When I was away from home I felt free, when I was home I was in another state, walking on eggshells and living in fear.

Once again we would move away, only to return with him pleading and begging her to take him back to give him another chance.

As she had with my father, she would end up feeling sorry and even offering an apology for something she didn't even do.

When I was nine years old I had gone to stay at a friend's house for the weekend.

When I returned home I found her sitting up in bed. She had a bandage wrapped around her head and chin. Soft words murmured from her scarred, swollen lips. She cradled her hand under her chin as she spoke. Seeing the bruising and swelling on her gentle face made me feel sick to the stomach. It looked so sore.

I cried seeing her like this, knowing how much pain she must have been feeling.

I could almost feel her pain in every part of my own body.

"What happened?" I asked... even though a part of me already knew.

"I fell down the stairs," she said, looking down and away from my pleading eyes.

"Please tell me the truth, Mum," I begged. I needed her to say it out loud.

Her jaw had been broken in three places.

"He kicked me in the face while I was on the ground," she later admitted. The redness of shame spread across her face and I was heartbroken.

Oh, Mum.

But it wasn't over. She was physically and emotionally abused. He controlled and manipulated her in every way, and she fell deeper into a state of despair.

Diagnosed with having psychotic depression she attempted to kill herself by taking an overdose of Valium and Serepax.

Luckily, she made a call that saved her life.

Whilst speaking to her boss on the phone, her meek voice was slurred.

Her boss suspected something was terribly wrong and called an ambulance. The police had to break into the apartment.

The doctor said that she was lucky to be alive.

She lived tormented by guilt and worthlessness, fighting her own demons as well as living a nightmare of abuse, she sought love from the outer world, sadly destroyed by her inner world of low self-worth.

Eventually, she went away on her own to sort her life out.

I felt the paralysing fear of abandonment and the vulnerability, struggling to understand why my mother would want to leave me.

Then, I became his prey...

I was under his control now. I feared if I wasn't the 'good child' I would be punished.

I adapted to becoming the peacemaker, although I was far from peace inside myself. He used this opportunity to groom me, when I trusted him, he molested me, abusing me emotionally, with manipulation and control. He violated my innocence at a time I felt abandoned, fearful and unworthy.

My struggle with trust has been real.

I value and need trust as much as the air that I breathe. I give trust in others freely. This is why I needed to learn, and become aware of healthy boundaries, to acknowledge the value of trust others show me.

He showed me his sick distorted perception of love that only he knew.

Then one day out of the blue, my life became even more dark.

Just like pushing a button to detonate a bomb, he punched me in the face for putting a cup in the sink whilst he was washing the dishes.

The hit stunned me.

I stood in shock.

Then an intense feeling of rage took over. Blood started to pump to my head, my breaths became deeper, the anger filled my entire body.

The impact of the blow triggered something inside me, and it really scared me.

I've had enough!

I felt like I was losing control of myself, because I wanted to really hurt him. Like he'd hurt my mum. Like he'd hurt me.

I had one of those moments from a movie where you see yourself actually doing something you know you would never do. I ran frantically towards the garage, searching.

Where is that hammer?

I imagined smashing the fork-end of the hammer into his skull.

I want to kill this bastard.

I had so much anger and rage inside me, and it was finally exploding up to the surface.

But that would make me no different to him.

I stopped in the garage, consciousness awakening me out of my rage. I took three deep breaths and escaped into the back yard.

Be calm. Breathe. Be calm. Breathe. Breathe. Breathe.

I did not want to hand over any power to him. I needed to take time to control my own emotions and be responsible for my actions.

I knew I had to get away from him. I was earning an apprentice wage, and within days, I moved into a room in a share house.

Freedom, at last.

It took many years for me to understand and forgive my mother for leaving me alone with that horrible man.

I could only have enormous love and compassion towards her, understanding I was not accountable for her actions and knowing she was acting out of desperation.

But how could I judge her, when my first relationship wasn't much different? Within a short time, I attracted a similar person to my stepfather, without knowing any different. I travelled down a similar path. I stayed in a 10-year relationship, and we did get married.

Eventually I found out he was having an affair. I was so naiive. I had trusted him and he was lying straight to my face. He basically lied about everything.

That was when I realised he believed his own lies. The most dangerous liars are those who think they are telling the truth.

Of course, the thoughts of, *'I'm not good enough'* came flooding in.

It wasn't until later I came to understand it wasn't even about me.

What kept me strong throughout this was that I believed I could not be held responsible for other people's behaviours or actions.

I can only be responsible for my own.

Sure, I am guilty. I have faults. I make mistakes. I have verbally lashed out and totally lost my shit, said hurtful things to get back at someone for hurting me…

And what good did that do? Absolutely nothing. Being hurtful only feeds the drama; we really don't want to be there.

I soon woke up.

Removing my rose-coloured glasses to see clearly, I was living a fantasy of a non-existent happily ever after and in total denial of what was really going on.

When I told him I knew of his affair, he said, "But you can't leave me! We are married and you're my wife!"

When I moved out, he followed me home from work one day to find out where I was living. He ran up to the front door and banged on it loudly, while I cowered inside.

"I've got a gun!" he screamed from the front landing. "I'm going to shoot you and kill your dog!"

Memories of my stepfather came flooding back, and the years of abuse my mother endured.

I will not go through this anymore.

I called the police and took out a restraining order against him. I totally cut any connection with him, and filed for divorce.

But despite the fact I knew it was for the best, it was far from easy.

The flood of feelings and thoughts come rushing in; coming to terms with betrayal and letting go and detaching from old beliefs.

I came to understand that sometimes the things that hurt us the most teach the greatest lessons in life.

Why?

Because I am stronger.

Because I had to be smarter because of my mistakes, happier because I've known sadness, and I'm wiser from all my lessons.

My father passed away at the age of 49 from pneumonia. I was 21 years old at the time. His passing brought about many emotions; loving him because he was my dad, grief, shame, and resentment for his unforgivable behaviour.

As I grew older, and lived through my own marriage breakdown, I looked at his behaviour with curiosity as to what he must have experienced as a child to behave in the way he did.

I never believed we were deserving of the way he treated us. He just didn't know any better. He acted from a place only he knew how to.

The man from my childhood had left this world, and now the man I had loved as a woman was also out of my life.

I felt lost and was seeking a new direction.

Being 'single' was strange, although it brought about a wild and true freedom that I had not experienced before. It felt good as I had discovered a new kind of confidence.

No put-downs.

I started to believe in myself and that I was worthy.

I stopped looking out and turned inward. I am not what has happened to me. The events in my life have shaped me into who I am, but they don't define me.

I am thankful. I have the ability to learn and grow from my experiences. I am grateful that this has strengthened me in more ways than I could ever imagine. I have learnt that the greatest relationship you can have starts with yourself.

Firstly, your friendship with yourself.

Your freedom.

Your honesty.

Trust in yourself.

Understanding yourself.

And most importantly, your connection with being truly present.

Tony Robbins had a profound influence on me. His desire and purpose to help others planted a tiny seed of inspiration which has flourished inside me.

And I'm inspired daily by the 'Soul Queen', Oprah Winfrey. I aspire to be just like her. I can relate to what she has experienced as a child, and I have enormous admiration and respect for how she has helped so many people by sharing her story.

In my journey of learning and evolving I found:

> That meant living in truth with each person in your life.
>
> It meant refusing to say or do something that you don't believe is right.
>
> Living in truth with other people means, that you refuse to stay in any situation where you are unhappy with the behaviour of another person.
>
> You refuse to tolerate it.
>
> You refuse to compromise.
>
> *-Brian Tracy*

Sir Richard Branson had just arrived in Australia to launch Virgin Blue airlines.

My eyes stay glued to the TV watching the six o'clock news, my undivided attention watching him standing on the wing of the plane, shaking a bottle of champagne, and my heart pumped with excitement. Popping the lid off the bottle and spraying the foamy bubbles everywhere.

I admired everything about him, his perspective on life, his passion and ambition for the success of the vision he saw for the future. Reading his book *Losing my Virginity* had sparked a passion inside me. I needed to work for his company and the energy was drawing me in like a giant magnet.

I made a plan, directed my energy and focus on what I wanted to achieve. I researched and gathered the information I needed.

I sent in my application and waited...

and waited...

I received the call I was hoping for, with an invitation to attend an interview.

I was shaking internally and beside myself with excitement, yet trying to stay composed to be fully present at the same time.

I set out with the confidence to be the best version of myself having fun, and being authentically me.

Then came the greatest news ever.

I was offered the job! "Congratulations, Peta," said Simone, the recruiter who had placed me. "I can see you're going to go far."

In a state of euphoria, my life changed in a moment. I found trust in my vulnerability and courage to follow a dream, achieve it, and having such gratitude for the opportunity to live it.

Working at Virgin was the dream I'd hoped it would be. Sharing reception duties with another lovely woman, we were at the hub of their Brisbane headquarters. "Hi, Peta!" someone would sing out every couple of minutes in the first hour of the day, as they all arrived at the office. It was like the family I'd never had.

I worked hard and we played hard, too. Regular events were the highlight of my life, and I met inspiring individuals on a daily basis. Sir Richard mingled amongst hostesses, pilots, admin and call centre staff as though he was one of the crew. He was down to earth, quietly spoken, and a true gentleman. I had seen him breeze through reception multiple times and at one party, I saw my chance to connect properly. "Hi, Mr Branson, my name's Peta. Bradie and I are the receptionists at head office. Can we get a picture with you?" He happily obliged and pulled us in tight for a happy snap.

The energy and culture he created was everything I had hoped for when I applied. Working at Virgin is one of the greatest highlights in my life. The humbling experience, meeting and working with such amazing people. The friendships and experiences shared will stay will me forever.

Beyond those years of highlight reel moments, I have been blessed with many more. In addition to years of professional success, I have been fortunate personally as well. My three beautiful daughters are my daily inspiration and my reason for not wanting to bring my past into their lives and our future. I want to be responsible for who I am as an adult, and I want them to know that they are enough as they are. They don't have to prove anything to anyone.

That is my message.

Ignite the passion inside you, trust it and don't let anyone stop you.

If I can do it, you can too!

When you truly believe in yourself, anything is possible.

CHAPTER 5

Nothing can stop a soul with a mission

Marta Madeira-Mulungo

"Mother, here is the baby; go home. I'm going to school to write exams. They start today and I cannot miss them. I have a great chance to pass."

"But..." protests my mother.

"You both will be alright, Mother," I reassure her. "I'll be right back as soon as I am done."

"But, what if she..."

I could not allow Mother to go into the rational worry mode she is usually in. I have a mission to finish this year.

Nothing can stop me.

Not even my two-week-old baby.

My mother looks at me, concerned. She glances at the baby asleep in her arms. She looks so peaceful, so calm and relaxed. Mother is not sure what to do in that situation. But I do. So, I take charge.

I can tell now is the perfect moment to give her a direct order.

I look straight into my mother's eyes and instruct, "Mother, go home with the baby. The last exam finishes at 8pm. I'll be home by 10pm."

I see my mother looking at her watch. 5:30pm. I know she is mentally calculating how long it would be until the baby's next feed. She is not yet on formula – we do not have money to purchase it anyway.

"Mother, don't worry," I say, touching her shoulder lightly. I look down at the baby and her little eyes are closed. I lightly pull away the blanket which has perfectly swaddled her, and it reveals a beautiful rosy face which lights my heart and takes my breath away.

I look my mother straight into her eyes – and manage to say convincingly, "I spoke to her. She will not wake up until I am back from school. She will not cry, you will be just fine."

"What?" says Mother. I see the shock in her face. "It does not make any sense, Marta, the baby will starve!"

I turn away and start walking in the direction of school. It is about a 25-minute walk from the Maputo Central Hospital where I had been hospitalised in the maternity ward for two weeks. I am lucky to have been discharged the day my final grade eight examinations started. I was not going to miss that opportunity.

I am feeling rather weak and a bit feverish, but there is no stopping me. I am like a robot on a mission. I know I have to do this. I fought so much to get to this point, and I am not going to stop just because the baby decided to make a debut into this life two weeks before my exams. I walk as fast as I can before my mother can recoup from her shock.

I have to do this. Mother always said education was important. At 14 years I have already figured out why it was important. My aunties, who were more educated than my mother and could speak English, had nice jobs, they travelled a lot and could afford nice shoes and clothes for my cousins.

My cousins always looked beautiful when they went to school even though they were wearing uniforms. They seemed to have a very nice glow in their skin, and I had always wanted that – not out of envy – but a deep sense of desire which created a strong determination that I wanted to be like that one day.

Right now, I had to wait until they were done with the clothes and shoes to inherit them. I wear secondhand clothes most of the time.

I want to have my own new clothes bought straight from the shop, not donated ones.

For that to happen, I need education; that is my mission.

As I become more clear about my mission, I pick up pace to the point I am almost running. Towards the end of the hospital building, about five feet away I see a long staircase gradually revealing itself. I find a perfect hiding spot below it and decide to peek at my mother.

I look back toward where I have left her. I am curious to see how she is handling things. I see her starting to walk towards the bus stop.

I feel relief and in some sense gratitude that Mother is with me every step of the way. I feel supported and this is all I need to continue my mission.

I come out of my hiding place below the staircases and realise then that my heart has been racing. I take a deep breath to clear my mind and reduce the tension I am feeling. Keep going, I tell myself. I continue to walk towards school now in a more regular pace. I lock my thoughts into thinking about school and the exams ahead of me.

I want to show them all that I can do this, that I am strong.

I have to make worth all the fight I put up in school, and the drama with the family, even the shame I put my mother through. If I do this right and pass my exams, I can show to everyone that I am fine, and my mother can rub it in their faces. All I need is to be there today, and for the next four days.

I know my beautiful little baby was in with me, she had been very quiet when I told her of my intentions. When I was done talking, she smiled at me. It was the first smile I had seen from her, and although her eyes were closed, it had been so comforting and soothing to me. There and then I felt I had a person of my own. I was not alone, and my mother had no choice but to tag along.

This is the perfect team. Me, Mom, and my little one.

As I approach school the drama of the past nine months plays on my mind.

*

Especially the day the shit hit the fan at school. I was in history class, and by then my belly was beginning to show. I did not know what was going on in my body, I just knew I felt sick all the time and I had way too much saliva to deal with than I could manage.

One day during class, the saliva became too much, I ran out of the classroom to spit. As I got back, the teacher stopped me and asked, "How long will you continue with that?" I was really confused with the question, and I honestly didn't know what was going on. All I knew was I had not been feeling my best and I was hard in the stomach area. The teacher grabbed me by the hand, almost pulling me, and she took me to the headmaster's office.

"She is pregnant!"

I was shocked at this statement. I swallowed the saliva that was already piling in my month. I almost choked. I tried to protest at the accusation, but nothing came out of my mouth. The teacher left me there and the headmaster just said, "There is nothing I can do." He added, "Go home and tell your parents to come and see me. Don't go back to class!".

"Why can't I go back?"

"Because school is not for pregnant people."

I was confused at what is going on, but the headmaster looked so serious that I could only obey.

I arrived home and there was no one home, as usual. Mom would be back from work around 7pm. We had no telephone at home. In 1984 only companies, rich people and some people living in the city had a landline. My aunties had a landline, which I sometimes used to call mother when I was in the city.

There were no cell phones, the word Google did not exist yet. Some houses around us had television sets, but very few. We did not have one at home. We, in fact, did not have electricity, so all I could do was go and play outside with my friends.

I dropped my school bag and ran outside. I realised the streets were empty because it was school time. I remember a friend from two streets back who was not going to school because her mother passed away and she had to look after the house. I went to her, but as she saw me, she ran inside the house and slammed the door. I wondered why she did that, and I looked inquisitively at her brothers playing outside and one of them said, "She's not allowed to play with you because you are pregnant." Then he added, "Go home and leave her alone, we don't want anyone teaching her how to make babies."

It was the second time in the same day I was accused of being pregnant.

What is going on?

I got back home and saw that this time, I was not alone. My brother arrived from school and asked me what I was doing so early at home.

"Well, I was sent home to get Mom to go and speak with the headmasters," I say. "They say I am pregnant. Alice's brother also says I am pregnant."

My brother, who was two years older than me looked at me, his head tilted. He said, "I think you are pregnant, everybody is talking about it. Why don't you just admit you are?""

"I am?"

"Yes, you are."

"Are you still dating that arrogant boy?"

"Yes, I am."

"Have you had sex with him?"

"Yes, I have."

"Then you are pregnant."

It sounded like a harsh verdict, one that I did not understand the implications of, so I looked at him with curiosity, but he did not go any further.

"Are you going to tell Mom?" he asked.

"Yes, I will, she has to go to school with me tomorrow."

I tensed at the thought of getting my mother to see my headmaster. His cold face when I left the school gave me an indication of being really in trouble. I ran to my bedroom and threw myself in my bed, cuddling in my pillow for comfort. Below it I felt a piece of paper I was very familiar with. It was a cutting from a magazine. I took it out, rolled on my back and gazed at it as I had done for the past two years.

That picture took me to the fantasy land; it brought me hope. It was a picture of a huge refrigerator which was open and advertised all sorts of nice food I had never seen in my life. That picture always made me dream and fantasize of a better life, of better possibilities, of something beyond the experience that I was living then.

"I want you, and you, and all of you," I said out loud, pointing to yoghurt, cheese, cakes, and other things I did not yet have a name for. Little did I know that right then, I was starting an attraction force so strong it would shape my entire life.

Below the picture there were some words I could not comprehend. My auntie had told me it was English. That picture lead me to the conclusion that, to have a better life, I needed to speak English.

At about 7pm, my mother arrived home as I was finishing to cook dinner. I looked at her lovingly, and I could see she was tired. It was quite a long walk from the bus stop to the house, so I let her settle a bit. As I was laying the table for dinner, I was placing the dishes next to her and she grabbed my belly and says, "Why is this so big? Is there a baby here?"

I was confused at this baby talk. Why would I be having a baby inside me? I remembered the lesson in biology class when the teacher was explaining the reproductive cycle of a woman, so it was women who have babies, not girls! *Mother must be confused,* I thought, after all she only studied up to standard four and I was in standard eight!

My brother entered the dining room at that time, and mother asked my brother if he knew about my pregnancy. "Yes, she told me today she was pregnant."

My brother turned to me and asks, "Are you pregnant or not?"

Remembering our afternoon conversation and his harsh conclusion, to my mother's surprise I quickly responded, "Yes, Brother, I am pregnant."

"Why did you not tell Mother?"

"She never asked."

"Well, she says she did," he responded as he looked at my mother for confirmation.

"No, she did not, she accused me of carrying a baby, but I am not."

"So, what is the difference?"

"Well, I missed my period, so I am pregnant, but I am not carrying a baby. That is for women; I am a girl."

This statement was followed by a long silence at the house, a silence that would go on for days. I could sense a sort of black cloud lingering around us as I carried on with my daily chores, and I began to realise that something serious was going on, but nobody was explaining.

During dinner everybody was silent. It was as if there was not enough air, and I was struggling to breathe, so I quickly finished eating, cleaned up, and we all retired to our beds with as few words as possible. The whole situation was well above my comprehension.

I wish someone could explain things to me.

The next day arrived and she usually would wake me up at about 5am to get ready for school, but she did not. I decided to stay in bed partly because I was not feeling well, and I was confused. Mother got ready and left the house and at that point I summoned the courage and energy to get out of bed. I went to check on the bus money that she usually dropped on the table for each of us, but mine was not there. Walking to school took two hours. I had done that many times to save the bus money for candies, but the headmaster asked me not to return, not without my mother anyway.

It was Friday. I was hoping that during the weekend I could talk about my mother going to see the headmaster with me on Monday.

Sunday arrived to a beautiful day. The sky was so clear, and I could feel the dark cloud around us dissipating.

Mother had always relied on me to help around the house. And I was good at what I did. I woke up at about 5am and noticed there was no water coming from the tap; the water containers had very low reserves. Without my mother having to ask, I fetched the 20 litre water can and went to the water well, about 25 minutes from home.

At the water well, there was a long queue. It was the perfect place to catch up on the gossip with the other girls, but it seemed like none of my girlfriends wanted to talk to me, I had a strong feeling that everyone was, in fact, talking about me – I was the gossip!

It began to sink that, whatever I did was very bad, but I was yet to find out what it was, exactly.

I started to feel a bit of shame. A feeling I became very aware of, for the first time. It felt like judgement, like rejection, like excrement, something to hide because no one wanted to have it around.

I used that rejection as a way to finish my water chore very quickly. Since no one would talk to me, I jumped the queue, fetched the water, and went back home.

I made seven trips like that.

My mother asked me how come I was being so fast, and my answer was, "Since no one wants to talk to me, I just stand in front get the water and come home." I could see the worry in my mother's semblant, but she would not explain further.

Mother never felt easy to talk to about complicated stuff to me. In fact, I don't remember ever having a conversation with my mother. I don't remember her explaining anything to me.

She talked like, "Do this... Do that... Come here... Go there!" We exchanged jokes and laughed sometimes, but I don't remember a mother/daughter conversation.

It was like that even though I was the only one who always stayed with her. My other five siblings had moments where they went to stay with their fathers or with other relatives. Not me. I was her rock. I was her support. I even had her mother's name, Marta.

It was about 2pm and I heard the sound of a car arriving at the door. I ran outside to see who has come to visit, and as I opened the gate I had an abrupt stop as I remembered that I was in trouble. Just a few days ago I had confessed to being pregnant.

I was used to my death squad showing up whenever I did something wrong, but I was far from accepting it. Those were the rare moments where I felt really angry and felt that I needed a father to talk to or to be talked to.

You see, my father had rejected me before I was born.Despite the fact that mother was his wife, he could not agree that he made her pregnant, so he kicked her out of the house before I was born; and because I look so much like him, sometimes Mother resented that and on rare occasions she would voice it. In those instances, I felt rejected by my mother also.

My death squad was composed of my two aunties and their husbands. Four adults to handle me when my mother could not. I knew what they were coming for, and they did their job. And their job was very confusing to me. It was not a conversation, it was not an explanation of what was happening and the consequences, it was not educational, it was not counselling. No, none of that. They arrived, judged, and passed a sentence. And left.

It felt scary and confusing, always. And now for the first time, I also felt ashamed, felt judged, and added more to the existing feelings of rejection. It really felt like excrement. You don't question it. It's bad, period!

As we all settled for the hearing procedure, my body was tense, I felt small and hopeless; I was gasping for air and my heartbeat was not consistent.

How did I put myself in that position again? I should know better.

The session went like this.

"You know what you did, and now you are pregnant. You are going to have a baby and as punishment you will now go to the farm with grandmother."

I scratched my head and my eyes looked up as I was trying to reach for the next thought. When did I not go to the farm with grandmother? Whenever I was on school holiday I went to the farm with grandmother and I loved it. I would plough, plant, and harvest. Sometimes I would go to the farm on weekends to help speed up things during harvest time. This sentence did not make any sense, but what did?

My mother, on the contrary, felt lighter. Maybe the fact that she did not have to talk to me about the pregnancy was a relief to her. I took the opportunity to tell her she was needed in school. She agreed immediately to meet me in school after work. I could almost see myself back in school where I belonged, despite the opinion of the headmaster and now, the death squad. I began to wonder what was my mother's opinion in that, but didn't ask her.

On Monday I arrived at school two hours before my mother. I let the headmaster know my mother was on her way. I parked in front of his office because I was watching him. I wanted to make sure he stayed out till my mother arrived around 17:30 hours as promised. I knew she would be there. My mother always kept her promises.

As I waited, I saw three pregnant girls go in and out of the headmaster's office, all three carrying books, which meant they were students. I was intrigued because I was told that pregnant people don't go to school.

One of them sat next to me on the bench just outside the headmaster and she started chatting with me. I learned that she was transferring to evening class because she was pregnant, and she was going to get married soon.

Right before my mother arrived, I had a chat with another one from whom I learned the same. So, it was possible!

My mother arrived as promised and I took her to the headmaster's office. As we patiently waited, the tension between me and my mother built up again. I could see that she was avoiding any eye contact with me. Finally, the door opened, and a young woman dressed in sneakers made a gesture indicating that it was our turn.

"Well let's not waste each others' time, shall we?" said the headmaster. "Your daughter is pregnant, and the rules say she is expelled from school."

Mother looked down, crossed her arms firmly, and did not utter a word. She seemed to accept the verdict. As she was about to leave, I stopped her and I looked at the headmaster and asked,

"Why can't I continue to study?""

"I have already told your mother; you are expelled because you are pregnant."

"I saw three pregnant women coming to your office today and they are all students and they are not expelled."

"Yes, but they are more than eighteen years old and they study at night; it's different, you can't study at night."

"Why not?"

"Because you are very young. Night classes are for adults."

"Then I will study during the day."

"You can't, because during the day is for young girls."

"What am I?"

There was a long silence. My mother looked at me with a mixture of admiration and pity, she did not know the confronting side of me. I was a nice girl at home. The headmaster also did not know what to do.

So, I asked him.

"I am in standard eight, which classroom should I go to?" He did not answer. Then I added, "I am going to look for one and join today." I opened the door and left his office, and I did just that. Without paperwork or approval.

I learned then that adults don't always know what to do. Sometimes they need a little help.

If I knew what I wanted I could always get it. This lesson has helped me in the rest of my life until today.

*

I stayed true to my mission of getting education.

After the baby was born, I discovered I was good in selling and since I did not have any products to sell, I would go to the local market and help the local business owners sell for a commission.

Soon I got enough money to start my own stand. I continued to go to school at night and also studied English. I earned a scholarship to go to Zimbabwe and learn English and completed a secretarial course. This scholarship came through one of my aunties who was part of the death squad. In fact, all members of my death squad have supported me and the baby in one way or the other. They were not bad people; they were adults with a complicated mission.

A great career with international organizations awaited me on my return. I was able to fund my university, finished a Bachelor's degree and then went for Master's degree in the UK.

I supported my mother always, and she supported me always.

Seven years ago, I started my own Consultancy business and later on discovered my passion for coaching. I help people transform their ideas into results. Just like I did.

*

The streets are busy and I cannot help but notice how happy and excited I am today. I have always found Christmas to be exciting and a time to really connect with family. I glance at the dashboard of my car and notice that it reads 19:55 hours.

It's a long drive to my daughter's house.

As we turn the last corner, we can see my daughter's house at a distance. There is only one other house with the lights on in the whole street and the other houses are still being built. It's a new promising neighbourhood, as we arrive at the gate, the automatic door opens, revealing three cars parked in the driveway. I push my car to park right behind the new Mercedes Benz. As I notice it, a big smile lights my face, still remembering the day my little one came to show off her new car.

"Hi Mom, come right in, feel at home," my daughter welcomes. Right behind her, her fiancé and my four grandchildren are tagging along to welcome us.

We go in the house and a long and beautifully table is set for our Christmas dinner.

I look around; the house still smells of newness. They moved in six months ago. I can see the pride in her eyes, and I can feel the pride in me.

My little rosy baby is now 35 years old. She owns her business, she built her own house, and she has three cars parked in her driveway.

I did good. We did good.

As all these thoughts and feelings are racing through my mind, I hear a car arriving and it's my son and his family. His wife, and my grandson. We are complete now.

We came a long way. I can still remember Christmas Day in 1999 when I had to rush her to the hospital to deliver her baby. On that day, I became a grandmother at 29 years old. At 50 years old, I am a grandmother of five.

It all worked out well in the end. My mission is well accomplished. I now realise that my big mission was to break the bone of poverty and create success in my generation. That mission has evolved so much and went on to become my profession and passion in life; I help my clients who are giving in to doubt and fear step into their power.

I look at the dinner table and my fridge picture comes alive, below the Christmas trees their presents await...

Thank you, GOD!

CHAPTER 6

From rage to redemption
Kenneth Nathan

The room is bustling with three or four doctors in sterile green clothing, covered from head to toe. One of the doctors looks at me as I enter the room and says, "Yes, who are you?"

The family friend who is with me replies, "This is one of Paul's children and he's here to visit his father."

"Well, okay, but don't touch anything because it's all sterile," the doctor says, holding a syringe.

I still can't see my father's face, because another doctor is blocking my view. But I can see the rest of his body and it is convulsing in harrowing pain.

"Come on Paul, settle down," the doctor is saying... then one of the doctors moves, and I see him.

I'm not ready.

I could never be ready to see something like that.

This is what somebody looks like when they've been burned alive.

His whole face and head is much larger due to all the fluid build-up and if I didn't know for sure it was my father, I would never have recognised him.

It is beyond my worst nightmare. It is more like a horror movie.

My whole body begins to shake, and I can't stand there much longer, so I rush out of the room and am comforted by a family friend outside.

I want to speak but I can't form the words. All I can do is stare at her, my hand on my heart. It is thumping so loudly I can feel it in my ears.

Is this finally the end?

*

My family immigrated from India to Australia in 1974. I was seven years old at the time and my father was a Christian Pastor. Our denomination sponsored us to immigrate to Australia to pastor a church.

We stepped off the plane in Sydney with high hopes of a better future and my father chasing his dream. We were in a new country, a foreign land not knowing anyone and without any support.

It's a brave move for anyone to relocate to a foreign land, especially with young children. Australia had only officially dropped its *White Australia Policy* in 1973 under the Whitlam government and opened its borders to non-European migrants.

Directly following Federation in 1901, policies were designed to keep Australia white and British, so neighbourhoods and schools were still pretty much white Anglo back then and we were exposed to racism and discrimination for the first time.

On my first day of school, a group of kids were following me around in the playground, laughing and calling me names.

"Choco-boy," they taunted.

"Where's your elephant?"

"Why aren't you riding your elephant to school?"

These were only some of the names and derogatory statements they were saying to me. I finally found a place to sit, where I just buried my head in my hands and cried.

Things didn't go according to plan for my father, either. What was promised to him at the church was never delivered, and he felt this betrayal deep down within.

Dad already had a tumultuous past with religion. My father had converted to Christianity from Hinduism in his late teens. I never heard much about my father's upbringing in India, only that he was disowned by his own father because he converted to Christianity.

So, the turn of events at work was felt even more deeply. Dad had to find other work to feed his family and we moved around Sydney quite a bit.

He survived a tragic car accident just a couple of years later, which added to his depression. He fell into alcohol and gambling addictions to cope with his own self-loathing.

There were times when I'd come home from school and find him drunk, lying sprawled out on the sofa. He never had many male friends to talk to or spend time with, so drowning his sorrows was a way he coped with his depression.

Sadly, it was during some of these times he would actually take notice of us and would get a little too rough wrestling with my brother and me. One of us always got hurt and we would call my mother at work in tears, complaining that Dad hurt us again.

Over the years I watched my father suffer from many health ailments and his daily dependence on medication grew, as well as his hospital admittances.

As a child it was fun to go through my father's bag when he'd come home from work. I was always hoping to find some chocolates but most of the time there were only bottles of pills.

Over the years I was accustomed to seeing my father erupt violently whenever there was conflict in the home. But when this happened, he was more violent toward himself than any one of us.

Whenever he was triggered, he would slap himself across the head many times and very hard until there was quiet from us.

Sometimes he also used items around the house to hit himself, and we would look on in horror.

Once when my father had picked my mother and I up from the train station, he was driving too close to the centre of the road. Some oncoming vehicles were honking their horns at us as they passed by.

"Dad, you're driving too close to the centre line," I said, getting nervous.

He ignored me.

"Dad!" I yelled.

He kept his eyes firmly on the road ahead, still driving perilously close to the oncoming traffic.

Unable to take it anymore, I grabbed the steering wheel to veer the car closer to the left side of the road.

A struggling and yelling match erupted and when we stopped at the traffic lights, Dad began hitting his forehead with open palms, again and again.

I looked around in horror, sure that other motorists were seeing this too. It was a quiet, yet emotionally damaging, ride home that night. But there were many days and nights like this.

Years later I came to understand how this form of self-harm toward himself stemmed from some of his own childhood traumatic experiences.

Dad never talked much about his childhood, but the bits and pieces I did hear weren't pleasant. In my early teens I overheard Dad talking to someone about a childhood incident where he interrupted his father in a conversation that he was having. This outraged his father, who slapped him across the face so hard, he fell to the ground and cracked his head open.

Dad grew up with so much unresolved childhood trauma that manifested in anger, and he brought that into our home.

Police and ambulance services were called on numerous occasions because of my father's many suicide attempts. Dad would try and drink himself to death, swallow pills, or use some form of self-harm to try and end his life.

I didn't realise it at the time, but it was also a means to try and control us. Because every time he attempted to take his own life, my family would have to drop everything and focus on him.

Growing up all I knew about intimate relationships was what I witnessed in my home, which was yelling and violent conflict.

I lived in survival mode for most of my teenage years, not knowing what each day would bring.

I was 18 on the night I was standing at the bedside of my father in the hospital emergency room – he had been burned alive.

Is this what burnt human flesh smells like?

Dad was working night shifts in the city and would catch the train to and from work. He usually parked his car at the train station and would drive the ten-minute journey home.

His memory is fuzzy from that night, but he remembered getting off the train and into his car, which mysteriously stalled shortly afterwards.

He got out of the car to check under the hood to see what the problem was.

He was just metres up the road from the railway station, next to a cemetery. There weren't many streetlights and the road was dark. It was a place you wouldn't like to walk alone late at night.

As he was looking under the hood, he felt someone grab him from behind and pull him into a tight bear hug. He couldn't see this person but the next thing he felt was something being poured down his back, and he knew immediately from the smell that it was petrol.

"What are you doing?" he asked, but got no reply. So, he asked again, "Who is this and what do you want?" but there was no reply again.

I couldn't imagine how scared he must have felt, not knowing what was going to happen next.

He was on fire.

As he lay screaming whilst being burned alive on the ground, he heard the laughter coming from both of his assailants as they watched him burn while fleeing the scene.

A teacher working back late at night at a nearby primary school heard my father screaming and called the police and then rushed over to assist him.

If she wasn't there, I'm sure he would have died, hideously burnt alive.

Dad survived this callous attack but was left with inner and outer scars for the rest of his life. He had already been scarred emotionally from childhood and other trauma, but this was much worse.

He was never the same again after this and I've always said I lost my father in 1985.

There were many nights where he would have these horrible nightmares reliving this trauma and would jump out of bed screaming and run out of the room.

This would awaken the whole house and one of us would have to hold him down and calm him down before sending him back to bed. There were many years where my siblings and I had to parent our dad.

This burning incident sent my family into further turmoil both emotionally and economically. The police never found those who were responsible for this crime and no motive was ever considered.

I still question why there wasn't a proper investigation and why the police didn't interview people who were closely associated with my family back then. Some things just don't add up about this crime.

Today I'm convinced racism was partly a motive and I'm still hoping and praying the cowards who were responsible for attacking my father will one day be exposed and justice will be served upon them.

The only way I knew how to cope with this trauma was to bury it. I never talked about it much with people even after they asked. It just brought back way too many bad memories for me.

I had learned to bury a lot of things growing up and never really had anyone who I could talk to. I read somewhere that what helps a young person through the turbulent years of adolescence was one significant adult.

But I never had anyone. I was also a shy young man and found it difficult to express myself, especially my anger. Years later what I buried resurfaced whilst I was living in the USA.

In 1991 I received a golden opportunity to study in the USA at a Christian College. I was quite a restless young man in a lot of ways back then and was searching for something. I also needed some direction and security in my life.

Attending a strict college with rules I had to abide by was something I definitely needed, as it brought me stability. I felt safe for the first time and had some direction and purpose, but I found it difficult to study. My brain wasn't attuned like that and I struggled throughout my college years writing papers and sitting for exams.

I also became envious of other students who I could see came from good homes and grew up in peace. Their lives were so ordered and restrained, which was something very foreign to me.

In 1996 while in my senior year, I attracted and married a woman who had also experienced childhood trauma. She suffered from severe migraine headaches and flashbacks during our very intimate moments. It's ironic how we attract the type of people who've had some similar experience to ours in childhood.

She would have nightmares and lived with major depression and anxiety. It was an unhealthy and volatile relationship which lasted four years. We both brought so much childhood baggage of suppressed emotions and unresolved issues into the relationship.

Both of us were accustomed to express these negative feelings toward each other in less than respectful and loving ways.

For me it had a triggering effect.

During my first marriage I started having these flashbacks and intrusive negative thoughts for the first time from my childhood. Every time there was conflict between my wife and I, it triggered me to relive my childhood traumas all over again. I would erupt in fits of rage which left my wife living in fear during the marriage.

There was a lot of yelling and swearing that included breaking things in front of her and punching walls. There were also episodes where I self-harmed and threatened suicide as a means of emotional manipulation and control over her.

In some ways, I was my father all over again.

I had never dated much in high school due to my lack of confidence and low self-esteem, and the idea of bringing a girl home and exposing her to my dysfunctional family life was too embarrassing to even think about.

So I entered college with no experience of romantic relationships at all. My first wife was pretty much my first girlfriend.

Unhealed trauma can negatively impact all relationships in so many ways. What we experience in childhood concerning intimate relationships is a picture of what we believe our own intimate relationships should be like. I just didn't know any other way.

My wife and I tried numerous counsellors and went to so many marriage courses and retreats, but the root cause was never dealt with, which was our post-traumatic stress disorder.

After four years of marriage things finally came to a head and we separated for the final time. It was during the separation when I learned my marriage was really over that I hit rock bottom.

All three of my siblings had also experienced marriage failure and I vowed it would never happen to me.

My marriage is different and I am different, I used to think.

The separation and divorce were very painful and forced me to my knees begging God for His forgiveness of all the things I did wrong.

I'd never felt so alone and I started having serious anxiety attacks. I would drag myself to the phone to call the ambulance whenever I thought I was about to have a heart attack. At the hospital I was diagnosed with having a nervous breakdown and I was prescribed anti-anxiety medication.

The weeks that followed were very difficult. I still lived in hope thinking my wife would return and everything would go back to normal again. Every time I experienced anxiety I would take these drugs and it would knock me out for a few hours.

Eventually I knew I couldn't go on like this anymore. I needed the support of my friends and family, so I packed my bags and returned to Australia in 2000.

Back in Australia I started searching for new meaning in my life. I was trying to make sense of all that happened and wrestling with my demons of guilt and shame at the same time. I was angry with myself and with God, asking why my life was such a failure and why he allowed all these things to happen.

This thinking tormented my soul and upon seeking medical help I was diagnosed with severe depression and was placed on anti-depressants along with my anti-anxiety pills.

Was I going to be just like my father and become dependent on medication for the rest of my life now?

Taking these antidepressants did help me feel a lot better but there were some side effects. They made me feel too good. My conscience became disinhibited and I went down the wrong path of promiscuity and alcohol abuse. (I would never try and shift the blame on such things as tablets for my behaviour and I take full responsibility for my actions, but I do feel the easy accessibility to depression medication today should be a cause for concern. I think there are other alternatives one should consider and trial before swallowing tablets.)

I began working as a youth worker with traumatised violent teenagers, where I witnessed similar behavioural patterns to mine from years past. I was also studying counselling and social work at the time and was learning more about childhood trauma and abuse.

Was this why my father acted the way he did?

Is this why I acted the way I did?

I was beginning to find the meaning and purpose I was seeking of why my childhood was so traumatic. I felt comfortable working with these kids because I could relate to the turmoil that they were experiencing. I knew well that raging storm going on in their heads.

But I was still living a wild lifestyle and still experiencing these intrusive thoughts and flashbacks from childhood, coupled with the shame and guilt I was experiencing from my marriage breakdown.

I cleaned myself up and in 2006 remarried after meeting someone off the internet. For a while, things were good, but it didn't last long, and we were divorced just over a year later.

There weren't any major issues in this marriage as there was in the first, and my second wife was a nice person, but it just wasn't a good match.

I had previously vowed I would never erupt in anger and violence again, which I didn't (and subsequently never have to this day). My second wife and I just weren't compatible enough with each other and it was a wrong choice of rushing into marriage again way too soon without getting to know someone. Yet again a symptom of my childhood trauma and attachment disruptions. (I don't want this to sound like my second wife was just a blip in my story here because I mentioned her briefly. This was her second marriage too and the breakdown of our marriage would have also painfully affected her.)

After the failure of my second marriage, my self-esteem took another hit.

I guess I'm just a loser after all.

I started to go back to my old ways of loose living.

The flashbacks continued and I started talking angrily aloud to myself, pretending I was addressing the situation or person(s) who hurt me from years back.

"God, why did you put my family and I through such terrible things?!" I would yell looking up at the sky.

These flashbacks and thoughts mainly occurred late at night when I wasn't able to sleep.

Looking back now I could see the reason for it all; because I was starting to awaken and shed the old skin away. What I had buried deep down within my soul was starting to rise to the surface.

But why was this happening only now?

I had finally come to understand how trauma can be intergenerational and what my father lived with in his head for a number of years. I also came to a better understanding of what post-traumatic stress disorder is and what I, and my family, still live with today.

I continued working in the community services sector with young people and in 2007 I got to put my pain onto paper. I co-authored an anger management course called RAGE *(Re-navigating Anger and Guilty Emotions)* that went on to win an award with the Australian Crime and Violence Prevention Awards.

RAGE is a simple six-week course which helps teenagers become aware of their triggers and how to express this anger in nonviolent ways. I used examples of my own past struggles and unhealthy anger patterns in writing this program.

Professionals who attended training in RAGE started labelling me as an adolescent anger and violence expert. A label I only partially accepted because adolescent anger and violence are symptoms of some deeper issues which require work with more qualified professionals. But my own traumatic experiences and explosive behaviours did allow me to be a bit of an expert in working with some of these clients.

In the years that followed I really started changing for the better because I was enjoying the work I was doing. It brought meaning and a new life's purpose.

I had a few short periods of lifestyle relapses, but 2016 was the tipping point.

I had a falling out with a close friend while holidaying together on the Island of Bali. Without thinking, I used some pretty harsh words and made fun of something that was of sentimental value to my friend.

"How can you say such terrible things like that to me Ken?" she said. "You really need to take a good hard look at yourself and your words or you'll have no friends left," she continued.

For 49 years I had been searching for the answers to my problems on the outside as a way of trying to fill this huge gap on the inside. My search included so many failed relationships, wrong choices, and swallowing pills.

But the answers were right there within, all along.

I left Bali early and returned home and started to reflect upon my life more seriously.

I was running a successful small business and turning 50 in a year and I knew I didn't want to be on these antidepressants any longer, as they numbed my mind and emotions.

I began reading books on spirituality and a new world began to open up to me for the first time. I was able to wean myself off the medication I had been on for over 10 years and I began meditating and doing yoga, which helped me tremendously.

This was an amazing spiritual awakening and it allowed me to have a new perspective on God and not just what's contained in the Bible.

I also came to understand this whole universe a lot better, and my place in it. I started smiling at everyone I passed by on the street as I discovered how connected we are to each other and to everything.

For the first time in my life I found inner peace, which surpasses all understanding. Outwardly I'm decaying but inwardly I'm being renewed each day.

Today I continue to write programs on tackling the problem of violence and other issues in children and teenagers and I have found my redemption and life's mission.

I'm now thriving as an author, trainer and keynote speaker all around Australia. One day, I'd like to go beyond our country and help more people around the world.

I'm a very different person now. Sometimes I pinch myself and say, "Who was that person before?"

I know there'll be some who will judge and label me after reading this but what stones can they find to throw at me?

*

I think back to the day it finally happened. I wasn't prepared for this day at all.

The year was 2008.

The phone rang at 7am.

"Kenneth, you better come over because your father is on the ground and he's not moving. I think he's dead," my mother said, crying frantically.

I quickly got dressed and drove as fast as I could to my parents' house. When I arrived two ambulance vans were parked out front.

And there he was.

My dad.

Lifeless on the floor of his bedroom.

I knelt down next to him and put my hand on his head. He was so cold.

But he looked at peace at last.

I lowered my head and kissed him on his cold forehead.

"Thank you for being a great father to us and for trying your best. I never got to tell you how proud I was of you.

I forgive you for everything."

There are so many things I never got to say to him.

Despite everything he had been through, my dad was also a compassionate and kind man who would do anything for anyone who needed his help. I knew he loved us. He just struggled a lot with his past.

And I could certainly understand and relate to that.

I've found new meaning and purpose as to why all these things occurred in my childhood. I still have these flashbacks of the past traumas from time to time, but I've learnt to manage them with the knowledge that these dark periods that intrude my brain are only moments and this too, shall pass.

I've found that meaning is something we have the freedom to create from whatever tragedies have occurred in our lives.

We can either allow these tragedies to break us or we can choose to use them to our advantage and create our life's purpose.

But whatever meaning you create should be unique to you and originating from your own life experiences. What you do with that meaning is what really matters anyway. Every single day, we have the choice to either thrive and fly or crash and burn.

You'd be so proud of me, Dad. I've chosen to fly.

CHAPTER 7

Onward and upward
Lisa Boorer

I don't have much time.

I feel apprehension creep up my spine as I grab my belongings, clothes, shoes, computers, certificates, and makeup, and throw them into the boot of my car.

I have warned the two office ladies what is about to go down, then I sit and wait for the inevitable.

The staff room at the back of the club has an eerie silence today. The off-white walls which are normally bright and inviting seem to be closing in.

My stomach is churning, my nerves are raw. I feel a tremble pass through my body as I sense her approach.

She walks in wearing her sharp, black suit, made-up perfectly, and holding a shiny black briefcase.

I wonder where she found that? It's been years since she's shown an interest in the business. A wry smile almost comes to my lips.

Her heels click clack on the shiny floor as she steps through the foyer with her cocky saunter. It bolsters the air of authority she carries with her everywhere. Today it's on steroids.

I detect a slight tremble in her hand and notice her eyes darting side to side – the only signals she is nervous. Otherwise she appears to have balls of steel.

My lips curl into a smirk as I silently thank the owner of our security company for tipping me off about the event about to unfold.

I stand calmly.

I can hear my own voice, clear and strong, belying the emotions racing through me. I have already removed the club key from my keyring. My fist is clenched and I can feel the shape cutting into my palm.

I slowly open my hand. It is steady as I slide the key towards her.

"Your demise will not involve my hand, but I will enjoy it when it arrives," I spit.

My mother looks at me and smiles, "I love you, Lee."

Bile rises in my throat at the sound of her saying that. I am deeply hurt, and my response comes through gritted teeth. "That's a bit rich coming from a person who doesn't know the meaning of love."

I turn and walk out the door for the last time.

Sitting in my car, I need to calm my racing nerves.

Just breathe. Just breathe. Breathe. In. Out. In. Out.

My mind is racing. How can a mother do this? She has fired me from the company from the franchise group that I have built.

I have worked in my family's Gold Coast strip club for ten years. Ten years of giving every ounce of my energy, my love, and my commitment to my family. My blood family, but also my extended family. The girls. The bar staff. The security team. We are a tight knit group, we make good money. We work hard. We play hard.

And it wasn't just the club. I have been working on expanding it into a franchise. I have studied, researched, negotiated, found the right people, done the right deals. I was going to make her a lot of money.

My mother hasn't been part of the day-to-day running of the club for a long time, but now that most of the hard work was done for the expansion, she doesn't want me to be a part of it. She wants it all to herself.

I knew she could be ruthless. I have seen her caustic nature served upon others, but didn't know how soon I would experience it personally.

I start to cry. Damn, I hate crying. It is such a sign of weakness. Fucking tears streaming down my face.

I wipe them away with my sleeve as my uncle's words ring in my ears. *She did the same to me. She does it to everyone. Take no notice, she will want to be friends again soon.*

Not with me. This time, I'm done. Permanently.

Right now, I need to make phone calls.

I need to read the letters she gave me again.

I need to ring my son and text the other one in the UK.

I need to let everyone I normally do business with know that I am no longer there, and who they need to speak to instead.

Rove, my husband, is standing outside the coffee shop on the corner as I park. He is anxiously wringing his hands together, his brow furrowed beneath his mop of dark ringlets, his full lips pulled into a straight line and his green eyes are barely visible, squeezed into slits of anger.

We exchange a brief hug and he orders coffee. He knows I prefer not to be touched when I'm stressed. It only takes a moment of kindness and I will break – a lesson I learnt as a child.

I can't afford to break.

As I sip my coffee, still breathing in and out, the cavalry arrives. Fast and furious texts have been sent and calls have been made… and now my extended family are sitting around me.

"Thank you all for coming," I say, drawing in my breath to steady my voice.

Sound positive.

"You are all probably wondering what is going on, but I want to assure you that everything will work out," I reassure them. Maybe I am reassuring myself.

They are all looking at me, wide eyed, taking it all in, waiting to find out their fate. A voice comes from the back. John is my gorgeous first born, hair the colour of corn silk, with piercing blue eyes and fair skin. "Mum, what has she done?"

I steady myself, trying to keep calm. I'm not sure if this will be the last time I see him, once he realises the impact of today's events. He has always been very close to my mother.

"John, she fired me. She is taking the club and the franchises I have been working on. I hear my voice rise as I add, "Peter is back."

My brother Peter was close to John for a long time, and I watch it sink in, his eyes wide and wild.

"Yes, it will just be the two of them," I reply to his silent question.

Sitting at the table amongst this turmoil and hurt, anger and hatred is my delightful baby girl TJ, quietly colouring in, seemingly oblivious to the drama unfolding around her.

I smile at her. *This is why I keep going.*

The rest of the day is a blur. My phone rings continually as the news spreads.

Sitting at home, I make coffee and sit alone with my thoughts. Dark, tumultuous thoughts. A lifetime of abuse, fear, anger, guilt, hurt, and betrayal sitting in the pit of my stomach like concrete – too heavy to move, no tools to move it, too defeated to care.

I turn the shower on and sit on the floor still clutching my coffee, in the distance I hear the sounds of a wounded beast, a deep guttural sound, followed by blood curdling screams, loud gasping sobs. I can't work out where they are coming from.

Eventually the sound of sobbing subsides, and the room has fallen into darkness.

I finally recognise the sounds – they are mine.

I see no lights. I have no direction. My hero just betrayed me.

It seems ridiculous but I hear my religious upbringing echo in my head… *Just like Jesus was betrayed for 30 pieces of silver.*

I crawl out of the shower, my body aching. The pain is real. My chest hurts so badly I can hardly breathe. I can't focus. I reach the bed and climb in, exhausted.

I sleep.

The morning arrives to more messages and questions than I have answers for.

Every dancer and staff member has texted me.

Why is Peter here? We hate him.

Your mum said that TJ was sick and that you had to leave to look after her?

When are you coming back?

This is totally fucked, why are they here?

I can't read any more. I know if I answer and Peter and mum find out they will fire the girls.

I just can't do that to them.

Who will go to court with them? Hold their hands at the doctors? Teach them to change a nappy or sterilise a bottle? Who will protect them when the client becomes obsessed?

My heart breaks for them. There is no one to do this now.

I will never walk through the club again, the polished timber lined walls, jet black carpet, shimmering mirrors, the beautiful curved marble bars, the green and blue neon lights. I will never again sit and watch a lap dance, quietly thrilled by the hunger in the eyes and hands of those who have paid for the attention.

I need coffee, I need cigarettes.

My beautiful girls. I have worked so hard to build this family. Every one of us works together and cares for each other.

We have a uniqueness which is foreign to strip clubs. We are family, and we stick together to the end. We are The Paulies Girls.

I can't see them. I can't say goodbye. I need them to continue to look after each other. I can't guide them, support them, hear them, nurture them... They have been torn from my arms.

A fresh wave of pain washes over me.

Bloody Cruella de'Ville and her mean sidekick.

The loss growing, washes over me like a tidal wave sweeping me into another abyss. I can't find the surface. Where is the bloody door? I need out of here, mind racing, no answers, no solution.

Another lifetime passes. I need more coffee, more cigarettes.

I lost my childhood to my mother... her accidents, her bloody religion, the need for her parents to approve of her, even if it killed me in the process.

The lectures of the Jehovah's Witness leader run through my mind.

You aren't respectful to your parents, Lisa.

The scriptures say that if you are respectful, all will go well with you. It is the only scripture with a promise.

I was 10 years old, sitting in a room by myself while being told I will be destroyed at Armageddon for being a wicked child.

I had answered with one question, "So where does it say that parents aren't allowed to abuse their children?"

"Lisa, the scriptures don't say that, they only tell you as a child that you must be respectful."

My nan's voice echoed in my memory, "In Bible times they would have stoned you to death. Elija called the bears down to eat the wicked children. If we lived then you would have been eaten."

My father beat me, kicked me, punched me, locked me outside in the dark and screamed that he wished I had never been born, yet here... I was the problem.

I must be the problem. Even God doesn't like me apparently.

Well, fuck God too.

I will never cower to my father. I will never surrender. He may hurt me physically, but I am smarter and quicker than he is, and one day, I will win.

I make another coffee, my mind still filtering through my childhood memories, trying to piece this all together.

My beautiful mummy, her petite figure, blonde hair that is never out of place, eyes the colour of cornflowers and her smile, which lights up the world as she sings and dances. I used to watch her apply her makeup, mesmerised. I saw men look at her admiringly as we walked past. I will never be as beautiful as her.

Then one day, in the living room, a body stretched out on a mattress, a mangled body, dry blood, bruising, blue, purple, black, green, a swollen face, bandages... She is not recognisable. *What have they done to my beautiful mummy?*

Rove's cousin Lissie arrives upstairs, "Hunny, you look like death warmed up, would you like some breakfast?"

I shake my head. "Lissie, I have stood by my mum, all my life, haven't I? I have bathed her, fed her, toileted her, medicated her."

I thought back to her long stay in hospital, after the attack. "I sat by her bed for three months, day and night. I slept with my face resting on the stainless steel table she lay on. I held her hand and told her stories of her childhood. I relayed all our happy memories. I sang her favourite songs. I read her the newspaper every day...

...I have put my money into the company, my heart and soul. I have put myself last, my husband and baby girl last. And now I have no job. I have been cut off from the people I have worked with for years...

...Why would she do this?"

Lissie nods. She has seen my entire family, the way they treated each other and outsiders, the cold unrelenting viciousness which lays just below the surface. The pure narcissism, the fear of not having enough, the fear of being homeless, of being destitute. Every action, every choice, governed by fear or greed.

We are and have never been a family, we were raised in a war zone, we were survivors or victims. I am not sure at this point which one of us is the victim and which one the survivor.

My brother needs to have it all, my sister will befriend whomever she thinks will win and will take care of her.

It will be a very short amount of time and my brother will cut my mum out. Surely, she realises that?

I love Lissie. She diplomatically doesn't say a thing, and just places toast and fresh coffee in front of me.

"Lissie, today is the last day I am allowed to feel like shit. Today is my one day of mourning. Tomorrow I will build a dream, execute a plan and be bigger, better and far more caring than those cold hearted sub-human beings that were once my family."

Lissies smile lights my determination to stay strong, to press on. She, too, was raised a Jehovah's Witness. Funny, it takes one to know one, and only we who have shared their abuse and brainwashing tactics truly understand the mechanisms within our own thought patterns.

I take my moment to grieve and then I speak to my husband and our accountant.

Together, we are going to buy a strip club in Brisbane.

Our own club.

It's going to be amazing.

*

And it is.

Months later, I walk in the doors of the freshly decorated club, ready for its first customers.

Small and intimate, the walls are a criss cross of gold metallic paint, with black and gold carpet, leather lounges with soft velvet cushions and bunches of fresh flowers.

"I am going to make this the best family strip club in the country!" I say out loud to the girls who have followed me to my new venture. I know with the right level of nurturing the girls will be loyal.

We create a fantastic environment. It is cultured, nurturing, fun, and a whole lot of crazy. Our regular clients have tagged us 'The Cheers Bar'.

I have printed out a sign and stuck it on the wall of the staff room, as a reminder for myself and the hostesses:

> **Each girl leaves here better for the experience, gaining self-respect, resilience, self-worth, knowledge and acceptance.**

Fifteen hours a day, six days a week. I am feeling tired yet still excited every day, then out of nowhere my body turns into a traitor.

I am bleeding.

It is too heavy.

It lasts for weeks.

I feel weaker every month. This is not right. This is not how my body is.

I see my GP. "Lisa, this is normal for a woman who is 40," he says. I leave his office still not feeling right.

Two months pass and it's getting worse, I book into the GP, "I want an ultrasound, I need to know what is going on; this isn't right."

A week later, Doctor Dot clears his throat, "You have 19 tumours, seven at stage three."

I reach for my phone to call Rove. "They have found multiple tumours. I'll be okay. I'll have a hysterectomy."

Silence.

"I'll be home within the hour. We can talk then," he says.

A few minutes later, my mobile beeps, a message from Rove.

I look over at TJ and smile, thinking about my wonderful marriage to her father. I got it right this time. He is my soulmate, my best friend. We have never even had a cross word. He's worried about me. I know his text will say, 'I love you'.

I open the message and my smile fades. I hear my cry, "Noooooooo!"

I stare at the screen in disbelief.

I am sorry, this marriage is over, I can't do this anymore.

I call, I can hear him crying as he speaks, but I can't make sense of what he is saying.

TJ and I arrive home. I am in shock from what the doctor said, and now I have to go in and try and piece this back together.

I don't understand. I don't understand. I don't understand.

"Rove, I just need to know why, when, who?"

He is crying, and hugs me tight. "I am so sorry, but I just can't, I can't do the club, I can't do the boys, I just can't do us anymore. I still love you, but I just can't," he says.

The pain this time... this betrayal... it is worse.

Worse than my mother.

I thought I had felt the worst pain imaginable, but no, there was more pain to come.

I love him with my whole being. I don't want to live without him.

I can't let go, I can't be in the same room, the air has been sucked out of my lungs, out of the room. I gasp to breathe, unconsciously knowing I hve to, desperately wishing I could stop.

Numb from pain and disbelief, the same day as my diagnosis, my marriage is over.

We separate that day.

I pack my clothing and some of TJs clothing. We are moving to the Gold Coast again.

My voice hollow, empty, just a faint sound in the distance.

I can see that TJ is confused. I need to reassure her that all is normal. "TJ, you and I will drive up and see daddy on the weekends." She nods and returns to her game.

Every Friday to Monday we play happy families.

She hasn't been told yet that daddy has a new girlfriend.

She was one of my strippers, the very last person I thought he would fancy. I had no idea they had been an item for some time before he ended our relationship.

My mind is in turmoil, my sense of self totally destroyed.

Who am I?

What is my identity?

I have no need to go on, life is cruel.

Three betrayals in three years, I must be the worst person alive.

My brother, my mother, and now the love of my life.

The day of the surgery Rove drives me to the hospital. He looks at me with those killer green eyes and a crooked smile and asks, "Would it be wrong to wish you a happy anniversary?"

Tears roll down my cheeks. "Yes it would be wrong. It's not happy, is it?" We sit silently and cry together.

The operation is a success, I am sore.

Physically and emotionally, I am destroyed.

Every day I wait and wonder if today will be the day Rove comes home.

I take up residency in the rocking chair on the front veranda of my Gold Coast home, a large three storey, white-walled Spanish style house with large terracotta tiles and huge balconies front and back. The double staircase leads to Lissie's quarters and the spiral staircase to my room. The house is set back on an acreage block surrounded by trees. It is totally screened from the outside world.

My safe haven, my house of healing.

For a year I sit there, every day, looking at the big tree in the garden. The one the kookaburras sit and sing in every afternoon. "For an entire year that bloody tree hasn't grown even one inch," I point out to Lissie.

*

One hot summer's day, my phone rings. "You need to buy the Gold Coast Bulletin. There is an article about Paulies. They have gone into administration."

I should feel a sense of satisfaction. Yet, I feel the need to help them.

Over and over, I ask and I ask, yet there are no answers. I know they are out there – I just don't have them.

How stupid am I?

How many people are going to betray me?

Why am I surprised? There is something terribly wrong with me. My own mother can't love me.

Why do I take people at face value?

Why are people uncomfortable with my honesty?

Why are people reckless with other people's feelings?

When will I work it out that I am not good enough? No one will ever love me.

God, I don't even know if I like me.

Searching and reading, drinking and crying, sharing and laughing, laughing and crying all at once.

My mind, a constant whirlwind, yet on the outside I am calm, my voice is steady. Those close see death in my eyes, others are fooled by the smile.

I have regained my strength.

As I look back, I have acknowledged that it has been one hell of a journey.

I hear TJ laughing. My little girl playing and laughing, safe and happy in our hideout, wrapped in the walls of our make-believe palace.

"I can't believe it's Sunday night," I say to Lissie as we sit on the veranda. The air is cool. We have lit the chimenea and the flames flicker and dance off the white house.

I sit cradling my Royal Winton teapot, matching teacup and saucer, full of port. Lissie has her bottle of red wine.

I notice my tree. It has grown a foot, a whole bloody foot.

The night sky is ink black, it embraces me with its calmness and blocks out the rest of the world. A smattering of diamonds demands my attention. Lulling me comfortably into my own nothingness.

"Look," I point out to Lissie. It's a falling star, a light bulb moment, my pure clarity.

Excitedly, my voice rises and falls as I recap the memories, moment by moment.

"Lissie it all makes sense, why didn't I realise it before?"

Everything and everyone grows when they have the right circumstances.

A smile creeps across my face. I've got it. I realise there are people who feel I have betrayed them.

My honesty at times makes people uncomfortable. I need to be conscious to use soothing words, upbuilding and positive.

I hear my Pop say, "Sissy, you can't put an old head on young shoulders." I smile to myself as his words fall into place. You need experience and knowledge to understand why things happen.

People who have betrayed me have done so out of fear, or hurt, guilt or pain. Those who are too afraid to embrace their own pain inflict it on others.

I now feel sorry for those who never take the time to know who they are. Just as my Pop said, experience has taught me that kindness and compassion are the only emotions I need.

I have forgiven myself for expecting others to behave as I felt was right. I realise that what they did, even if it was unkind to me, allowed me to choose to walk or stay, be bitter and stunted, or be thankful and grow.

I finally realised that for every pain I have suffered I have also been able to create or accept opportunities for growth, for adventure, for new friends and new experiences.

In spending time with them, I could see my blessings.

Each person who has entered my life and inflicted any sort of pain has taught me something about me I didn't know or hadn't acknowledged.

That old saying is ringing in my ears, "We should count our blessings, but we should also make our blessings count."

So now what Lisa, now what are you going to do?

I see Lissie sitting, smiling, knowing. I smile back, comfortable in my safety, her love and support, my home of healing. "You know, I love my girls. I spend time with them every day, I happily share life skills and life lessons with them. I never judge them, I just nurture them."

Lissie nods, "I know you do. I have watched you for years give and expect nothing, you don't ever judge and even if you do, no one would guess." I smile at Lissie, she is my rock, my soul sister.

"Lissie, if it hadn't been for you and Tony, my ever so intelligent, witty youngest son, taking care of TJ and I, we would not have made it this far."

I was finally able to reveal my feelings out loud.

Because that's the secret.

We are here, to show love, kindness, compassion, wisdom, insight, acceptance, and damn, just be a good bloody person.

My mother's and Rove's betrayals allowed me to put myself first, to follow my dream.

I stand and thank them both. Without their pain I would not be standing here today, looking up at these huge sandstone arches.

My University. A big dream I had long ignored, until now. I will walk out of here in 13 months with an MBA.

Without their betrayal I would never have made the time to invest in me... Yet here I am, my whole body tingling. I pinch my leg to check it's not a dream.

God, that hurt! I laugh as I walk to my lecture room.

I forgive those who had inflicted pain on me.

I forgive them because I forgive myself.

CHAPTER 8

Awakening woman – from shame to freedom
Camilla Constance

"You're a slut, Camilla. Everyone says so."

His measured tone suggested concern. It said, "I am worried about your well-being." It was patronising. It was deeply dishonest. It was a candy-coated rock that landed in the pit of my stomach with numbing shame; shame I had been running from my whole life.

Part of me wanted to curl up and hide.

But another part, a powerful queen, roared inside, *"First they dragged us from our temples, then they burned us, and it's STILL not over!"* She raged at a society that still sought to control and limit me, to control and limit women.

Swallowing the pain behind my anger, I bit back the harsh words that would have stripped the flesh from his bones.

These occasional weekends together were too precious to waste, so choosing calm over fury, I breathed deeply, flooding my body with fresh oxygen, fresh energy, new and empowering belief systems.

"Who is 'everyone'?" I asked.

I didn't need to. I knew it was mainly his tight group of old school friends. I was too opinionated, too fiery, too passionate, too sexual, too intelligent, too quick witted, and never impressed enough by their entitled, mediocre, male selves.

"You know who, Camilla, people in my life......people I value even if you don't." His voice cracked a bit. It mattered to him that his people approved of me. He didn't want to defy them to love me.

In the beginning I hadn't challenged their authority, I was just another lonely woman in an unhappy marriage; low hanging fruit just waiting to be picked. He had picked the fruit with every expectation that I would seamlessly move from the home of one man into the home of another, kids in tow.

Fergus had relished being my knight in shining armour, waking me from my decade of darkness, quite literally, with a kiss. In these heady days of a new relationship it was tempting to convince myself that I would be happy in the new, shiny tower he offered me.

But I had also done far too much learning and growing to believe in fairy tales.

My journey of self-exploration had awakened a ravenous hunger for sexual freedom and adventure which, while challenging to his conventional vision, was completely essential to my growing identity as an independent and powerful woman.

I couldn't return to putting a man's comfort ahead of my expansion.

And I felt sure that my sexual magic would bind and strengthen us through all the difficulties ahead.

"Well, I can't control what they think of me, I can only control my behaviour and my choices... and right now my darling... I choose this."

I reached up for his lips and started nuzzling him softly. I moved my body against his, carefully brushing my hardening nipples against his skin, teasing his mouth open for longer, deeper kisses.

Our love making was indulgent and languorous. In the dark of the night, under the eaves of his little cottage, we dissolved into each other, banishing judgement and shame from the world outside.

With our sexual energies flowing around and between us, I whispered spells of enlightenment.

Our love would be expansive and freeing. Not for us the stale misery of control and possession, boredom and lies, jealousy and fear.

We would keep our beautiful and vibrant sexual relationship alive by granting each other freedom to explore and grow, safe in the knowledge that we would always have each other and our deeply honest love.

And in that final explosive moment Fergus cried out, "I fucking love you, Camilla."

"I love you too, Fergus" I replied, holding him tight, feeling him nest in the embers of our fire.

The glorious alchemy of his body, our words and our combined energies soothed me. I felt loved and safe. *This is where I belong*, I thought, and in his arms, to the sound of his contented breathing, I fell gently into sleep.

"Good morning, gorgeous." His smile stretched from ear to ear. He had a post-sex bounce in his step. He radiated relaxed confidence.

"Mmmmmm. Good morning, my love," I moved to sit up and receive my cup of tea, "I slept so deeply last night. You were amazing. Sex was sooo good."

"It's always good with you, Camilla," He chuckled. "I am intoxicated by you." His tone grew a bit more serious, "You break my heart and challenge me in ways that I don't always find easy, but we have a connection like I have never known and you drive me wild!" With that he jumped onto the bed with boyish abandon.

"Careful!" I giggled, mindful of the steaming liquid in my hands.

This was the man I loved. Relaxed, happy, confident, playful; free of the social judgements and constraints which seemed to choke him in his everyday life. My Fergus.

The man I alone held the key to.

As I took the last few sips of my tea, he slid down the bed, positioned himself between my thighs and started kissing me. I looked down to see him looking back up, all twinkly eyes and beautiful smile as his tongue awakened my body.

"Fuck!!!" He cursed. "Have you seen the time? I have a call with that coach and didn't you want to get home to see your kids before bed?"

"You crack on with your call, Fergus," I suggested. "I'll creep out when I am dressed and packed up...... I'll be as quiet as a mouse." Our eyes locked in amusement, we both knew discrete quietness was not my forte. "Promise."

As I tiptoed down the stairs, I heard that his Skype sesssion had started, a question coming out of his computer's speaker grabbed my attention; "If I could wave a magic wand, what would you desire from your relationship with Camilla?"

He barely hesitated before replying, "She moves here, sorts her divorce, gets a job... she'll be busy."

"And what does that gain you?" the coach asked.

"We'll be normal, like everyone else. I'll look after her,' he replied with blasé certainty. "She'll be content."

Normal??? He was given the opportunity to desire anything he wanted, anything. He could have chosen 'extraordinary' and he chose normal?!

My head throbbed. *Look after me?* A red mist consumed my body. I wanted to scream, to kick him, to pummel his normal chest, *I am not a child!* My queen roared, *I don't need to be looked after!!*

It was all a blur until I heard the familiar rattle and cough of my car's engine. I pulled out of Fergus' driveway and headed for home.

Home. Real life with the kids and my husband, Bill. I could feel my eyes welling up as the guilt of separation from my family overwhelmed me once again.

Bill had acted with incredible kindness and understanding when I had told him I had fallen in love with someone else. The pace of our separation was slow, deliberately so, to give everyone in our family time to adjust. We were doing it our way, with kindness and honesty.

It wasn't what I had expected when I married my university sweetheart. I had expected to be a loving wife and mother in the heart of a happy home. But we had failed to cherish each other as we threw ourselves into the overwhelming task of creating a picture book family life.

We lost each other as we strove, year after gruelling year, to meet completely unrealistic expectations, until eventually, we were two strangers sharing a house.

Every morning, as I dragged myself out of bed, I had fixed a determined smile on my face to hide the unbearable loneliness inside.

Every evening, as I did the washing up, I had gripped the kitchen sink, drawing on its solidity to strengthen the rod in my back. Rigidity became my safety.

Every bit of life was sucked from me: all of my vitality, spark, zest and spirit as I was pulled into a place of deep darkness. I hadn't wanted to go on.

A high brick wall on the school run had suggested itself as an easy way out. I could almost feel myself putting my foot down on the accelerator, turning the steering wheel ever so slightly to the right and shutting my eyes...

But I always had at least one child in the car with me.

My climb out of depression hadn't been a choice. It had been a necessity. I was responsible for bringing three young lives into the world and they needed a healthy, happy mum. Bill understood this better than most.

But was I now in danger of asking too much from them?

How can I take them away from their dad? Their home? Their friends? I questioned myself. *How can my love for Fergus withstand the pain we are going to inflict on so many others? And for what? For a man whose greatest desire in life, his magic wand desire, is fucking NORMAL?*

Normal... I had tried normal. I was terrible at normal. Or rather, normal had been terrible to me.

Normal was my father giving me away, a piece of property, to my husband in a ceremony presided over by yet another man.

Normal had dried up our sex life and any attempt to cherish me.

Normal had consumed every ounce of energy and happiness and joy I had ever had.

Normal had nearly killed me.

I had absolutely no desire to exchange normal with one man for normal with another.

"I want extraordinary even if he doesn't!" I shouted out loud for no-one and everyone to hear.

The striking outline of Dartford Bridge loomed ahead, the half-way point on my journey home, taking me from Fergus' world back to mine. They were distinct worlds though and as much as I loved my weekend bubble with him, how real was it to think we could turn an occasional bubble into real life?

My heart and body yearned to be with him. He made me feel safe in a way I had never felt before. Neither in my childhood nor in my marriage. I loved my children with a passion and a fierce resilience that had kept me alive during the darkest months, but I had never felt safe, not until Fergus.

But he wants me to be normal and normal isn't safe. Normal is an illusion. To keep the illusion we lie and lie and lie to each other. And deceive ourselves. For the sake of normal we sacrifice truth, self-acceptance and ultimately love. I can't live like that again.

Who gets to decide what normal is anyway?

I could feel the prick of tears against my eyelids. I needed Fergus in my life, but I couldn't see how I could stay alive in the life he desired for me.

Worse, I feared I could never be normal enough for him. When the thrill of the new relationship died off, as it inevitably does, I would still be too passionate, too loud, too opinionated, too sharp and always just too bloody sexual.

He was so kind and sweet, so utterly decent; he deserved to be loved by a gentle, normal woman, not someone as challenging and difficult as me.

"Mummy!!!" The children flew out of the door when they heard the car on the gravel. Dream, wagging her tail furiously, pushed them aside to greet me first. I had made it.

I relished the smell of freshly washed hair as I hugged their warm bodies goodnight, feeling myself melt into their trust. I loved these three children more than anything in the world. I vowed silently, again, that I would not cause them any pain in my bid for happiness.

I was tired when I finally got to bed. His last message of the evening said,

Goodnight my darling Camilla. IFLY. Fx

The morning was still dark when my phone pinged, waking me. In a sleepy daze I reached over to my bedside table, flipped it open and read,

Boof!! Good morning! I can't wait to see you my gorgalicious darling!! It's been such a long weekend without you sweetness. Xxxxxxxxxxx

Simon. The "problem". The man who saw a woman in chains and wanted her to be free.

Fergus hated Simon. "Find a hobby," he'd suggested for the long weeks apart. "Compartmentalise, it's what I do." He hadn't expected me to choose sexual exploration facilitated by the internet. But I have never liked team sports and knitting bored me.

I could have cheated on Fergus; it would have been far easier to cheat than tell the truth. It would have been normal to lie. It's what everyone did. But I had experienced the pain of half-truths and lies, and I didn't want that.

So, I chose honesty. It hadn't been easy. I had made mistakes. I was operating without a script and worse, against a sea of hostility. Normality, I discovered, had an army of defenders, including some of my closest family and friends.

*

"Come on kids, your bus will be here soon!!" Another frantic morning; none of us moving at the speed of the kitchen clock.

"Mum where're my shoes?"

"Snug? Dog bed?... Lunchboxes... TEETH... c'mon!"

At last they were all on their way in a flurry of coats, kisses and goodbyes. I watched them walk up the muddy track towards the village green before returning inside to tidy away breakfast debris.

20 minutes darling. Xxxxxxxxx

And then he was with me, his presence filling the kitchen. I flew into his arms and he held me as if I were the most precious being in the world. "I have missed you so much, my darling," he said squeezing me tightly. "Radio silence weekends are murder for me."

He manoeuvred my body out of the kitchen, up the stairs and into my bedroom. Within minutes he had removed my clothes, in a nanosecond he'd released the catch of my bra one-handed.

It was *his* trick; one he was ridiculously proud of. I loved his deftness and the fact that he had, at some point in his life, decided that this was an important skill to learn.

It was time well spent. It made me feel like a goddess.

I think it was on our third 'date' that I saw his soul. We had been in bed for hours enjoying the newness of each other and the powerful intensity we created between us.

Our eyes were locked as he moved, slowly, inside me. He was holding me with every part of his being as he gently released layer upon layer of trauma locked deep inside my body.

In a moment of complete surrender, my eyes fixed on his, I saw his pupils spring wide open into deep, dark pools perfectly ringed by a bright white light. I felt myself drawn into his inner sanctum. And everything was completely still.

Within minutes of the most profoundly spiritual experience of my life, I had had to race off on the school run. It was later that evening, as I cooked the children's supper, that my phone pinged:

> Today was exquisite. You are exquisite. When I made love to you this afternoon I looked into your eyes and saw straight into your soul. Xxxxxxxxx

I froze.

He'd had the same experience as me!

I stood and stared at my phone, hugging my still-tingling body with delight until the smoke alarm alerted me to the fact that supper was cooked.

A year on from that magical moment I was, if anything, even more intoxicated by his presence, energy, wisdom, and kindness. His path to my door had not been an easy one. I saw the pain etched in the lines around his eyes, but magically it had given him a curious mind.

My Mondays with him healed me, reset me, and made me feel that I could truly be accepted, and even loved, for the woman I was, rather than as the woman others wanted me to be.

"So how was Fergus?" He enquired as we drank coffee, our bodies entwined.

"The usual," I replied, unsure how much to disclose. "He reported that his friends think I'm a slut."

Simon let out a deep, pained, sigh. "Darling, I think, maybe it's time to understand he is never going to accept us." He took my face in his hands so that I was looking into his eyes. "Fergus is going to make you choose."

"But I don't want to choose!" I exclaimed, fighting back tears, indignant that any man thought he could assume control over me again.

"I know you don't, darling. But not everyone is as comfortable with different as you and I are," he said softly. "I won't make it difficult for you, my love." He did that thing that only he can do with me, he held my gaze and quieted my protest before it could leave my mouth. And then he kissed me.

Outside it rained, inside I danced in the light of our sex. My body tingled and pulsated all over as he pleasured me through wave after wave of orgasm, to that place where I experience myself as purely divine, where I feel at one with the Universe, with Spirit and with the deep yearnings of my soul. This was love, love for me, love for him, love for existence.

It was less than a week before I saw Fergus again. His text had read,

I have a job near you on Friday, can I steal you away for one night? Fx

I was in the kitchen when he arrived. I heard his car before the dogs did and rushed to the door as he stepped out of his old, battered VW. *"He looks so tired,"* I thought as I bounced towards him with a stupidly broad smile.

"Hi, Fergus," I heard the eldest say behind me.

"Hi, matey," replied a weary Fergus. I smiled; I loved that they all got on so well.

"Coffee?" I asked. He nodded, jaw clenched. There were no hugs. He didn't take me in his arms. He just sat down heavily at the table. My stomach knotted.

"How were your clients?" I asked breezily, desperately trying to earn a moment with his beautiful, twinkly eyes. Tortuously, he kept them down, fixed on his tablet, a barricade between us.

I pressed on with cooking. I loved having him at my table. Him, there, in the middle of all the hurly burly of family life. It felt so good. So normal! I could feel my body settling into the rhythm of domesticity. *I could actually do this,* I tried to persuade myself.

Once supper was served, I went up to my room to pack an overnight bag. Fergus followed me up and closed the door behind him. I thought nothing of it.

He sat on the chair in the corner of my room, not my bed. The knot tightened.

He hunched over and examined wringing hands. The tight knot had grown into strong cramps. My throat was dry.

"Camilla, I need to talk to you," he started in a pompous, strangled tone.

"Okay...."

He didn't look up. He carried on wringing his fucking hands. He was a pitiful sight.

"I can't go on. I can't do it anymore."

I froze. Fear draped its cloying cloak over my shoulders, eating its way into my bones.

"I love you, Camilla, but you are breaking me."

Fight, Camilla.

Make him see sense.

Talk him round, persuade him.

Make him love you again.

The voices in my head were loud, panicky. No part of me thought I could survive this. The cloak tightened its hold on my breath, my body, my heart. Fergus was my safe place. He was where I belonged. I would surely die without him.

"Camilla..."

Why the fuck is he using my name the whole time? He sounds like my mother, not my boyfriend!

I wanted to scream at him, "I am your darling! Call me darling!" But I was gripped by a frozen, stunned silence.

"Camilla, are you hearing what I am saying?"

His question required an answer, I gave him the only one I could muster in that moment, "I'll give him up," I whispered, "I'll be yours. I'll be whatever you want me to be."

He let out a long, pained, sigh. "We both know it's too late for that. If it wasn't HIM," he spat, "it would only be somebody else. It's too late for us, Camilla."

"All the promises... do they mean nothing?" I pleaded passionately, "All our plans, our dreams..." My voice petered out as I had the dawning realisation that he had never meant any of it.

He had allowed me to dream of a future with him which he had never intended to grant me.

It had all been lies.

"HAVE YOU EVER BEEN HONEST WITH ME?!" I screamed, launching myself at him.

"Camilla, calm down," his voice laced with fear.

"YOU HAVE NO FUCKING RIGHT TO TELL ME TO CALM DOWN, YOU MEASLY TOAD!"

The weight of the cloak dragged me down. I collapsed in a heap on the floor. I was vaguely aware of him stepping over me on his way to the door.

And then he was gone. My safe place walked out of my life without a single backwards glance.

On the night he left I remember the children coming to me, stroking my hair and comforting me until I was able to sit up. Then as they ran me a bath, they scurried around the house collecting every tea-light and candle they could find.

"I never liked him," declared the eldest. I knew he was trying to cheer me up and I loved him for it.

"Mummy, he was never worthy of you," my daughter said a little more diplomatically.

I was numb for so many weeks that I was grateful when the pain kicked in. At least I could feel something.

I walked. I cried. I wrote pleading letters I never sent. I filled page after page of my diary. I slept. I meditated. I self-pleasured, transmuting the agony of pain into the ecstasy of orgasm.

Simon came over whenever he could and held me as I cried. He has had more mascara on his chest than can be healthy for a man.

In Starbucks one day, my beautiful girl presented me with a pen and paper, and we wrote a mantra. We spent a summer dancing around the kitchen, laughing as we chanted these words,

I am beautiful

I am brave

I am loved

I am love

I am a FUCKING GODDESS!!

*

Christmas 2019, impatiently early, I knocked on Bill's front door. The youngest, rubbing still sleepy eyes, opened. "Mum, you're……..early?!" he exclaimed.

"What's this?" came an amused voice from behind him, "Your mother early? That's unheard of!" Bill, all smiles, hugs and handshakes ushered us in. "Happy Christmas guys, come in, come in."

His new kitchen smelt like Christmas, an evocative mix of pine needles, turkey roasting in the oven, strong coffee, and the latest addition courtesy of teenage boys: Lynx deodorant. We sat down at the old kitchen old table still marked by childhood projects.

"D'you take milk in your coffee, Simon?" Bill asked.

We ate delicious food, we drank a little bit too much wine, we played card games and charades. My heart was full to bursting as I soaked in all the love, laughter, friendship and family. I was where I had always wanted to be.

We are not a nuclear family according to the script. Instead, we are happy.

In the end I didn't have to choose between a loving family and my sexual freedom.

When I rejected the shackles of convention and stood loud and proud as a shamelessly sexual woman, I unleashed my true power.

A power that is kind, compassionate, patient, loving, brave, sassy and bold.

A power that is the bedrock of our genuinely happy family.

My fear of flying, my fear of truthful sexual expression, had brought deep unhappiness to myself, my husband and our children.

Then one magical year I owned my slut and freed us all.

CHAPTER 9

The monster in the room

Annette Densham

Curled up on a chair, lost in breadcrumbs dropped by Agatha Christie, trying to put together clues faster than her famous moustachioed Hercules Poirot, something catches my eye.

A movement.

Ever so slight.

A jerking motion.

Although I am unsure of what the movement is, my stomach rolls as if on a ship in the middle of a wild storm. My senses prickle, meerkat ready, poised to flee the stalking vicious hunter eager to tear flesh from bones.

"That's hit high in the air, down towards mid-wicket. Will it carry the boundary? That's six. What a fine shot..." Tony Grieg shouts in the background, as the battle rages between Australia vs England.

The hairs on the back of my neck prickle. That sick feeling you get when you know something is not quite right makes my stomach lurch. I look over hesitantly at my grandfather, the only other person in the room.

His eyes are slitted, lizard like, predatory and steely, focused on me, not on Greg Chappell as he approaches the wicket. Dressed in blue Speedos, and powder blue and white trimmed terry towelling short set, I feel more like a cheap bathmat, not an object of intense interest.

"Um... what are you doing, Pop?"

He ignores me. His right hand jerks up and down in his lap, his breathing laboured and hard, panting in a way I'd never heard someone pant before. Heavy. Frenzied. Steamy.

Frozen in place, I will the chair to swallow me whole, to get me away from the unit where we are spending our summer holidays. My eyes dart to the room my Nan is napping in.

Please wake up, please wake up, please wake up, I chant in my head, hoping she picks up on my fear and gets up.

My eyes are drawn back to Pop, in his chair. His movements quicken. His hand pumps, a piston on race car, speeding to the finish line. Peeking through his hand is his penis. Hard in his grasp. The veins popping out, throbbing, engorged with blood. Growing up in an all-girl household, men were an unknown quantity. I've never seen a naked male body, let alone an erect penis. My 12 years on the planet has taught me all men are good for is causing pain, hurt, and heartache.

His breath catches in his throat, a low, resonate moan escapes his lips. His body shudders. Shivers... and shudders again. Then stills. He sighs; his eyes heavy but holding me in his gaze, pinning me to my chair. Tears leak from my eyes, blinding me to his scrutiny of me, but I can still feel the intensity of his stare. Suddenly, the invisible hands holding me, trapped, let go.

Released, I flee to the beach, as if being chased by an army of zombies, eager to devour me.

I stay out until the sun hit the horizon, the last of its heat gone and the mosquitos start feasting, me as the entree.

Returning to our unit, on our first EVER holiday, I slink inside, a thief in the night, guilty, on edge, hoping to see my Nan in the same room. The fragile security I've built in my head, crashes around me like the massive white-tipped waves onto the beach.

I take refuge in the tiny twin room I share with my sister, curl up, tight, in a ball, locking out the world, a flimsy haven away from Pop's perversion.

What started as an idyllic Queensland summer has descended into turmoil and angst. My little heart broken, shattered like glass as it hit the ground, swept cavalierly off a counter. I try to reconcile the man I looked up to, with the creepy monster ogling me with his eyes as he vigorously masturbated. I have become a tasty, tantalising morsel, with my maturing body, perky, taunting buds for a dirty old man. The air around me, vacuumed into a void of uncertainty and fear.

*

Two years before, my breath had been stolen for a different reason. As we rolled down the long driveway, a majestic castle, framed by a big old pink trumpet tree and the crystal blue swimming pool twinkling in the hot Queensland summer, rose before me. Disguised as a two-story house, verandas gracefully looking over the front yard, the lush native bushes and plants welcomed us with overgrown, outstretched arms to our new home.

After years of bouncing between cockroach infested rentals, with blistered, buckled lino, Mum standing guard every night, to stop earwigs crawling over us and living with dodgy men my mother thought were 'father material', we had a place to call home. Finally.

"Get out of my way," I'd yelled at my little sister, as we jostled for pole position, eager to be the first in the front door, to get dibs on the best bedroom.

"Mmmmmuuhhhhhmmmm, Annette hit me!" she screamed, as I elbowed her in the ribs, my attempt to prevent her from getting in front of me.

For once, mum is on my side. "Annette gets first pick this time. You picked first last time," our referee declared. I shot my sister a triumphant glare.

"That's not fair," my sister whined.

"Yes, it is," I gloated. "You're adopted anyway so you don't really count."

She punched me hard in my right arm. Room selection forgotten as we declared war, again.

Up the wooden stairs, through the first living space, down the hallway, I paused at the doors of two bedrooms, side by side. My breath caught, "Wooooooooooowwwwwwww," a gasp of wonder exhaled from my throat. The room to the left was the most beautiful I'd ever seen. Three windows opened out, overlooking our new neighbour's front yard and a cul-de-sac surrounded by gum trees and paddocks.

While it was an ordinary room; four walls, windows, carpet and a door, just like any other in a suburban home, it was special because it was mine. All mine. My own bed. My own wardrobe. My own space with a door I could barricade against an annoying little

107

sister and a nagging mother. A place I could retreat to and bury myself in books and music.

This haven was made possible by my grandparents. My mum's parents. They sold their Tasmanian home to 'rescue' mum, a winsome gypsy on a hapless journey seeking peace and safety.

Some of my favourite memories had been holidays with our grandparents. Nan dressing us in our best to have morning tea with the CWA ladies, fawning over two little blonde angels. Trailing Pop as he tended his prized garden, pointing out the different plants. Swirling our hands in the pond, with warnings of not to lean too far in, in case we fell. Curling up in front of the fire, munching on crumpets and vegemite, as Nan read *The Jungle Book* to us.

My mum was a bit of a gypsy… moving from man to man after my father left when I was three years old. By the time I was 10, we had lived in over 45 houses. Some for as little as two weeks.

One night, mum sat us down. "Girls, Nan and Pop are coming to live with us. I've found two houses and you get to pick which one we move into," she explained.

"Really?" I breathed. "We get to pick?"

"One has a granny flat where I can live, and you girls will be upstairs with Nan and Pop, or the other one we'll all live together, and it has a pool."

"The one with the pool!" we both shouted. A no brainer decision: a house with the pool was the obvious choice…and it meant, finally, I would get my own room.

Moving in with my grandparents meant no more latch key kids and vegemite on toast and tinned tomato soup for dinner. It meant friends we could keep longer than a heartbeat. A real Christmas tree. Posters on the walls.

Nan and Pop were our lifesavers. A haven. A place to have a 'normal' childhood instead of the chaotic and violent filled one we had lived in our short years; Mum sought safety and refuge in the male kind, often to her detriment… and ours.

Every afternoon when I arrived home from school, a yummy treat – Iced Vo Vos or homemade tea cake – was waiting to be scoffed down, dinner on the table at 6pm and my new blue Holly Hobby bedspread, in my freshly painted room with its cream coloured walls and matching curtains. I'd pinch myself to make sure it wasn't a dream. We made friends with the kids in our street, enjoying afternoons of front yard cricket and Marco Polo in the pool, and caused havoc by damning the creek trickling at the end of our street.

It was our sliding door moment. We'd weathered being dumped by our father; the man who said he loved us, chronic health issues (that's a whole other story), a string of abusive and violent men, and fleeing halfway across the country from my birthplace in Tasmania to Queensland, to this place of safety.

The magnificent home, with the swing set in the back, abundant passionfruit vine regularly sucked dry, and our own rooms, was the doorway that let the biggest monster of all into our life. Our grandfather.

In the summer of 1982, the monster, who had laid dormant as he quietly scoped out his prey, reared his ugly head. Not in an act of outright violence or aggression, but like a slow festering tumour, eating away the body's organs, insidious, terrifying, and uncontrollable.

The holiday, at Caloundra, in a unit situated moments from the beach, started out as idyllic as I could have imagined. Waking up to the peaceful sounds of waves hitting the beach, catering for ourselves (Nan was the queen of offal and leftovers), roaming the beach, collecting shells, and building sandcastles, until the sun set. It was the most exciting thing that had ever happened to us.

After a couple of days of frolicking in the sun, the rush of excitement dissipated, and afternoon naps were in order. Except for me and Pop. He was keen to watch the cricket as Nan and my sister dozed in their room. In the chair, opposite Pop, I was in prime position to be the object of his lecherous focus.

*

Our beach holiday ended with a quiet drive home. For me, I came home a different person. The energy was sapped from my soul as I wrestled with how to handle what had happened. I dragged my feet through the screened-off patio where we often had afternoon tea, Iced Vo Vos and lime Cottee's cordial.

The house had changed. Life took on a different light; the rose-coloured glasses warped into dirty sepia tones. What was a sanctuary, had become a prison. I started to notice the whispered fights between mum and her parents. To feel their judgement and disappointment in mum, palpable, a cloying cloud of poisonous fumes.

Her room, a Pop-homemade screened creation, at the front of the house, away from the rest of the family, reminded me of

Flowers In The Attic; a family imprisoned in an attic, hidden away from the world. It was bitterly cold in the winter. Mum, under the covers in bed at eight at night, layered with clothes and her red and blue trimmed fleece dressing gown, because it was too cold to sit on her chair.

There were shadows everywhere; dark, gloomy corners, crawling with uncertainty and looming disaster. My only mission was to never, ever be alone with my grandfather. It consumed me. But Pop was everywhere, a malignant presence, trying to get me alone.

As a kid, I loved reading Agatha Christie and Nancy Drew novels. I inhaled them. Books were my best friends. They didn't judge or criticise. They never made you feel unsafe. And they were great teachers. I would get Nan to take me to the library so I could research spies and strategy.

I got good at avoiding Pop. Where he was, I wasn't. If no one was home but him, I'd be somewhere else. I joined Little Athletics and trained regularly to be gone in the afternoons. I went to swimming training. I was at the neighbours. I roamed the neighbourhood, getting home as the sun slid beyond the horizon. I made friends with the neighbourhood boys; who made me feel safe; their token sister. Just to not be alone with that man.

That once golden cave, the room of my dreams, was now a fortress. The door, a barricade, protecting my virtue. I was sure if he got his hands on me, nothing good would come from it.

Starting high school meant the walk to school took twice as long as primary school. A blessing in my book; I was gone from the house longer. As I set off to school that first day, in 'the frog suit'; an ugly green uniform with pointless tartan sewn-on tie and heavy material that did nothing to hide the growing sweat marks under the arms from the steamy Brisbane summers and my Princess Diana haircut, I was eager to make new friends and see my primary school pals.

It had been a lonely Christmas break, spent locked in uncertainty and fear. Knowing what Pop did was wrong but that saying anything – dropping a bomb like that – would wipe out civilisation. I was desperate to tell someone, to share this dirty, terrifying secret, so that I was not alone.

Life ambled on. I stayed out of his way. I tried to stop kissing him goodnight; a ritual in our house. "Goodnight, Nan." Kiss on the cheek. "Goodnight, Pop." Kiss on the cheek. My goodnight kiss for him was the barest touch my lips on his suntanned, weathered cheek; swooping in, a ninja with a feather touch. His smell sickened me; Brylcreem, wood chips from his lathe, soil from pottering in the garden and Peter Jackson dark blue cigarettes. A pungent, stomach-turning stench.

"Night, Nan. Thanks for taking me to softball today." She was sitting on the olive-green fabric couch with the wooden arms, popular in the 80s, knitting, readying bits and bobs for the church fete. I walked purposefully towards the hallway.

"Night, Pop," I added brusquely. My foot had barely touched the section of carpet, in the hall, leading to my room.

"What about Pop?" Nan asked. I had nothing. The words I wanted to say caught in my throat, a tangle of fish bones silencing me. I kissed him on the cheek.

In the years Pop tormented me, he'd never said 'Don't say anything.' It was a given. I instinctively knew saying anything would cause too much pain and strife for Mum, and I was prepared to carry that for her.

My efforts to avoid Pop were not always successful. When it rained or I had to carry too much to school, Nan would get him to drive me. I would protest, happy to walk, desperate to walk but unable to offer a reasonable excuse. She'd insist – I suffered horribly with recurring ear infections and Nan didn't want me to get sick.

The first time I'd been alone in the car with him, without the rest of the family, I hopped into the grey Holden Premier, with its bucket seats and gear stick on the wheel, in the front. Click, clack went the seat belt, forgetting I'd be sitting arms reach from him.

Left out the driveway, now bordered by pristine gardens with trimmed, well-kept bushes, tended with dedication and love from Pop, we headed to school. I was late, flustered and totally engrossed in the latest Stephen King novel, *Pet Sematary.* I'd moved on from Agatha Christie, finding her stories vanilla after reading *Salem's Lot*, quickly followed by *The Shining.*

Flicking through pages as fast as I could, eager to finish the chapter before I get to school, I hear zzziiiiiipppppppp from the driver's seat. Keeping my head straight to the front, fixated on the journey, I looked out of the corner of my eye. Pops penis was hard, enveloped by his left hand, with his right hand gripping the steering wheel, as we cruised down the long street to school. His movements frenzied, time is short before gears need changing or lights turn red. He came in his hand, using his handkerchief to clean his mess... and drove on as if nothing happened.

"Where do want me to drop you?" he asked.

"I don't care. Anywhere. Here," I blurted.

"Do you want me to pick you up after school?"

"No." It was all I could do not to vomit.

He pulled into the dusty dirt driveway between the senior's hall and our family church... the other side of where I needed to be. The car had barely stopped before I fled, racing as fast as I could, as far as I could, to get away from him. Shaken, I locked myself in the dingy toilet stall, its walls etched with 'for a good time, call ....' 'Tina is a slut' and love declarations 'Jody loves Tim,' sobbing, sick to my stomach and mentally beating myself up for being so stupid.

Lesson learnt. Back seat. Right behind him so he couldn't see me in the rear vision mirror. Scooch down. Out of sight.

He still wanked on the way to school when he drove me by himself. He never said anything, and he'd always try to catch my eye in the rear vision, getting off on my fear, as I made myself as small as I could.

My schoolwork suffered, from an A student to who-gives-a-shit, talking back in class, smoking down the creek, stealing money from Mum and Nan's purses, stealing from shops, wagging school and being the queen of detention. No one seemed to notice. The festering shame and guilt, eating me up from the inside, hurt. It hurt deep into my still growing bones. Tangled sheets and haggard eyes in the morning, dreams too horrible to remember, haunted me throughout the day.

The end came after Nan and Pop returned from their Sydney road trip.

It'd been Mum, my sister and me for a month. Bliss. Peaceful. Calm. Safe.

When Nan and Pop returned home, Mum changed. I have no idea what happened, but she took it out on my sister and me. It went on for weeks; picking at us for every misdemeanour – beds not made with nurse's corners, dishes not washed properly, grass on the floor, toothpaste in the sink. She'd scream at us like a banshee. Not talking to us for days, ignoring us when we'd say good night.

One night, I'd had enough. I was tired of being her punching bag.

"AaaaaaNNETTE," she screamed.

I knew I was in trouble. I was normally Annie. I racked my brain, trying to think what I'd done wrong.

"Yes, Mum," I called from my bedroom.

"Get HERE!"

I dragged myself reluctantly to the kitchen, her glare laser like, cutting and harsh. She's a rigid, size 12 steel pole. I waited for her to acknowledge me.

"Why have you not dried the bench?"

"I did."

"You did a shit job. Look at it. Look AT IT!" She screamed the last two words at me.

I snapped. "Shut up. All you do is yell. You don't care what happens to us. You made us live with a dirty old man who can't keep his dick in his pants…" The words poured out of my mouth, cascading off my tongue, bitter, painful words trapped too long in the cage of my mind.

The reprimand she was about to lash at me gets caught in her mouth. She stopped. Blinked. Gulped a breath in, "What did you say?"

It spewed out of me, all the things Pop had been doing, in body-wracking sobs. Snot dripped from my nose, sopped up by my shirt sleeve, rivulets of tears soaked the neck of my t-shirt. I collapsed onto the floor, a wrung-out rag, spent.

She gathered us into her arms. "I'll fix this," she said.

Within a week, we'd packed and moved into another rental in the same suburb.

Life moved on. It always felt to me the whole thing was swept under the carpet. Nothing was ever said. We never talked about it. Never addressed it. As if words would feed the evil as breath does lungs starving for oxygen after being underwater too long.

*

Pop was diagnosed with cancer in the 90s. It has been many years since I thought of him. After we left, I had little to do with him. Just the thought of him turned my stomach.

I made a promise to myself I would never let what happened to me and my sister happen to my children; that they could always tell us anything. Secrets are cancer that infects lives; festering, leaching colour from the other chapters of life. No matter how painful or destructive the secret is, the light must shine on them.

Mum rang one afternoon. I was at my desk at work.

"Poor old Billy is dead," she said. "Pop is gone." The cancer had taken its course.

"Good," I said. "I hope he rots." I hang up, not wanting to indulge in the fakery of lamenting the passing of this horrible human. Conversations with other family mourning his death made me cringe as they waxed lyrical about what a good bloke he was. My nan had taught me, "If you don't have something nice to say, say nothing at all." I honoured her wisdom and said nothing.

*

I grew up in a family who embraced the old Victorian ways of sucking up the bad and negative, putting on a brave face and getting on with life, regardless of how the poison festered inside.

If life is a roller coaster, then the first 25 years of my life was the scary loop-da-loop. I made terrible choices that changed the course of my life.

Despite the pain and turmoil of my younger years, I always see the good in others, which is probably why I got taken advantage of so often. I have an enduring faith in other humans and look at the world through rose coloured lenses. I always felt I should have been more damaged, but I guess when you grow up rough, one more dint in your armour is just another dint in your armour. If the armour holds and life's axe cannot cleave a gaping hole in your torso, you can get on with living. That I did. I found joy where I could and enjoyed the moments of light, despite the darkness that lingered in my heart.

My life changed when I met my now husband, Earl. I was 25 and had decided there were no good men out there and if I was still single by the time I was 28, I would pack my bags and travel the world seeking adventure and mischief.

The universe works in mysterious ways... or does it? I found a good, loyal and honest man. I took him to meet Mum and she called me after. "He's really nice. Maybe too nice," she said. I laughed. It was ironic that Earl being 'too nice' triggered warning bells for her; I don't think any man had ever been nice to her.

We've been married for over two decades now and have two sons – Zayde and Qwyn. We have our moments but still love being with each other and fill our time together with rock concerts and festivals, comedy, and travel. We're secretly waiting for our kids to be gainfully employed so we can leave home and backpack around the world.

When my first son was born, almost 20 years ago, I realised I did not want the past holding my future hostage. I had lived through a lot in my short life and I knew I didn't want to be like my mother.

I invested in personal development. Despite it being through the notorious Amway education system – and I hated the 'happy clapping' – I got so much out of the books and CDs they recommended.

Don't get me wrong; I hated Pop for a long time. I was glad he died. Yet, I wouldn't be the person I am now if I hadn't lived through him.

It was enlightening to delve into all the ways I had sabotaged my past because of THAT moment in my life. I realised the damage my mother had inflicted on my sister and I with her choices. That without intending to, her decisions had consequences on our lives long past our childhoods – the men we had relationships with, the alcohol and drugs taken, and the choices we made that left a lot to be desired when it was our turn to adult.

The chapter of my life with my grandfather is only one chapter in my life. There are so many more that are filled with good times, great friends, and momentous moments. The biggest lesson life has taught me is my story shapes me; it doesn't define me.

The past 25 years have not been all sunshine and rainbows; bad things have happened; but I am better equipped to weather those storms. I am stronger, more resilient, and can find the funny in just about anything life throws at me.

I have two children who are healthy and well adjusted, a happy marriage, and a thriving business. I can't help but pat myself on my back and think...

You've done good, girl.

CHAPTER 10

Un-broken

Ivan Brewer

I don't remember a time before pain.

My life is lived in vignettes. In impossibly slow, blinking torments, changing scenes randomly from one to the next. A somnolent daze lived to the metronomic rhythm of medication like the casual echo of a ticking clock.

Wake up. Tick. Pain meds. Breakfast. Tock. Happy pill. Lunch. Tick. Pain meds. Dinner. Tock. Pain meds.

A clawing, breathless, suffocating reality, replete in Penumbral darkness, darker than dark.

Time meanders marked out in random stakes and the anniversary of my death. I feel so alone. A cocoon filled with nothing but endless pain, reverberating, tolling without end.

I lay alone, in a darkened room, decrying everything that is lost to me, my hopes, my dreams, my aspirations. My image of what I thought life would be. My image of who I thought I could be. Alone whilst my wife and children's life continue, without me.

How I hate this room. How I hate to lay prone 20 hours a day, a prisoner of my bed, a prisoner of my life. I am so tired; I can't sleep. I haven't slept more than four hours a night for a year. How I crave it. Peace.

How I pray to close my eyes and never wake up. How I pray for an end, as I close my eyes and dream of taking a life. My own...

As I stand still, the early morning sea breeze buffeting me, a gentle daggle of salty water upon my pain creased visage, the memory of my darkest days feels close at hand in the pre-dawn light. The memory of ending my life being more palatable than living it.

The first tentative hints of a new day often remind me of those terrifying months after my surgery, and today is one of those times.

The sunrise reluctantly unfurls its promise and I turn to plod unsteadily upon the wind-swept sand; blood red and black like a gushing wound, the new light wrestling with the old shadows.

Quite the metaphor for my life I realise; where I have come from. What I have gone through. What I go through. I can taste it still, the urgent, palpable need for an end, but it has forever lost its allure.

I rarely walk in the morning. The pain is high, and it confuses the rhythm of medications that ebb and flow through my veins.

But sometimes I do, just to prove to myself I can.

A wave breaks thunderously upon the foreshore's pediment, tessellating the shining rock with foam, streaming away into the early morning darkness. The first hints of the sun's rays a gleaming, glittering mosaic.

It is beautiful.

I breathe long and deep of the salty air, a soft moment in a long run of hard days.

I remember asking "why" not so long ago; why me? A desperate, feckless shout into the void. But I received no more than its caress in reply. Not even judgement.

The fickle tempest of Fate owes no answers.

Today is a milestone day; one to ruminate upon, and mark in passing. It is the last time I will see my specialist, as my care is coming to an end. It has been more than two years, but time has passed in bitter spurts and stalls, and I have little to no sense of it at all.

I know now that I won't ever get better. I know now that despite the pain of recovery, despite the commitment to rehab, that no matter what I do, I can never escape. Pain is my new reality, my every day, my every waking moment, without end. My pain is chronic and it all but consumes me, a livid, vivid nightmare weighing upon my shoulder.

I remember the last time I saw him. It was a bitterly cold, wet winters day, and his opening words will forever echo in my mind.

"You are lucky to be alive."

My wife gripped my hand a little tighter.

I hadn't known what to do with lucky; when every waking moment is filled with unbearable pain and suffering it echoes a little hollowly.

"Get to be alive" was more apt, I had thought.

He was peering at the latest MRI image, his crystal blue bespeckled eyes sympathetic to what he saw.

"Here you can see the screws, and the pins; they look great," he continued, "You can see the bone growing over the "scaffolding" here, and here. I'm very happy with that. You are healing well."

"It was a success then?" I had asked.

"The surgery went well, but no, we didn't get the result we were after, did we?" he replied solemnly.

Wincing as I shifted in my chair for the 20th time,

"No, I guess we didn't."

It had been six months then. Six months since I had woken to find myself enshrined, captured in this tortured and wretched intimate embrace.

Seeing the network of metal in the back of my neck had made it very real. I tried to speak, but my voice broke with emotion and no words escaped my lips.

Can I pick up my son?

I had been sternly warned that if I walked hand in hand with my son or daughter, and they tripped and fell, I had to let go. If I didn't, I would tear the network of metal out of my neck. I could lift no more than the weight of a bottle of milk, and even then, not without pain.

Tears flowed as I managed the second time to ask my question.

"Yes," he answered. "You probably couldn't damage it now if you tried. Though I don't suggest that you do."

"But why does it still hurt so much?" my wife had asked in a whisper.

He didn't know.

I rushed home, cheeks damp still, to collect the kids from school. It's something of a blur, but I do remember, in stark detail, the moment I crouched down, the moment I reached out. The moment I picked up my son, the warmth of his embrace, the tickle of his messy blond hair against my cheek. His cry as I stood, his feet dangling.

My overwhelming love for him was finally made real.

Time had stopped. Oh, how I had missed that. Something so simple, something so mundane. Something I had expected to be months away still.

In that instant I felt something, something beyond my pain-bound reality. The softest mote of hope, the knock knocking against my walls, a delicate whisper from beyond. I felt my son's heart beat against mine, and the brutal dissonance of my pain quietened just a little, a gentle note of joy heeded in its place.

That was truly where my story begins. The story of my rebirth, of my recasting. In acknowledging the battle which lay glistening in tears and torment before me. With the dimmest glimmer of joy amongst the darkness of absolute despair.

My son has been a talisman throughout my recovery. He was just five when I was rushed into surgery. He didn't, couldn't understand what was happening. The day after Anzac Day he came in tow with my wife and daughter to see me.

His little face fell apart, his eyes a-glaze, his easy swagger stopped mid-stride. I will never forget the moment he first saw me. I had piping and monitors everywhere, lay in a morphine daze, pain etched deeply upon my face.

I was barely conscious.

My daughter pushed past him, and came to my side, hand thrust into mine. She was all smiles and caring, unperturbed and unchanged.

"Hi Daddy," she said, full of life and innocence.

She never left my side. Every day after school she made my wife take her to see me, and she stayed as late as she could. My son never returned. This wasn't what his Daddy was supposed to look like.

Two years; a long time and none. It was a dream that saved me. As I wished with all my soul for succour, I had awoken with a gift.

Upon waking, I understood that my life no longer belonged to me; it was mine to give, but no longer mine to take away.

It belonged to my wife, to my young son, to my daughter. It was theirs now. And forever.

This new perspective has subtly changed the trajectory of my life. It no longer led inexorably to my death, to a surcease of suffering. If I am to live, I thought, it must lead me to endure. It must lead to more.

And it has led me to the question I have been striving to answer ever since... but how?

Pain and trauma have changed me irreconcilably. Yet the idea of me, my internal reference point, the image I had held in my head of who I was, had not changed. This template was for a fit and athletic man. If I was out of shape, I would simply gravitate back to my ideal. I would play sport, throw myself into activity. I would expend energy and focus, and I would again return to that ideal.

But this anchor, this subconscious representation of myself is no longer possible.

This was what I could never be again. I was changed, forever imperfect and flawed. This 'template' had not just eroded and aged, it was utterly destroyed. It no longer existed. Could not ever exist again. That version of me, that very definition of me had died the day of my surgery.

I truly, deeply hated what I became. I couldn't look in a mirror. I couldn't look upon my weary visage. I had stopped shaving. It was too painful anyway, and I no longer wanted to recognise the face peering back at me. It was a year before I shaved again.

I had died, but I had nothing to replace 'me' with.

I had not consciously understood that at the time; I was mourning everything that was lost to me. Existing in the in-between of where I was and where I thought I had to be.

The space my lost self left became an opportunity for me to be born again. To recast, to reform what was possible; a new, empowering and enervating self-image I could strive to meet, I could strive to become, and be constantly moving towards.

This was a tremendously empowering existentialist realisation. It made me present; I turned my head from the magnetism of the past, to live unapologetically in the now. My language changed. I no longer think of what I can not do, but contrive to ask "how?" How can I do the things that are meaningful to me?

This was my rebirth. It was a rend in the veneer of my pain. And I had but to tear it open...

A woman and her dog jog towards me, a dark shape against the emerging blue-bright sky. She stumbles upon the sand, and pants, her mid-sized dog, a silhouette in the soft light, looking up at her in admiration. I can't help but smile; if love could be personified, there it was leaping and tugging upon its lead.

Running is something no longer afforded me, and I sigh in ironic lament; I always hated running. But it tastes differently when I can no longer sample its bitterness.

I remember with a smile telling my Physiotherapist that I couldn't and wouldn't be doing her exercises anymore. The surprised, and then delighted look upon her face. I had learned that baking bread was better suited to me; its insistence to keep to a schedule regardless of how I was feeling made me progress.

Functional rehab she had called it.

I had no idea what I was doing at first, had only a cheap and dusty $70 mixer that had never seen daylight, but I began anyway. I purchased a Kindle version of Paul Hollywood's book *How to Bake* and was hooked.

Within days I had purchased a bread tin and within weeks was making bread from scratch. Within a month my family no longer purchased commercial bread and two years later I bake four to five loaves of bread every week. Baking became the nexus of my rehabilitation; post-surgery I had lost all the muscles in my upper back and neck. I had no trapezius, and the absence of these supporting muscles meant the screws and pins in my neck worked alone.

Baking is terribly painful, but the rewards I receive far outweigh the cost. I learned to time my bake so that a fresh loaf of bread would be coming out of the oven just before the kids came home from school. Both under the age of ten, they argue for their turn at the crust, and make such a fuss about how much they enjoy the still warm slices of bread. They give me a role to play. I am no longer just my injury. I have become our family's baker.

Baking became my rehab. It was only a short 15-20 minutes of actual hands on kneading in a three to four hour process, but when bread needs to be leavened, proofed, knocked-back, baked and pulled from the oven I had to do it, regardless of the pain. It was the perfect rehab schedule. Within months I had rebuilt some of the muscles in my neck.

This came to represent the return of my recovery into my hands. I had begun to break free of the iron-cage and take control. I had changed the paradigm, and there was no going back.

My medical team was becoming a circle of sub-contractors in my mind. They worked for me. And I had little patience or forgiveness; they either served me and aided my respite, walked beside me in my recovery, or they were fired.

I was finally regaining some control; less a piece being moved around someone else's board, and more chartering my own destinations.

My trauma connects me, it binds me to those I am near. I am hyper-sensitive, existing within this ecosystem of emotions; a boiling, roiling turmoil.

Stress is a terrible burden I can not bear to bear. My own, or that of those around me.

Pain empowers moments and tries to define and make them permanent. This is a ready danger, as my life can personify the pain I experience; I become a victim, a martyr. Noone else can deserve more pity or sorrow. Noone else can experience more suffering.

I don't complain. I don't want to be defined by what has happened to me, nor by what I can no longer do. I fight to define myself, and be defined by others, as more than just the trauma I have experienced.

So, I choose to no longer live to the beat of another's drum. To instead always seek my own cadence. My own rhythm. I can no longer be my giving self, as the price of admission is simply too high, and I have such a small amount on offer.

Another bitter-sweet lesson learned the hard way.

I have forced myself to shift, no matter how unnatural, to become beholden to no other, but to myself and to those that matter most. My life is now more like a series of transactions where I inquire the price before I buy; I invest pain and get a reward or return. I have too little to waste.

It may be intellectual, emotional or spiritual. Out of necessity, I can no longer do that which offers me nothing. The only exception is my immediate family circle; my wife and two young children. But they are a precious and constantly giving joy all by themselves.

I had learned so much, but pain was my final battlefield. Surprisingly enough, it was beauty wherein the answer lay.

Pain and trauma colour my life, and I exist a step removed from reality. I don't have direct access to it and the world is not at all as it seems to be to me. I often mistake what I see and experience, filtered through my altered state, for reality as it is.

This is both an opportunity and a torment, for if reality is adulterated, I have the power to change it too. I can choose what it is that I see.

Pain batters me, washes over me wave upon wave, a brutal oscillation, an undeniable force. My pain never ends, can never end. It is me who must change in response to the pain. Even though I am a vessel sealed tight, and nothing gets out, I realised I am porous inwardly, open and diffuse; Pain cannot escape, but I have discovered how some succour can seep in.

I have discovered that an endless array of beautiful moments exist but a step beyond my preconceptions of reality. To engage them, to be free for but a moment of my torment, to find again a taste of my blissful dreams, I am learning that I must 'unself'.

Philosopher Iris Murdoch defines what we call beauty as "an occasion for 'unselfing'." She writes:

> *"Beauty is the convenient and traditional name of something which art and nature share, and which gives a fairly clear sense to the idea of quality of experience and change of consciousness. By giving attention to nature we can clear our minds of selfish cares."*

This meeting of the natural world on its own terms detaches me from my daily life. 'Unselfing' was another powerful revelation. It bound together so many disparate elements of my palliation into an at-hand assuaging salve to be applied when needed.

As Murdoch prescribed;

> *"Take a self-forgetful pleasure in the sheer alien pointless independent existence of animals, birds, stones and trees."*

I had discovered that the key to unlocking myself, the key to my un-becoming, existed without. With my inner 'self' becoming 'unselfed'. Through an agency entirely beyond me.

For pain screams a little less loudly when I become lost to it in the natural world's glorious symphony.

My search for solace grew, and I found it again in art and its implicit escape.

Art has brought me closer to the truths I chose about myself. Its munificence is a manifestation of freedom which steals me from my pain-chained daze. It sets me free. It makes life bearable, it provides a pause, a stillness, to which to escape. For when I was truly enraptured in art, be it man-made, or natural beauty, it would not be denied.

And the pain waned.

Music has an undeniable power to move me, to open my heart and take me otherworldly to a place I can never see on my own.

My pain is muted, its screeching decibels dulled when I am captured by music, and I seek it out in my most telling times. To exist outside of myself, for but a moment, is a most glorious respite.

I have reframed my moments of pain to be fragile and short-term. They will no longer define me. Even were they last weeks at a time, my chosen reality is now what I move towards.

I now live my life deliberately. Consciously. I refuse the banality of Pain. I choose, for without choice I become what I am by default – broken. I have promised myself that my disability will be the best thing ever to happen to me. I have promised myself it is a gift.

Intense physical and psychological trauma is seared into my soul; a dark, miserable stain upon the very essence of 'self'. It will never fade; it will never leave. And whilst I can never be 'fixed' I have chosen to be un-broken.

Where does all this leave me today?

Out in the open.

I am far beyond the expectations of the medical team and the specialists around me. I am unfettered and free. My pain is permanent, my disability severe, but my function, that which I can do, is limited only by me; my tolerance of pain and perseverance through the day to day.

I fight my body daily, hourly, minute by minute, and I always lose. I spend my reserves wantonly, with reckless abandon, and I am punished. With ruthless efficacy.

My spinal cord is permanently damaged. It bears the marks of a 3cm long compression so severe it was less than 1mm from severing completely. I have been gifted with an impossibly rare disease, which turned the ligaments in my neck to bone, and which steadily compressed my spinal cord to all but a slither.

I should not be alive.

But I get up again. I rise. Always battered and bruised. Calluses earned, blistered returns on tenacity, worn like a torn and tumbled cloak.

To fight once more.

I have grafted my former goals, from my past life onto this one, and have found some new; I crave to do a PhD in Hospitality, I want to sing in front of an audience, I want to master professional public speaking, and I want to continue to write.

I want to help others master a life of misery, a life simply not worth living, and to thrive. For if I can climb out of the depths of the abyss, others can too.

There is nothing more my specialist can offer me, but good luck. It has been an intimate journey we have shared, and as I turn once more to the blinding dawn, I know I am ready. I am ready to walk along, without him. The ready embrace of my family is all I need.

I have long hidden in the shadows; it is past time I cast them.

CHAPTER 11

Why me, why not me?
Bisi Osundeko

"Please wake up, my waters just popped," I say with a sense of urgency.

My husband Mayor rolls over and rubs his eyes. "Water?" "Water?" "Which water?" he asks.

"Look, dear, this is serious," I say, and emphasise pointing to my protruded belly which is fast deflating.

He sees the soaking wet towel. "Oh my God, what happened, Bisi?" he asks.

"I can't feel the baby move anymore so we need to ring an ambulance straight away."

"Bisi, Bisi. Why is this happening? Are you in pain? You seem calm!!" Mayor screams with his hands on his head.

He then starts speaking in tongues... several languages... but I am concerned about the fact that time is already ticking and the towel I am holding tightly to my body is already getting badly soaked as well.

"Honey, please be strong and ring an ambulance right now," I plead.

I have already started searching for information on urine leakage in pregnancy online and I think that what I am experiencing is normal.

The team of paramedics arrive with the expectation that I am due to deliver right at home.

"Mrs Osundeko, can you feel any movements in your belly?" the paramedic inquires, holding me with the expectation that I am going to collapse at any minute.

"Actually, I'm not really in pain... this whole thing feels surreal," I reply.

"Bisi, can you feel Joseph moving?" Mayor asks.

"Erm, I can't feel any movement or maybe our baby is still moving but I can't tell," I say.

"We have come prepared to help you deliver your baby right here at home. How regular are your contractions?" the second paramedic asks.

"No... In fact... God forbid. I will not deliver my own baby prematurely!" I scream while holding on to my deflated belly.

"This baby will make it to term. Please don't treat me like a sick woman. My legs are working, and I can walk to the ambulance," I plead, moving around as if trying to dramatise how strong I am to the paramedics.

"Bisi, we really don't have any time to waste," Mayor says, and then turns to the ambulance crew and says, "Thank you so much for coming so quickly. Please, how fast can you get my dear wife to the City hospital?"

In the ambulance, reality starts to hit me. I know the hospital well, and I am already familiar with the neonatal unit.

But I'm not ready to do this again. I really expected my current pregnancy experience to be completely different from my first.

"I am so scared," I say out loud, to nobody in particular.

They rush me into a delivery room and one of the doctors comes over to examine me.

"Sadly, your amniotic fluid which ought to be a source of support for your baby, has completely leaked when your waters popped at home," the doctor explains while holding a stethoscope to my belly.

"I understand that my colleague has already enlightened you about premature labour and I also understand that you are not new to the neonatal unit," he adds, with a tone of comfort.

"Is there anything you can do to help?" Mayor says, stammering.

"Well, we can give an injection that will delay labour but considering that all your waters have gone, we are not sure about the results," the doctor says.

"Oh Lord, please help us," I whisper.

This is even more painful than my first experience with Joy.

A couple of days after, I am still in pain and sing all the time in my native Yoruba language. The other pregnant ladies on the ward look so startled and I forget they have no idea what I am saying. It's been 12 years since I left Nigeria but the words come so naturally. I start looking at the clock, and the pain starts increasing. At this point, it isn't just my belly that is aching badly, but my head, my entire body.

Fear grips me.

I fear that my life is ebbing away. My body is trembling, and I throw my hands on my belly as if I am pleading with my body to hold onto my precious baby. I am dashing through the room erratically as if in a dance as I continue to sing Yoruba gospel songs.

Suddenly, I feel as though my legs can't support my body. I am staggering and losing my balance.

I gather all the strength I can.

"Please help me. I need a nurse. Please help," I say to whoever is passing through the ward.

One of the nurses suggests they should get the foetal heart monitor to check if the baby is still fine.

Lo and behold, as soon as they check, commotion starts in the maternity ward. Every medic within the maternity ward runs towards me. Everyone starts running helter skelter. Nurses, doctors, serious looking people in scrubs, suddenly come to my rescue.

"Her baby seems to be in serious trouble," one male doctor says as they carry me into a bed.

"Bisi, we are taking you to the theatre straightway for an emergency caesarean operation. Your baby must be out right now," a senior doctor says with a lot of panic in his baritone voice.

"I'm afraid we won't wait for your husband to get here because this is about saving your own life as well," he adds.

I pray in silence. God, you let me down, I don't want to go back to the NICU the second time, please just take me home.

Lord, I'm young and I don't have enough strength to manage another disabled child.

At this point, it seems my baby has been delivered within slip seconds because it is such a quickie caesarean.

"We finally found his heartbeat," one of the surgeons says, rejoicing.

I can hear all the conversation in the theatre but am way too sedated to fully understand what everyone present is saying.

I am drifting in and out of consciousness.

The environment in the theatre feels very serene, yet it feels as if I am in a bit of a tussle with someone. I don't want to wake up because I feel as if I am enveloped within so much uncertainty.

Over a long distance, I hear my name.

"Bisi, Bisi, please wake up," Mayor is crying. "I love you, please come back, my dear. The doctors said that the sedation ought to have left your system by now," he says.

I open my eyes.

"She's finally awake, she's awake," Mayor says, his eyes wet with tears. "I'm so happy to see her eyes open."

For a minute, I can't understand why Mayor is so overjoyed.

I attempt to touch my pregnant belly, but my hands can't move.

It then dawns on me that I am no longer pregnant. As if in a dash, I suddenly regain my memory.

"What happened to our son?"

"What does our son look like?"

"When did Mayor get to the theatre?"

"Who is looking after Joy?"

I ask Mayor multiple questions, one immediately after another, without waiting for him to answer the previous one.

The excitement suddenly drains from Mayor's face.

"Don't worry, they are looking after our baby," Mayor answers, as if trying to censor my questions. "For now, your own wellbeing is all that matters to me," he adds.

The suspense is huge; I can't understand the mood in the theatre.

"Relax for now please. We will take you to the neonatal intensive care unit (NICU) to see your son," a female doctor says as she walks towards where I am laying.

Mayor looks at me and we both gaze at each other.

This is our second baby and I remember that we desired our baby boy to complete our family.

As I am wheeled towards the NICU, the familiar environment starts playing out to me. I feel numb.

I want to cry but my tear ducts are dry.

Why am I walking this same path to the NICU again?

A nurse then points towards a lone incubator.

"That's your baby boy, Mrs Osundeko. Will you like to touch him?" she asks.

I look at her without saying a word and then look at Mayor.

"Your baby is too fragile at this moment to be carried but we can open a side of his incubator for you to touch him," she says in a reassuring voice.

I hold onto Mayor's hands tightly and we both move towards Joseph in silence.

He is so tiny, yet he is slowly moving within the glassy incubator. Mayor and I stare at Joseph for hours without knowing exactly what to say to each other.

Joseph's situation looks a lot more complex than Joy's did at the time.

This is the beginning of our second experience in the NICU.

During our time there, Mayor and I always pray with bereaved families even though it certainly wasn't our job to do so. Our empathy for others grows during this period and I discover that I am always moved by the plight of other families of sick children. Comforting other parents unconsciously brings me comfort and I start to discover my purpose because I derive fulfilment from helping others.

There was a couple that I can't ever forget; they'd lost their twin babies. We see them crying along the corridors. No questions asked, we just go over to hug them. Nobody refuses a hug at such trying times. We had formed new friendships within the walls of the hospital because it became our new home during those terrifying months.

Joseph is poorly and doctors often remind us that his chances of survival are slim.

*

I thought back to the last time we were in the NICU – when our first child, Joy, was born.

On the same day she was born, as soon as I left the labour suite, a team of doctors had called Mayor and I into a room for a meeting.

"We are sorry to let you know that your baby has Down syndrome," one of the doctors had said. Standing beside him, the others were nodding in the affirmative.

"It is impossible for my beautiful baby to have down syndrome or Down syndrome, whatever you call the syndrome," I argued.

"Our baby looked perfect to us and she was already smacking her lips, showing readiness to breastfeed," Mayor said.

"Are you making a mistake?" I asked.

"Did you notice that a midwife looked at your baby and she left the delivery room to call one of the doctors?" said the same female doctor with a tear in her eyes. There was sadness written all over her face.

This isn't the sort of welcome to the world I imagined for my beautiful baby whose presence was all I was waiting for to soothe my aching heart after losing my mum a month before my due date.

I continued to shake my head in disbelief while I was taking a look at each of the doctors, one by one. A part of me wanted to question their medical qualifications and the credibility of what they were collectively saying.

"Are you sure that my baby has Down syndrome?" I asked.

One of the doctors who rarely said anything then started to explain, "We actually have a robust method of identifying babies who are born with this chromosomal condition."

"By the time we took Joy away from you to the neonatal unit, we examined her eyes, creases in her palm, toes and other facial features and it all pointed towards this same syndrome," another doctor said, this time with a louder voice as if trying to reassure Mayor and I as regards the accuracy of their findings.

One of the doctors tapped me as if trying to check that I was alright.

"We then sent a sample of your baby's blood to the laboratory for confirmatory tests and this test also confirmed our diagnosis."

"No, no, no, this can't be true! Jesus, Saviour, please help Joy, help us!" I screamed with tears running down my face.

I clung to my chest. I felt violated. I felt surprised that while Mayor and I were put into another room after we left the labour suite, they were busy testing my precious baby as if she was a specimen.

A flurry of thoughts filtered my mind.

"We understand that you did not expect this news," the doctor announced, as if trying to wake Mayor and I up from our trance-like gazing, crying, and praying.

"So, where is my baby?" I cried.

"She is currently in the neonatal intensive unit for sick babies, even though she was born four days overdue. Her lungs are not working the ways they ought to, so she is under a head box as well receiving oxygen," the doctor explained.

"What is all this?" I asked as if I had just been robbed of a precious possession.

"One of our nurses is ready to take you and your husband to the NICU to see Joy," one of the medics replied. "Also, please don't forget that a representative of the Down syndrome association is also coming to talk to you and she's coming over with some literature."

I started crying loudly and the doctors looked at me as if they didn't expect me to still be crying after all the wailing.

"We don't want to be forced into this club of special needs parents or any association. We have no experience of parenting a special child, please," cried Mayor.

However, the doctors were already on their way out of the room that we were in. I looked around and started to worry about my daughter's future.

Mayor and I held each other as I was led into the NICU. It felt as if we were walking into uncertainties. We were so afraid. We had a million and one questions.

Joy was a big baby, considering that most of the babies in the NICU were premature. We really felt out of place. As the weeks went by in the hospital, I started attempting to breastfeed Joy but her breathing problems meant that she had to be tube-fed.

After some weeks in the hospital, Joy was finally discharged to go home. All the excitement that comes with having a new baby had subsided and we simply felt exhausted.

Being strong was the only option Mayor and I had.

During our time in the hospital with Joy, one of the nurses enlightened me about skin to skin care for babies and I was gifted a kangaroo care top which helped to facilitate bonding with Joy.

Unknown to me, that discussion was sowing a seed into my entrepreneurial future. Working or running a business was the least on my mind at the time though. I had no sleep. I was very afraid. Within such a short space of time, my weight plummeted though my eating was poor.

Prior to having Joy, I had set out the perfect future where I would simply let my mum help babysit Joy while I had my sights set on some top environmental firms in the Midlands that I was aiming to apply to for jobs.

I started to feel inadequate. I felt that if I was unable to nurture a perfect baby within my own womb, then I had failed completely. All the amazing academic achievements, scholarships and awards didn't matter to me anymore because based on my cultural Nigerian background, children were viewed as major achievements too.

Sleep deprivation made me feel like a zombie. I was constantly forgetting the days of the week or what time of the year we were in so I really couldn't imagine myself attempting a structured work system.

The perfect future to me was one where I was gainfully employed with a great company. Without a doubt, I started questioning my decision to have my first baby whilst I was still in the university for my Master's degree.

Though Joy was planned, her disability was not planned. Unknown to Mayor and me, that was only the beginning.

Joy later had tons of diagnoses added to her main diagnosis. Apparently, some of the conditions like hearing and visual impairment were linked to her trisomy 21 (T21) diagnosis also known as Down syndrome. At that time, it felt as if the doctors were saying that something was wrong with every single part of her body.

Whenever the phone rang, I would wonder what the next diagnosis was going to be.

We were told to expect that Joy was going to have an open-heart surgery to repair the hole in her heart.

Yet during that time Joy was home, in the midst of the medically induced chaos, I slowly started to bond with Joy properly. I realised that she was first of all, *my baby*; before all the diagnosis happened. Mayor had to go back to work because there was no other way our family was going to be able to survive financially if both of us didn't work.

With Mayor's encouragement, I slowly started brainstorming about businesses I could run from home. The options were limited because then in 2007, I didn't know anything about website construction or social media marketing, so I started from scratch. I looked into childminding, online trading, and weekend markets.

I also experienced so much kindness from Dr Liz Marder. She often visited our home and would come upstairs into my bedroom to console me, when I was crying due to Joy's feeding problems.

Dr Liz later invited me to a support group. Something big shifted in my mind the very day I took Joy to the social event, a support group for families who have children with Down syndrome in our city.

The event was like a carnival. There were kids running around. Little kids, big kids. All these children have Down syndrome, yet they were so diverse.

Kids in wheelchairs and lots of kids without wheelchairs.

I went back home feeling as though something significant had happened to my mindset. I didn't feel alone in this new special needs parenting terrain anymore. This was the start of my love for support groups for parents of disabled children. I started looking forward to creating happy memories with my precious baby Joy.

I discovered that there were tons of other families with children like my daughter.

*

It was two years after Joy's birth that her brother was born. After lots of months in the hospital, Joseph was discharged home. Although Mayor and I boasted to the doctors that we were keen to use our parenting experience for Joseph, we were quite scared. We had become used to the nurses and doctors being around, and now we'd be on our own.

Both Joy and Joseph were on oxygen at the time, so our home was like an extension of the hospital; only that this time, Mayor and I were the doctors. Joseph was also sent home with a tube that was inserted through his nostril into his stomach for his feeding. The feeding tube was like a little upgrade from the jejunal tube that was used in the hospital because his internal organs were not digesting food.

Around that time, when I was bonding with Joy and Joseph at home, I was struggling with the piece of clothing I'd been gifted in the hospital.

I need a sling which will allow me to be hands free.

Looking back, this was my eureka moment. I researched the baby sling options available in the market, but nothing appeared to meet my needs.

I drew inspiration from my African background and the traditional way I had been taught to nurture and carry babies on my back.

I brainstormed options, and with Mayor's support, I bought a sewing machine.

My business, *Joy and Joe Baby*, was born right there at home within my conservatory in the middle of my super chaotic life, childminding business, and special needs parenting.

The feedback I received from some of my early customers really opened my eyes to the fact that I was a people's person. I derive happiness from seeing others happy and fulfilled.

Around that period, I also started to experience isolation, mainly because working from home meant that sometimes my only face to face interaction in an entire day was with my children and husband. I saw a leaflet from the community association where they urged residents to participate in the community meetings.

This was the start of my community activism. I started attending these community events with a view to combating the sense of isolation I felt, and I met people who lived around me.

During that time at the community association, I saw they had no website, so I volunteered to help them design and create their website. I used the knowledge I gained from creating my own new business website.

A few miles from where we lived, I also found out that our local children's centre had a lot of group or play activities for children but there was nothing for disabled children and their families. After a discussion with a staff of the centre, I then started by sitting in the meeting room on my own. Then the following week, another parent of a disabled child came, and I slowly built the special needs support group from there.

This was like a whole new world to me. I began to feel a lot more fulfilled from the inside and my happiness radiated to the outside. I felt as though my life had a new meaning. I was so happy that I was able to contribute something positive to the lives of other families in addition to discovering my calling in life.

Through this support group, my understanding of our ability to thrive in the midst of challenges gave my life a whole new meaning.

I now look forward to every single day as a chance to positively impact the world around me. Though this was a corner in my city at the time, I felt as though I was touching the lives of millions.

The experience that I've had so far with my own children proved to be very useful when it comes to counselling the parents who came to me for advice. During the time that I was overwhelmed with Joy's many diagnoses, I didn't realise that all the experience was going to be useful for other families in the future.

I enjoy talking to people, listening to them talk about their special needs and entrepreneurial challenges, and offering my expertise and experience as a way of encouraging them. Through that, I organised a festive party for all the disabled children in my community and it was a huge success.

Over time, Joseph came off the feeding tube and started feeding orally.

Joy started nursery school and she was thriving beautifully.

All these in spite of their disabilities that I was initially so scared of.

My marriage grew from strength to strength.

My business continued to grow from strength to strength.

My self-esteem and confidence continued to grow from strength to strength, too.

I have gone on from a person who merely survived each day to a fulfilled person who has gained a superb level of clarity as regards her direction and purpose in life.

I have gone on to become a person who other parents saw as a treasure of knowledge because I unashamedly owned my challenges and I'm always more than willing to offer my entrepreneurial and emotional support to special needs families where needed.

My children have gifted me in ways they will never know, and I am truly grateful.

CHAPTER 12

Breaking the chains
Charlene Kay Fouts

I bury myself in my closet under 103 stuffed animals, shivering, but trying not to breathe or make a sound.

If I can just be still and strong, that terrifying, huge black snake won't find me.

I fight to stay awake as long as I can but sleep always finds me.

I soon awake to a strong smell of alcohol and cigarettes.

I can feel the huge snake coiling around me, picking me up, and when I open my eyes, I see its slippery, shiny skin hovering over me while being held by its enormous body.

I scream, but my mouth is covered as it wraps itself all around me, covering my mouth and choking me. It tells me to shut up and be still or I will be hurt worse. It threatens to kill me if I ever tell anyone. It lays me down on the bed and goes inside of me.

Terror consumes me. I close my eyes and stay as still as I can, although my tiny five-year-old body trembles uncontrollably. The pain is tremendous, and breathing is difficult.

I cry and scream for help.

But no one ever comes.

Where's my mommy? Why won't anyone save me?

If it is just a nightmare like my mom tells me, why am I always bleeding and in so much pain?

*

When I get out of that house as a teenager, I think I will finally be free.

But the same kind of men as the snake in my nightmares still find me. And again, they are real. They continue to demean and wear me down.

It does not matter what their social status is, they are all horrifyingly brutal, encompassing physical violence, rape, and total dominance in the relationship.

After seeing my boyfriend out with another girl, I go home and pack his suitcase and throw it on the front porch.

I sit up in bed, with the covers up to my chin, shivering.

What will he do when he gets home?

I hear the car door slam and thundering footsteps as he comes to the front door, and the loud thud as he boots the suitcase I've left for him.

"Where are you, Charlene?!" he roars.

I hold my breath as he punches the door open and tears into our room, ripping me out of bed.

"What the fuck are you doing with my stuff, bitch?!" he spits, pushing me against the wall and holding me so tight around my throat, I can feel the air being sucked out of my lungs.

Everything seems to move in slow motion, and I can see myself being hit, again and again. He throws me to the floor, kicks me, picks me up and throws me again... but I can't really feel anything.

I am numb.

He pulls me roughly to my knees, and I see him reach behind his back. I see the familiar glint of his shiny Colt and all the remaining energy drains from my body.

Thwack!

The hard metal of the gun slams hard into the side of my face. Then he puts it in my mouth.

"You're going to die," he whispers.

Just do it.

But the end doesn't come.

He changes his mind and throws me onto the bed to take his rage out on me in another way.

*

I spend my life running and trying to appear as perfect as I can.

I was taught as a child there was no one that I could count on. I had to be quiet and figure it out myself.

I watched my sister have babies at the age of fifteen and I saw the terrible way that she lived, and the horrible life the kids grew up in, an endless cycle of trailers and different men coming in and out of their lives.

I know what it was like to grow up in a terrifying environment, and I do not want to bring a child into that kind of world.

I imagine a home and love and meals, cleanliness, and stability, a husband who loves me. But to me, that is just a dream, and don't imagine it is possible to accomplish.

*

At just 20 I find myself sitting alone in an abortion clinic for the second time.

They herd us into a small, dark, airless room. It is time to take the pre-procedure medication. I pull my knitted cardigan around my shoulders. Is it even colder than last time?

You can smell fear and heartbreak, but no one dares to utter a word.

"Evil, selfish, murderers!" bounces off the lonely, lifeless walls of the clinic. I know there are protestors outside. They just don't understand.

I picture the faces of my mom and sister telling me what a piece of shit I am. I walk to the window and some of the other girls tell me to stay away from it.

But I want to see them. I stand in front of the window and peer through one of the blinds. I can see their faces. They are so angry and full of hate.

Except for one lady. She is kneeling down in the grass and praying. She looks up and I see her eyes. She is looking right at me, but there is no way that she can see me behind the blinds. Her eyes are so full of love and she never stops praying.

She looks right at me and smiles.

I call her Mrs. X. She has a glow all around her and I believe she is an angel. I will never forget the incredible love I see and feel in her eyes.

I feel inspired to pray, too.

God, if you'll even listen to me, please forgive me and ask my baby to do the same.

I believe Mrs. X is an Angel sent to take the babies home.

Please take good care of my baby.

At only 21, life has taken its toll on me.

I still smile and try desperately to be smart, beautiful, and successful. If I can just be a little bit better…

I have lived through incest, brutal beatings, rapes, and by then, three abortions. My life is falling apart, and I am struggling to piece it together.

I am invited to a church and find my way to a counselor named Gary.

He spends years helping me face the reality of the sexual abuse by my parents, and this is where my healing begins.

Gary spends hours with me as a kind and trusted confidant. He helps me unravel all the terrifying experiences I could never bring together and face on my own. He teaches me how to love myself and to trust God with both my life and my horrifying experiences.

"God never lets anything in our lives go to waste. Someday he will bring everything together in your life for good," he says.

Gary helps me face my fears and stand up to that snake which dominates my nightmares.

And finally, it happens.

I dream of the snake's death.

It is a beautiful summer day and I am walking down an old dirt road. There is long flowing green grass with little purple flowers, just like the ones my Aunt Vella and I used to plant. A beautiful red dog runs beside me in the grass, leading the way.

From a distance, I can see a man standing on the side of the road. His arms are stretched out and he is holding an enormous, dead, black snake. It is much bigger than him, but no longer scary. It is Gary, and as I walk by, he says, "Never Again."

I wake up and know I will never have that terrifying nightmare which has plagued my whole life, ever again. With the past firmly behind me, I don't have to carry that guilt and shame around with me anymore.

I know the truth, and it sets me free. The giant snake has been slain forever and God will never allow it back in my life again.

One weekend, Gary arranges for me to go on a trip to stay at one of his best friend's houses in Tennessee. After driving down a little dirt road, I see a driveway open up to a ranch and a beautiful home with a cozy loft set in the middle.

Just down the road sits a little white church that I walk to. The beautiful stained-glass windows are forever etched in my mind.

I sit in this church for hours. I pray and write letters to my three babies I have aborted. I pour my heart out and I beg them to forgive me. When I am finished, I step outside to the little graveyard which borders the side of the church.

The sun kisses my face as I stand peering at the long grass and weeds which have overtaken the tombstones. It somehow comforts me to think that time has forgotten this peaceful little place. There is a quiet calmness and beauty, like nature stopped to join me.

I press down the grass and made a spot to sit down next to some tombstones.

The rustling of my papers is all that can be heard as I lay them aside. I choose a peaceful spot and pull the grass and weeds. There is just enough room to dig three small graves.

I read each letter aloud. *I'm so sorry.* The letters seem to float in my hand, and I watch the orange flames reach for the sky as I burn and release each paper separately into the graves.

Tears burn my face and suddenly I can hear the birds chiming in, giving beauty and testifying to the lives of my babies. They finally have a peaceful, charming resting place.

When the funerals were over, I lay down next to their graves and thank God for their little lives and the love and mercy he has for me. Mrs. X is kneeling down at a distance in the little graveyard. I would know those loving eyes anywhere.

*

I am still in my early 20's when I start a home for unwed mothers.

I want a safe place for women who want to keep their babies to learn how to take care of themselves and their babies. It takes me five years to get Paracletian, Inc. up and running.

I make an apartment in the top portion of the house where I live, and it is such a joy to see the girls thrive with their babies.

I eventually moved away from Paracletain, but it still exists today. I still get to see some of the girls and their grown children, and it's one of the greatest blessings I have ever experienced.

*

Despite the work I have done on myself, and my plight to help others, I still found myself struggling with relationships.

I was a flight attendant, and one late evening on the plane we had to take down a man who was beating a woman. We struggled to confine him in seat belt extensions, but the entire time, the woman who he had beaten so badly was fighting us to save him.

Over the next few days after the incident, I started feeling very angry and had nightmares of this woman with half her face barely hanging on, fighting me. I kept screaming at her and telling her that we were trying to save her life, but she wouldn't listen. I woke up in a pool of sweat and tears and realized that the woman was me.

I was still excusing domestic violence as if it were not present in my life.

I went to a church I had gone to periodically over the years and asked the pastor for help.

He arranged for me to meet Pat, an amazing counselor there. I had thought I had been healed and didn't need this anymore, but I came to realize that healing is a lifelong journey.

As we grow, different layers are removed, and we continue to become more free. Pat talked to me about loving myself and that little girl who was still inside of me, afraid and helpless, waiting on me to set her free.

One night I had a dream I was in a cute little house. It was different than the home that I live in, but I knew that it was mine. It was small and needed to be organized and some TLC, but it was mostly nice... except for a hole in the wall outside of the kitchen.

There were hundreds of people there in the small space. I wasn't afraid of them. They were mostly having fun and trying to fix things, but I just wanted them to leave.

I only remember seeing a front room, the kitchen behind it, and a small room that was walled in off the kitchen. There was a hole in the wall, and you could see what looked like a bunk bed and two old, baby dolls. I had a really uneasy feeling about that area. It was dark and dirty.

I kept telling people to leave the house, but no one seemed to be listening to me and I was tired, so I went to sleep.

When I woke up, the people were still there going through my things, but I noticed Jena, a girl from my church in the corner of the living room, on the other side of the wall of the kitchen. She had made a beautiful stand that went from the floor all the way up to the ceiling. There was a metal pole in the middle and iron baskets which were layered all the way to the top, probably five huge baskets. Each basket was overflowing with fruits and vegetables and the whole corner was illuminated.

After this, I woke up and felt exhausted.

That little house represented my heart, the place where I really do live.

It was mostly clean, except for that one little hole in the wall. That place which gave me a sick and uneasy feeling. Maybe I could hang a picture over it or have one of those many people who are around, patch it up?

Everything else seems to be okay. Oh, except for the hundreds of people who are overcrowding the place.

Over the years I had faced overwhelming abuse and had been taken advantage of over and over again. I desperately needed to rid my heart of the hundreds of people who were running freely in it.

I took a heart-wrenching walk through the pages of my history.

There were so many people to take care of. There were so many people, I exhausted myself trying to fill this huge void of desperately wanting to feel needed.

If only someone could just see me, really see and know me…

Because of my incapacitating requirement to be useful and needed by others, I opened myself up to unspeakable pain by being easily manipulated and used by people.

If I could do, or be, just a little bit more, then I could fix everything.

This also put me in a position of trying to control others in an unhealthy way to get my own needs met.

The first thing I had to tackle was ridding my house of the crowd. I started with addressing each person in the house individually. I made them get in a big line and I sat on a comfy sofa and talked to each one of them one by one. I replayed every memory and looked them straight in the eye. I told them what they had done to me, or I asked for forgiveness for what I had done to them.

There were some people there who just represented good memories and I thanked them for their help along life's rough journey.

The house got less and less crowded as I escorted everyone out the front door, one memory at a time, good and bad, in order to regain a sense of peace and balance.

Finally, it was just me and God.

Although there was still that hole in the wall which needed to be looked at. It terrified me to even look in its direction. My first instinct was to find something to cover it up and just make everything look pretty.

I gained the courage to walk up to it.

I looked through the hole into a very dark little bedroom. It was a bare room with no carpet and no paint on the walls. It was musty, damp and very dirty. There was only a bunk bed and two dirty, beat-up old baby dolls with no clothes on were laying on the top bunk. I picked one up and wiped the dust off it.

I felt nauseous as my eyes scanned the entire room. I could feel a presence, but my eyes did not want to meet what was hiding in that room.

As I closed my eyes, a wave of overwhelming emotion gripped every part of me. It would be so easy to turn around and go into another room, but I took a deep breath and opened my eyes.

There was a little girl in a nightgown, crouched and trembling in the far corner of the room. She had her arms wrapped around her knees and just stared blankly at me. She was dirty and disheveled. Her eyes looked so sad and empty. She terrified me and I wanted to run. This wasn't something I could look at.

The little girl seemed so weak and pathetic, useless in so many ways. She was really messing up the whole house just by being there. I tried to ignore and hide her for so many years, but God stood beside me as I peered through that hole in the wall. He took my hand and filled me with an unbelievable peace and love.

I knew I had to tear down that wall down and rescue that terrified little girl. I could hear the song, *The God Who Stays* playing softly in my ear.

I realized all the terrible things I had been through in my life were not in vain and that I was never alone. God was always there with me, waiting for me to see him and let him in.

It took every ounce of courage I had to pull that drywall down and walk up to that little girl.

At first, I couldn't do anything but sit down beside that beat up, dirty, and hurting little girl. I sat quietly in the dark, dirty room with her. I didn't want to feel her pain, to remember the overwhelming fear, terror, and loneliness which embodied who she was.

I spent my whole life trying not to show anyone her weaknesses, but I knew that God made me who I was for a reason, and he works all things together for good.

If I couldn't love, respect and protect her, my life would have no truth and no real love. I would also continue to repeat the vicious cycle of abuse I had kept experiencing.

I prayed to God to give me the strength to look at this little girl, and to love her. I held her hand for a while. She was trembling. It seemed like hours before I could utter a word, or even look at her. My eyes were fixed on the two naked baby dolls which were still lying on the bunk bed.

I knew that if I was to see a little girl right now being beaten or raped, I would not just sit here. I would not ignore her. I would protect her and fight for her. I would be infuriated and would run to her rescue to help her and do as much as I could for her. I would hug her, and I would tell her that everything was going to be alright. I would tell her that Jesus loves her, and he can and will restore her life.

Why could I imagine helping a stranger without even a thought, but never consider loving, helping, and protecting myself, that scared little girl?

It was time to face her, to tell her how sorry I was for treating her like everyone else did. I could not stop or change what happened to her in the past, but I could love, protect and acknowledge her pain now.

I threw my arms around that little girl and cried so hard that my breath escaped me. I could see Jesus sitting on the floor across the room. He was always there, even in my darkest, dirtiest places. He was the ghost who used to sit in the closet with me as a little girl. He waited for me to invite him to be with us. I picked up the little girl and I held her in my arms, hugging and comforting her.

I asked Jesus to hold me, and to show me how to love her. I told him that I was afraid of her, but I didn't want to be afraid anymore.

Jesus sat with us. He held me while I held her. I felt safe in that awful room, being held by Jesus, while for the first time I acknowledged and held that frightened little girl close to me. I scooped her up into my arms and I carried her out of that dark, miserable room, into my home.

I cleaned her up and got her some new clothes. We sat on the couch and I told her how sorry I was for ignoring her. I told her that I knew her pain. I knew how helpless and afraid she was, and that she'd done the best she could. I told her that nothing that happened to her was her fault, and that I was proud of her and that I loved her.

We walked outside to find the tree that Aunt Vella and I planted many years ago. It was very big now. Me, little Charlene, and Jesus sat and laughed and played under it. Aunt Vella was right, God can always be found in nature.

When we went back in the house, we cleaned up the bedroom and threw away the old bunk beds. We put in French doors where the hole used to be, and we cut out a large window to bring the beautiful sunshine in.

We painted the walls lavender and put down beautiful white carpet. We put a big, fluffy purple sofa in the room, a writing table and chair, and a big round white bed, with big, fluffy purple pillows. We also put two large bookcases full of books in the corner.

When we were done making the room beautiful, we walked out into the living room and saw the huge baskets in the corner illuminated and overflowing with fruits and vegetables. It was an amazing sight, beaming with an incredible white light.

*

Jesus always loved us, and he created me to be a confident, loving, beautiful woman. He chose me before I was born, and he created me for a purpose. He knew all my days before they came to pass and I know that he can take my story and use it for good, for life, and for strength.

There is nothing we can possibly go through in life that Jesus isn't aware of. He is always there. He is always waiting to be invited in to restore our lives and heal us. He wants to pour out his blessings on us; all we must do is ask.

I have written a book about all my life's experiences to share with other victims to offer hope in their journey. I've also started a Non-Profit organization called Healing Acres Never Again, which focuses on Christ-based recovery for people who have experienced trauma from incest, domestic violence, sexual abuse, rape, and abortion.

I have come to realize that healing and learning to forgive and love is a lifelong journey.

Sometimes facing ourselves is the hardest thing that we ever have to do.

Learning to love and forgive our younger self, and not trying to cover up our weaknesses, can be the key to finding our freedom.

And now, I am free.

CHAPTER 13

My catalyst for joy
Gabrielle Conescu

Our beloved cat Bella loves to spread herself out on the blue-grey pebblecrete path, lazing on the warm, course coir welcome mat at our front door.

Not this day.

This day, I am greeted by a sight which stops me in my tracks.

Bella is sitting upright, confident, comfortable, smug – mercilessly toying with the mouse positioned between her front paws.

The mouse stares up into Bella's face, hypnotised into submission, knowing every effort to move away will be thwarted by those paws. It keeps very, very still. This moment is all that exists. I've never thought of a mouse as beautiful before, but this little creature is gorgeous. It seems so small and defenceless, quivering with fear. I peer into those large shiny eyes and my heart melts.

Suddenly, I have an epiphany.

Oh my God, this little mouse is me!

"Bella! NO!"

Aghast, I snatch Bella up and dash her nasty game.

*

The job description leaps out at me from my computer screen. I read it a few times just to make sure. I've been job searching with very clear goals in mind – long term job security, stability, and assistance with my pressing financial commitments. This job ticks all my boxes.

This job is perfect. My skills and experience meet all the criteria.

I have applied for more than eighty positions with little response. They say ageism doesn't exist, but I'm not so sure. I'm ecstatic when the Recruitment Agency puts me forward as an ideal candidate. I feel validated at last.

The application process is rigorous. I am being thoroughly checked out by my prospective employer with loads of interview questions and testing. I am thankful I have great referees.

The phone rings. "Good news! You are the successful candidate."

Woohoo! Everything seems on track for my goals. I set my resolve that this is the job to see me through to retirement.

On my first day, Sybil, the woman who would be my boss, smiles as she enters reception to greet me, making me feel immediately at ease. She beckons me to follow as she showed me to my desk.

I sit down, my hands caressing the new stationery meticulously laid out ready for me. Daylight streams in through the window, which looks out onto the street. The view from my desk is the blank wall at the back of the room. Not the best, but I feel pretty good.

There are three of us squashed into the little office – our boss Sybil, the administration officer Connie, and me. I notice I am the only person with her back to the door.

We'd gotten off to a good start, finding some common ground during initial discussions. Sybil's efforts to make me feel welcome go above and beyond anything I've experienced before. The attention makes me feel really special. You can't help but notice her vivid blue eyes. I feel drawn in by her stories about all the stages of the project up till now. I am particularly impressed by the progress made. There is a lot to absorb and I am keen.

"I'm delighted to have you join the team, Gabrielle," Sybil enthuses, flicking her long, straight, almost-black hair away from her animated face as she speaks.

"I was brought in by the CEO to help him develop this project. Connie and I have done all the work up till now and now he's handed it over to me. I've created your role as an extension of the work we've been doing. You'll accompany the lawyer and me on site visits. Your job is to observe, learn, and write reports on our return."

This all seems reasonable, although as the first person to be trained in this newly created role, I feel a bit nervous about the amount of data I am to review. I am confident my experience and enthusiasm will overcome my apprehension.

Sybil speaks about our work with an air of exclusivity. I've never been subject to so many rules and boundaries around how we operated. No speaking about what we do, even to upper management. That was **her** job.

"Our work is really confidential. You don't understand the politics and could get yourself into trouble if you say the wrong thing to the wrong person, so don't talk about any aspect of the project. No answering questions or giving out information to anyone! Leave the talking up to me and you'll be safe."

OK.... no talking about the project. I get it.

But the behavioural directives don't stop there. Her helpful advice is peppered with warnings about people.

"Don't be too friendly with the other departments. We must maintain a professional distance."

"The politics are too complicated for you to understand. Just know that every conversation you have in this building, I will know about it."

"Keep a safe distance from Human Resources (HR)," she whispers, leaning in my direction. "The HR Manager isn't to be trusted."

The talking goes on and on. Apparently, danger lurks in every corner of the organisation. Sybil seems convinced all of it is true and is determined to make me feel the same way.

Wow! I better tread carefully.

It all feels very controlling, but I need my pay cheque. I need to hold on to this job. Debts need to be paid and I have a high interest property loan looming over me, which I can't afford to default on. Even a few weeks without work would cripple me.

As I settled into the role Sybil makes me feel involved in every conversation she has with higher management. My ego is taken to the dizziest of heights.

Three months later, I fall to earth with a soul-crushing thud.

Sybil is going to have an in-depth conversation with her boss the Chief Operations Officer [COO] in the next room. Before going in, Sybil fills Connie and me in on every little detail of her expectations. As she leaves to join the meeting, Connie and I are in an upbeat mood.

Excitedly, full of enthusiasm, and with no malicious intent, I do something very out of character.

I sit in Sybil's chair for a minute and lean near the wall between her desk and the COO's office to see if I can hear how well the meeting is going.

As soon as I do it, Connie's demeanour changes. She turns back to her computer, head down, working. I pick up on the vibe pretty quickly and move back to my desk.

Oh, shite! Lesson 1 – do not listen in on Sybil's meetings, ever.

I feel really bad. How could I make such an error of judgement?

When Sybil returns to the room I own up with an apology. I feel it's the right thing to do.

"You did what?" She slams her files on the desk. "Are you trying to spy on me? How dare you!" As fury takes hold, her voice shakes with rage. The rest of what she says becomes a blur.

In a nano-second, my glory days of being the shiny new team member are over.

I feel shamed, belittled, embarrassed.

Sybil and Connie are tight. They understand each other. In our small room of three, there is an undertone I can't quite pinpoint. The realisation dawns on me – I am alone.

From that day forward, I feel like I am walking on eggshells. There is no opportunity for clearing conversations. Everything I say and do is observed. My failures become fodder for Sybil, who keeps tally throughout my probation period, meticulously preparing my Performance Reviews.

I recall one such transgression. Sybil is out of the room when I ask Connie, as administration officer, to do something. Her frosty response makes me realise my mistake fairly quickly and I never ask again. But I am not going to be let off that lightly.

Sybil pushes the organisational chart for our team of three across the meeting table. It is a small chart with three boxes arranged in a pyramid shape. On top is the Manager box. Underneath the other two boxes which read Administration Officer and my position. Sybil points from Manager to Administration Officer.

"This is the communication flow for this team. Do you follow?

It does not go this way," she said, pointing from my position to Administration Officer.

Geez. Wouldn't it have been easier to simply say that when it happened?

"Do you understand?" she repeats.

It feels like the walls are closing in on me. It is perfectly clear. There is no use trying to apologise or explain when I do something which doesn't fit the desired behaviour.

Everything seems to be my fault. The way Sybil speaks to me makes me feel stupid. She speaks fast, makes constant changes.

She often replies to my questions with, "We spoke about that last week."

Why don't I remember that?

Confused, I start second guessing myself.

I have to choose my words carefully. They could be skewed to mean something entirely different to what I said.

Following a field visit one day, a simple observation about the lawyer's response to a question is reported back to him as though I had a very strong objection to his behaviour. This leads to an awkward distance between us and is only one of many such incidences with him and with other team members.

Each incident chips away at my confidence.

I become isolated. Sybil's behind the scenes manoeuvres have successfully driven a wedge between me and every other member of the team. Conversations stop as I enter the room. There is no-one in the entire building I feel safe to talk with about the predicament I find myself in, so I clam up, withdrawing into myself.

I become a vigilant observer.

As my self-confidence plummets, I become more and more anxious about my ability to perform tasks, with occasional reporting errors appearing.

My three-monthly Performance Reviews become torture. I feel like a naughty schoolgirl. The memory of Sybil sitting opposite me, leaning towards me with a superior sneer, pointing with her pen to my listed misdemeanours haunts my dreams for days after.

Somehow, in spite of it all, I pass all of my probation appraisals and at the end of the year my annual salary increase is approved. The good days keep me going.

I live in hope that Sybil's boss will intervene and put a stop to what is going on. Surely, he has to know. I cling to the hope that if I keep my head down and do my job, everything will be okay – despite it all, I really do love the work. But it seems I am invisible to him. With a busy, high-demand role, he rarely comes into our office. When he does, he seems anxious to leave quickly, and Sybil's assertions that he is uncomfortable with 'older women' makes me disinclined to reach out to him for help.

This woman is a genius at control.

Renovations mean our team is moved to a new open plan space on another floor. Sybil, being a Manager, has her own, glass-walled office. She can see us, and we can see her.

Released from the proximity of our three-person office cell, I am only too pleased to be able to work by myself in the open plan space. My workstation is my haven. I do my best to keep to myself, only ever entering the glass space if I am required to do so or need direction on a task.

Sometimes, my entry is met with a happy "good morning". Other times, a withering stare and disparaging comment. I never know from one moment to the next which it will be.

When is someone going to sort this woman out?

There are plans to grow the team. When Sybil is given the go ahead to recruit a new person, in a similar role to mine, I shudder. Clearly, no-one is coming to sort her out.

How much more of this can I take?

Our new colleague is Janice. Janice shares Sybil's insatiable appetite for conversation. The two of them spend hours, days, weeks, inside the glass walled office. I can see Janice's ego rising, just as mine had when I first started. We are meant to be working alongside each other.

I try to warn her, gently, carefully. "Janice, it might be wise for you to maintain a little distance. Be careful and be mindful what you say."

Janice turns her face away from me, dismissing what I've said as preposterous. I smell the superior tone in her caustic reply. "What, Sybil? I doubt that, Gabrielle. Sybil is really lovely."

My gentle warning only serves as fuel to convince Janice that Sybil is right about me. I am the team 'problem'.

Janice isn't reserved like me. Social and outspoken with her ego inflated, she defies the limitations Sybil tries to impose on her, making herself known and establishing friendships with lots of people, including those in high places.

This refusal to be dominated becomes her undoing. Not long after Janice's three-month review, the love fest begins to unravel. Unwilling to be the passive, dominated mouse, Janice speaks up at meetings and presides over situations as they arise. Sybil is losing control and is not amused. What ensues is war and it is ugly.

Janice is shunned and denied access to meetings and a smear campaign against her is directed by Sybil. The exclusion I had experienced pales into insignificance to the treatment Janice receives over the next two-months. Janice thinks she can rely on the friendships she has built up to save her, but that is not to be. Ultimately, Janice is given the news she hasn't passed her six months' probation and is escorted out of the building.

But she does not go quietly. Janice is armed with mud to sling and does not hold back.

"Sybil is a bully. You should see what she does to Gabrielle," she protests to HR and to anyone else who will listen.

I fight hard to keep myself out of the firing line. I cannot afford to lose my income.

But Sybil has laid her groundwork in discrediting Janice over her performance well in advance.

Because of timing, everything Janice said is treated as a grievance.

While Sybil's performance is looked at, Janice's warnings appear to go ignored. Then again, maybe not. It has been a very rough year and mud sticks.

It is time for damage control. Sybil suddenly becomes mentor and best friend to everyone, rallying the troops and fostering relationships with a procession of people through her office.

During that time, I bask in the sunshine of knowing she needs me on-side. For a short while at least, the pressure is off, and I enjoy my work.

Whew!

After the sunshine comes the rain.

Sybil is given the go ahead to recruit again. This time for two new people in roles like mine.

She's going to get rid of me. I have too many bills and debts. I can't afford to lose this job.

An undertone of nervous tension churns my insides. My head in my hands, words fail me. Who will be the casualty this time?

One of my new colleagues clues into the situation fairly quickly and eases herself out.

Phew!

The other, Carmel, is in for the long haul and good at her job. Sybil swings into action, taking every opportunity to discredit Carmel.

Here we go again!

After more than two years of this madness, I am really struggling. I sit at my desk paralysed with fear. My work requires intense focus and I can barely think straight, but still work hard to perform.

I feel my distress increasing, and desperate for someone to intervene, I phone the HR Manager, intending to ask for support. In our conversation her very first words are, "I must warn you that everything you say will be documented and put on record." I flash back to my first day and Sybil's warning, "Don't trust HR." Fear kicks in.

"Never mind," I mumble, hanging up the phone.

My anxiety skyrockets and is with me 24/7.

I am not myself anymore outside work, even on weekends. I complain about work all the time. My partner, Rudy, grows tired of listening to me moaning about my dilemma, but I feel trapped by the financial bind I am in. I have to hang in there.

Unable to stop the wheel turning in my head, I become antisocial and emotionally reactive. Feelings of inadequacy and shame hang over me like a dark cloud. My yoga class is the only ray of sunshine in my week.

I notice my fearful thoughts becoming paranoid. I don't like the person I am becoming.

My paranoia is a reflection of what is happening with Sybil. Convinced there are traitors amongst us, her behaviour spirals out of control.

Sybil chairs new 'Unpack the Team Culture' meetings.

During one such meeting, her controlled demeanour suddenly shifts. She locks us all in the meeting room, the conversation descending into a stream of accusations.

"Some of you have been having negative 'Rest Room' conversations. I'm going to weed out who it is. We are not leaving this room 'til someone talks."

We all look at each other. Nobody speaks.

She's really losing it!

Everything we do becomes overly complex. Sybil demands a paper trail for every conversation we have.

She insists I come up with suggestions and when I do, she rolls her eyes, ridicules me or discounts my idea. My colleagues remain quiet, not game to open their mouths for fear of getting the same treatment. Later, Sybil presents my ideas, framed another way, as if they are her own.

As she wreaks havoc, she tidies up all evidence. The job of recording team meeting minutes is shared with my colleagues. Sybil alters them. When we rebel, team meetings are cancelled.

As tension mounts, a string of consultants are brought in to assist Sybil with her management style. We are required to complete questionnaires. With so few of us, we feel vulnerable, knowing it will be easy for Sybil to identify our responses.

Shortly after, in a quiet moment, Carmel comes to me and says, "I am so sorry and deeply apologise for having caused you any upset."

Confused, I ask, "What are you talking about?"

Carmel says, "I've been in Sybil's office. She's very angry. She said everyone in the team has complained about my behaviour. She said I've been disruptive, and I've upset all of you."

It is simply not true.

I feel like I am being psychologically stripped down and the organization is allowing Sybil to do it.

Carmel and I are both feeling it. Carmel says, "I feel like I'm in some sort of weird science experiment."

Performance Review time comes around again. I feel shocked as Sybil hands me a copy of the Performance Improvement Policy (PIP). To me it reads like a detailed plan of the path to termination.

It's my first PIP meeting with Sybil and HR. My long-held hope that someone in authority will put a stop to Sybil's reign of terror is dashed. I am powerless, expendable – an animal trapped in a cage.

Sybil launches her attack. "These statistics show you are behind with your work. Because you are so far behind you are letting the entire team down. They are all under pressure because of you. I want you to tell me when you will have these reports completed."

Her tone is authoritarian, accusatory... condescending. Time stands still.

Every paranoid word ever spewed from that mouth flashes across my mind. Alarm bells ring out through my entire body. I stare at both of them.

"What's really going on here, Sybil?"

Sybil is quick to interject. "Gabrielle, we're *trying* to help you."

I look at the pair of them in horror. All I want to do is run.

The six-week plan to **help me** is set. I am to come up with a work plan for keeping myself on track.

I can't understand the statistics Sybil is using in the PIP meeting. Despondent, I secretly share this with my colleague. She quickly provides me with team stats she's been charged with managing all year. They show I am on track, and I've completed more work than in the previous year.

Sybil's statistics are a lie.

My motivation starts to drop. What started as an incredibly exciting job opportunity, slowly unfolds into the weirdest and most traumatic experience of my life.

Then at long last, after months of working at it, I get on top of my financial situation and repay enough of my loan to relax. Thank you, universe. The financial pressure is off. I've had enough.

Do I need to be here working for a woman who is making me feel more incompetent than I have in my entire life?

I go to bed on Sunday, dreading the morning meeting at which Sybil has promised to review the progress on my six-week plan. The last thing I want is one-on-one time with her.

My eyes flicker open.

FUCK! It's Monday.

Fear runs through my system like a power surge.

I don't want to be the mouse anymore. I'm done with feeling this way!

Today will be a turning point in my life. I cling to the safety of my blankets as I mull over my choices. The notion of placing myself in a meeting with Sybil makes me shudder.

I turn over in my cosy, safe bed.

There is no escape. If I go to work today, she'll be ready.

I reach down deep within myself and grab hold of my shredded dignity.

Not today. Not ever again!

My partner Rudy dials her direct number. "Gabe is sick and won't be in."

I exhale a deep sigh of relief.

I don't have a plan. All I can do is take one step at a time. I set an appointment with the doctor.

Tears tumble as I shed a little of my weary tale. Anxious days and restless nights have been part of my daily existence for too long. It feels strange to have someone listen.

Doctor Jane nods. "I want to reassure you, what you are going through is normal given what you've been experiencing. This kind of thing is rife. I have people coming to see me every single day."

I gasp. "I had no idea. I thought I was alone."

Doctor Jane prescribed time to rest and sleep medication, but I resolve to heal the natural way, even though I have no idea what that looks like.

Unsure of what to do, I surrender to my higher power and from then on take action on the guidance I receive. Call it instinctual knowing.

I knew this voice would guide me home.

In the few days of respite allowed by my medical certificate, I scour the internet and find a career coach in my vicinity.

We meet in a café. I feel immensely relieved to find her. The words I have held in for so long pour out. I just keep talking and crying in the café.

She is only too familiar with this story and nods her head as she listens. She asks, "Has HR advised you are entitled to have a support person with you for all of these meetings?"

I think for a moment. "No." They haven't.

My coach asks me a lot of questions, then warns, "I work with people who are taking their employers on over similar situations. If you choose this path, be prepared for the long haul – it's very arduous."

With her current knowledge, she helps me understand what I have control over and assures me whichever choice I make, she will guide me through it.

I choose to exit my employment. Even though I am full of fear and a blubbering mess in the final HR interview, by the time I am done, it feels like a triumph.

I have taken back my power.

Despite this small victory, I feel like a wreck. The haughty shrill of her voice, firing words like bullets, haunts me. I am incensed – with her, with the organisation I have worked for, with society, and with the world. I'd believed what society said – If I am good, do all the right things, I can expect a good life.

Society lied.

*

One day, I saw a sign for an art class, and somehow knew it was something I had to do. I enrolled on the spot. Exploring my artistic nature became an incredible new adventure, creating inner space in which to breathe. At once, I knew, I belonged here. I would never leave.

Then I took on new studies in Leadership, Coaching and Mentoring. What I learned blew my socks off. I'd spent my life trying to succeed in areas that weren't naturally my strengths. This incredible knowledge helped me unpack what had happened and got to the core of who I really am.

There, lurking in places I'd tried so hard to avoid, were intuitive gifts I didn't know I had. I can't tell you it was easy, but I can share how liberating it was.

As my awareness grew, I realised that for most of my life I'd been handing my power over to other people. I looked up to people, put them on pedestals. I believed they knew better than me. It took me to hit rock bottom for me to want to own my real power.

From the day I picked up the paint brush, I felt a new sense of optimism. Art was a bridge to my inner world and my ability to express myself. For years this had been missing.

I am free to be the Artist I was destined to be. My joy and expression of my deep appreciation for nature and the beauty is reflected in my paintings.

I'm on a mission to raise the profile of Art in our day to day world through my workshops and presentations. Art is a valuable, under-utilised resource that crosses boundaries and brings people together.

People come to my workshops with very little belief that they, too, can be creative. Seeing their looks of amazement when they discover they can, is incredible.

Last week, I participated in a public painting session. While I was working, I looked up to see Sybil sitting across the road, looking right at me.

I felt nothing. No terror, no angst, nothing.

This mouse is thriving, finally free of her tormentor.

CHAPTER 14

Me and the man behind the mask

Charleen Siteine

"Think twice. Being evil comes with a price, better think twice, 'cause evil comes with a price..."

I am startled in my sleep by loud sounds of heavy metal music playing. It's the theme song from his favourite TV series, Lucifer, playing in the background. He is pacing up and down the hallway, mumbling to himself.

"If she knew my feelings, she would be awake right by my side... I love her more than anything, but she keeps choosing to put me second. Why does she continue putting us in this position?"

I quietly reach over for my glasses, which are sitting on the side table next to me. I need to clear the blur in my eyes. I can see the redness and puffiness in his eyes, the frown on his face.

I let out a loud sigh because I am feeling so tired of seeing and watching him when he is like this.

He is draining all my energy and I barely have any left for our baby, Harper, let alone myself. I look inside his side table and straight away it is so obvious what could be wrong.

He's run out of drugs!

I know he'll be in one of his funny moods today, because of the way he's now sitting. He is stiff as a statue with his eyes still glued to the television screen. His arms are folded like he doesn't want to be touched.

I decide to join him in the living room, carrying Harper.

While I am singing nursery rhymes and playing peek a boo with Harper, I try and get Chris to join in with us. This is something he would normally do happily, but this time he's just not in the mood.

I try something new to turn his negative energy around… and cheerfully give him a good morning hug. His arms stay limp by his side, and he gets up to walk away without responding.

My brain has accustomed itself to get into this mode every time Chris enters into his kingdom of doom and gloom. It really doesn't make life any better or easier for any of us. I am constantly walking on eggshells, not knowing what each day will bring.

Especially because he is one person with me and a whole different person with others.

I sit on the couch contemplating what to do next, but at the same time trying to keep Harper quiet as best I can. I don't want whatever he is thinking or feeling to be triggered by loud unnecessary noises, which is proving to be rather difficult, given she's only eight months old… Babies make noises.

"Sssshhh, baby girl," I say, quietly.

He returns to our bedroom and even though it is the most gorgeous beautiful day outside, my insides don't portray that same warm feeling. If anything, it's the total opposite. Sitting there in silence is killing me inside.

Maybe I can ask him about work. Oh no, he'll get annoyed about that. Maybe if I talk about our upcoming two-year anniversary his tune may change and then he can focus on that… Maybe??

He has no motivation or drive to go to work or do anything productive with his time.

Usually he helps me out with Harper or is outside doing work on our house and even helping his friends… but today he just doesn't want to do anything. I get why he doesn't but time and time again he selfishly just thinks only of himself.

I am standing in the warmest part of the house, staring out the window, having mummy cuddles with baby girl Harper. I feel so cold, alone and anxious. I can see children playing and laughing outside, birds chirping, the outside world going along with its day… Meanwhile I am stuck here living in this toxic nightmare where I am feeling and wishing that I was in another place, a happier place just like the children that I can hear innocently playing outside.

Inside, Chris is wallowing so deeply in his own pitiful moment, he doesn't care about anything or anyone but himself.

While deep in my thoughts I am startled again.

Bang! Bang! Crash!

I hear the hard slamming of doors and raging banging of cupboards.

Why does he always do this?

My heart is beating rapidly and I can hardly breathe, but I build up the courage to go to the kitchen where he's making himself a coffee.

"Are you okay?" I probe.

The look he gives me is enough to stab me in the heart.

I can feel the hollow vibes he's sending out to me, like I'm meant to have superpowers to read his mind and know what is wrong with him.

Do I just let him be and wait for him to come to me to tell me what's up with him? Oh gosh, give me strength, please!!!

I'm frustrated… racking my brain to try and work out what's wrong.

He walks away from me into the spare room. However, I'm not ready to give up on changing his mood and ask him as lovingly as I can, "What's wrong, honey?"

This time he responds. There is so much rage and craziness in his big brown eyes as he comes up close and starts screaming at me.

"You're cheating on me!!" he roars. "I go to work and fuck knows what you are doing behind my back when I'm not here!

He is out of his mind! I try to remain calm and ask him, "Where is this all coming from?"

He yells back at me, "Don't you dare answer me with a question!!"

What on earth is he talking about?

"I moved from my family and friends so you can be near yours, and you think I'm cheating on you? Really?" It's ridiculous, but in my stress, I laugh loudly. Too loudly.

"You're just a bitch!" he says. "You chose to come back here, Charleen!" he says.

I've had enough of his behaviour and something inside me snaps.

"Oh, here we go again. Is this one of your mind control tactics, Chris? You always resort to this when you know I am right about something... and you call me a bitch? Wow."

I prepare myself for what will inevitably come next. Standing there with my hands on my hips with no fear, watching him act like a toddler having a tantrum because he isn't getting what he wants. All that is coming out of his mouth isn't much of an insult for me anymore because I have become immune to his angry verbal abuse.

Childishly, but aggressively, he says, "You're the dumbest bitch I've ever been with!"

"Oh my goodness, Chris, **GROW UP!**" I yell, angry and frustrated.

He spits in my face and says, "You dirty dog."

How did this become my life?

I can't take it anymore. I'm lost and confused. He's become so angry lately and I haven't done anything. "Do us all a favour and just leave!" I shout. Without thinking, I raise my hand at him, as though to slap him.

Whack!

The punch comes out of nowhere and sends me flying.

Cradling my right eye, I pick myself up and lock Harper and myself in the bathroom.

I start having flashbacks of my mother telling my sisters and I, "Once a man hits you, you leave him!"

I am laying uncomfortably, fully clothed, in the bathtub. Harper is sitting on my lap, innocently wiping away the tears rolling down my face, using her cute little hands.

I am shaking my head, feeling a mixture of emotions.

I have to leave him... But he needs help... But I have to leave him.

Chris was so different when we met. He was a tall, tanned and extremely handsome man who said all the right things and did all the right things too. He was like my dream man come true. His intelligence blew me away... His kind and loving nature towards me was unbelievable... but the thing which earned him the sign of approval and made me fall in love with him was how he opened up his heart to my young children. The bond he created with them was truly something genuine and special.

I remember that day when I was cleaning up in the kitchen and he asked me, "Can we talk about something important?"

I had dried my wet hands with a tea towel next to me, and went to sit down at the dining table where Chris was anxiously waiting for me...

As I sat down, I had nervously said, "Yes, of course. What is it?" My heart was pounding and my head was spinning, trying to figure out what he wanted to talk about. He was sitting in front of me, holding my hand, with a big smile on his face. He was breathing deeply, in and out. I could see how nervous he was.

He said, "I don't know how to say this without mucking up, so here I go... I love you so much. You know that, right?"

"Yes," I'd said. *Where is this going?*

"You also know how much I see your kids as my own, right?"

"Of course," I had replied.

Again, he breathed deeply, in and out... I was doing the same because I didn't know what else to do or say to Chris to make him say what he needs to. It was so hard to know what to expect from this conversation with him, especially because he wasn't giving me any kind of hint as to what it was all about.

"What is it?" I had asked. The anticipation was killing me.

He finally blurted out "Let's have a baby!"

I was speechless. We'd only known each other for three weeks.

"Are you sure?" I said.

Four months later I said, "I'M PREGNANT!!"

Hearing Harper giggling loudly, I am quickly snapped out of my memory, facing the reality of what my life is like now.

Things have changed so much, and it is filled with so much heartache and misery. I have grown to hate my life with him in it.

I even contemplate taking my life because I am so miserable, but when I see my daughter smiling and hear her giggles, I snap myself out of it. I need to try harder for her.

Maybe one day Chris will soften his heart and allow me to see my family again.

Over the next couple of days I look in the mirror... My right eye has swelled and a nasty black bruise appears. I try to cover the bruising with make-up but it's painful to touch, and I get dizzy multiple times a day. It's like being on a merry go round that just won't slow down for you.

As he casually walks past me with a smug look on his face, he acts like nothing has happened.

"I can't even go anywhere looking like this," I tell him. "The right side of my head is throbbing, and it won't stop. I need to go see my doctor." I feel like something is really wrong.

"Don't worry about what others will think, just tell them Harper headbutted you."

He wants to blame our daughter?

"Why can't you ever acknowledge when you have done wrong, Chris? Why, Chris? You stand there looking at me like you are Mr Perfect, when that is so far from the truth."

It's so typical of him to try and put the blame onto someone else for his mistakes. I was told by so many people that this is how Chris is, and they warned me and made it so clear that I would end up like this with him. In my euphoric state at the time, I chose not to listen to any of them. I thought they were all lying to me.

Feeling so much deep frustration within myself, I wish I had listened to these people because everything they told me that would happen... happened.

I feel like such a stupid fool... but I have to be strong for Harper and just keep on moving forward for her.

Finishing up his advice, he says, "You don't need a doctor, take Nurofen and go sleep it off."

Bastard.

Tears are rolling down my face because he is so blasé and carefree about the whole thing. He obviously doesn't love me.

I can't believe the nerve of this human being, refusing to take ownership of what he did to me. And now that I have to endure this unbearable pain because of his hard fist to my face, he refuses to take me to the doctor.

He keeps telling me I brought this upon myself... But, did I?

I convince myself it's my fault I'm in this situation with Chris. It is my eighth time coming back to him so of course it is, right?

I had come back over and over again, expecting a different result, but sadly, nothing ever changed.

"At least I live to see another day," I say to myself.

Days go by and my bruises are starting to fade. The sun is shining, the birds are singing, and I am feeling very optimistic for a better and happier day as I go about my usual household duties and making sure our bills are paid.

That is when I notice two unfamiliar transactions on my bank statement.

What are these for?

At that moment he walks through the door home early from work. I am puzzled as I'm surprised but make a conscious decision in my mind to not make a big deal out of him coming home earlier than usual. Instead, I take this opportunity to bring up my findings on my bank statement.

I casually say to him while he is pouring himself a cold glass of beer, "Mr Smith, you have some explaining to do..."

"What are you on about now?" he says aggressively.

I show him the two unfamiliar transactions on my bank statements... but before I could finish my sentence, he abruptly interrupts me, all defensive and says "I have had enough shit at work. I don't need this shit from you."

This time I don't hold back my thoughts and I say "Why are you getting angry? What are you hiding?"

"Ha," he says. "I'm not hiding anything from you, it's the other way around!"

He walks over to the spare room carrying his work bag. As he unzips it a familiar scent comes out of it; It's his 'happy stuff'.

I am standing there rolling my eyes at him watching him inhale with disapproval, but of course he just ignores me as usual.

I have lost so much because of him and his mind control and manipulation, his lies and deceit, his drug addiction and his abusive language and behaviour.

I can't take it anymore. I really can't. What can I do to have an impact? What will make him take notice? He needs help.

Feeling unafraid, I convince myself to grab his stash and run out of the room holding onto it so tightly he starts running after me yelling at me, "Give it back to me, you crazy bitch!!"

I refused and yelled back at him, "Please, you need to get help, you have a drug problem!!"

He catches up to me and aggressively grabs my wrist and snatches his stash out of my hand. "You bitch!" he yells.

I quickly run over to the spare room and see the rest of his happy stuff and throw it on the floor, spilling it everywhere. I don't want him to have it anymore.

Then, standing steadfast and unshakeable I demand, "Tell me the truth about these bank transactions! Who were you really with?!"

At the same time, Harper wakes up from her nap and as I am about to pick her up, he grabs her.

"Give her to me!" I cry, but he refuses.

Harper starts crying, and it escalates quickly. He gives her to me to settle her, but he's full of rage because of what I have done to his bowl of drugs.

I am holding Harper and turning away to shield her from his anger. But I am helpless against his rage. Chris lunges towards me. He grabs me and puts his hands around my throat, choking me until I can hardly breathe.

He squeezes my throat, hard. I am gasping, breathless, trying to pull away. I must protect my baby.

He pushes me towards where I tipped his stash, shouting at me, "Pick up every single bit of that shit up!"

Again, he grabs Harper off me as I try gathering all his drugs from off the floor with him yelling at me like I'm an animal who has disobeyed their master.

While I am scrambling on the floor, he says, "I don't deserve this, I'm leaving you. I can't do this with you anymore! Harper needs stability in her life, and you can't give that to her."

No! Don't take my baby!

I cry loudly, begging and pleading, kneeling in front of him. Sorry. Grovelling.

"Please don't take my baby away from me! I will make things better for us and I will never disobey you again, I promise... but please don't take my baby away from me!"

He ignores my pleas and walks out of the room with Harper in his arms. He grabs his keys and wallet and heads to the front door.

I run after him, screaming, "Give my baby back to me!"

The neighbours who live two houses away from us hear my cries, and rush out, asking, "What's going on?"

Hysterically, I beg them, "Call the police. Please. That drug addict won't give my baby back!"

The neighbours invite me into their home, trying to calm me down and call the police at the same time.

A few minutes before the men in blue arrive, Chris brings Harper back to me because she wouldn't stop crying while she was with him. As she reaches her arms out to me, my tears turn into smiles.

I let out a sigh of relief, but at the same time I see tears rolling down Chris's face. I see the sadness in his eyes as he slowly lets go of her. "I will love you always, Chicken," he says gently to her. Then he looks over at me and says, "I never wanted it to be this way for our family."

I look into Chris's eyes and respond with the same words he used on me once upon a time not that long ago. I whisper closely into his ear, "You really brought this upon yourself, you know?"

Within seconds a police car turns into the driveway, and two officers step out of the vehicle. They want to question the both of us in separate rooms.

I sit on the couch, tapping the tips of my fingers on my phone, anxiously awaiting my turn. My legs are shaking uncontrollably. Minutes later, the police officers come and talk to me but instead of questioning me they say, "Chris is not in the right frame of mind to talk to anyone. Do you have friends or family you can go and stay with? Or would you like to return home to Brisbane?"

The neighbours piped up with their strong German accents, "We will help anyway we can."

Thank you, I mouth silently to them.

The police go to get my belongings from the house, but return saying that Chris has asked to see his daughter again.

The police ask my permission, and I say, "Yes, he can see her for a minute."

Afterwards, I take Harper back into the neighbours' house so I can start making plans for what to do next.

They ask me, "Have you got all your identification and details?"

"What for?" I ask.

"To book your flights back home to Brisbane," they reply.

"Please, you can't!"

The kind older man takes me in his arms and says, "You need to go home and be with ALL your family, okay? No man is worth your tears! You need to go and keep Harper safe, okay?"

With my watery eyes I look at him and just nod my head.

*

Walking through the gates to board our plane I am holding on tightly to Harper when I feel my pocket vibrate. I reach for my mobile phone and instantly see it is a message from Chris. Then a second message, then a third, then a fourth... The messages don't stop.

Where are you?

Please come home

I need my beautiful girls

I'm going to get help for what you did to me

I love you

For a moment I pause... *Should I stay?*

But then I think back over the things he has said and done, and the advice from my mum, and I know I can't. Leaving might be the hardest thing I could ever do, but it would also be the bravest.

I look at my beautiful baby girl and am quickly reminded why I shouldn't give him another chance.

But despite being in a place filled with so many people around us and security guards doing their job, paranoia kicks in. I can't stop looking over my shoulder.

What if he finds me?

My heart is pounding. I'm so eager to just get on the plane and away from here. As I'm cuddling Harper, tears are rolling down my face. A stranger next to us offers me tissues but I jump off my chair thinking they have a whole different agenda. What's wrong with me? I am scared.

"All parents and children first please," I hear over the intercom.

It's time.

Anxiously standing in line, I am watching other parents and their children. I see their happy faces and joyous smiles and I hear the excitement in their little voices about going on a holiday or special trip.

Meanwhile, I am standing here feeling exhausted and tired with Harper. I am eagerly wanting to just get on the plane and rest our weary heads but instead I break down and cry uncontrollably.

Why did he have to change?

*

As the plane touches down in my hometown, I look at Harper as she stares at me with the cutest smile on her pretty little face. Smiling back at my baby I say, "We're home, sweetie."

I am feeling overwhelmed and scared at the same time as I am about to be reunited with my mother, who I have not spoken to in a very long time.

As we walk through Arrivals I am greeted with my mother's wide-open arms. She pulls me into her embrace and says, "Welcome home, Daughter." I get all emotional and cry in her arms.

We walk through the door of my parents' house and I am filled with emotion. Sitting in the lounge I see five sets of beautiful eyes staring back at me, wide-eyed and very surprised.

My other children.

They have been living with my parents while Chris and I tried to work out our relationship, because I didn't want them to be exposed to the drama… but with all Chris's lies, manipulation and anger, the time had dragged out much longer than anticipated.

I have missed them so much and cried for them in bed most nights.

And now I was home.

None of them, except my eldest, knew that Harper and I were coming home, so this is a massive surprise.

My handsome sons quickly run over to me and give me the biggest hugs. My beautiful youngest daughter is holding onto my mum's hand tightly, looking unsure if I am really standing there. My gorgeous eldest daughter, who knew I was coming home today, is standing there, speechless. I know this is a lot for her to take in. I go over to give her a hug but as I do, she reaches her arms out for Harper instead and hugs her with tears rolling down her beautiful face.

*

It's been a rollercoaster ride these past few years and the time since I reunited with my children, but as I sit here watching my adorable little blessings, hearing them laughing and playing happily with so much joy with one another, I am content.

I reflect on all the endless counselling sessions I went through.

I reflect on how I have rebuilt my relationship with my family and friends and even made new friends along the way who I wouldn't know had I not experienced this horrific time in my life.

I reflect on the endless sleepless nights and anxiety I'd feel whenever I went out with my children.

But I look at how my life is now and how truly blessed I am to be able to tell my story because sadly some don't survive such an ordeal.

I'm sad that my daughter was not able to have a close relationship with her father, but I did what I could to make it work, and finally realised there was nothing I could do. I have to protect her, myself, and my other children from the negative impact of having him around.

I survived the rollercoaster of disasters which came from living with him.

I survived the lies, the anger, the deceit, the trauma.

And today I am stronger, smarter, secure.

I'm a better mum and a happier person, and I want to pass my learnings onto my children. Especially my daughters.

"You are beautiful. You are strong. You are worthy," I say to them. "I will always be here for you, no matter what, and you can always, *always* walk away when you are not treated right."

I have shown them that eventually, after trying and falling down many times, that this is exactly what I did.

I survived.

I am worthy.

I am beautiful.

I am here.

CHAPTER 15

The best time to change is now

Brett D. Scott

"Hi Brett, this is Lyn."

My admin manager never calls so early in the morning.

"We've just been audited, and we have a problem."

This doesn't sound good.

"Over the last 18 months, you've managed to overcharge us by $50,000."

Silence.

"What?" I don't really get it. *Overcharge?*

"Yes. Our prices already have GST included, but you have added it on top... so, between all our clients, you've collected roughly $50,000 more than you should have since you started with us." Lyn sounds calm but I can feel the tension in her voice.

Fuck.

"You're going to have to pay it back."

Telling your wife you owe 50k is never going to be an easy task.

Telling your wife who also happens to be three months pregnant, is even harder.

I have no backup plan, no other job, no major assets I can sell, no savings, no business yet operating, a bad credit history… and of course, a baby on the way.

I'm feeling sick to my stomach. I want to run away. I want to curl up in a ball.

Can I make this go away? How did I let life get this bad?

Things hadn't always been such a mess, but slowly, over time, I made bad choice after bad choice, and finally, it's all caught up to me.

*

I'd spent years as a Hotel Concierge in both Melbourne and Sydney and then with Europcar as their Hotel Account Manager, which started out great, but over time wasn't fulfilling enough.

It didn't help that I was partying way more than I was working. Thursday blended into Monday in a haze of booze and party-pleasing pills, followed by a three-day hangover and sleep deprivation.

Not a winning combination.

But then I discovered something I could put all my energy into. I could finally become the proper entrepreneur I knew I could be.

In 2002, I got one of my best mates, Kon, to help me start a Melbourne-based magazine. It was a rebirth of a publication a fellow concierge used to operate – *Concierge Magazine* – and from that moment on *Blueprint Media* Australia was born.

Catering for the hotel industry, the magazine became fairly successful.

"Hey Carlos, this is Brett Scott. I'm running Concierge Magazine and we'd love to do a feature on the Black and White Winter Ball you guys are running in July. Can you give me an exclusive?"

I'd known Carlos in the decade I'd spent as a concierge in Melbourne and Sydney.

"Of course, my friend," Carlos had said. And he was true to his word. We ran a three-page feature and attracted thousands of dollars of advertising to go along with it.

My ability to form great relationships served me well, and with all the people I'd worked with and helped over the years, I had a plethora of contacts to call upon when doing featured events.

It was a winning formula.

The magazine started making significant money fairly quickly, so we decided to expand into Sydney and Brisbane. More locations meant more money, right?

Turns out that's not always the case.

We attempted to grow too quickly and stretched ourselves too thin. In early 2005 the wheels started to fall off, and we had to offer it to a bigger publisher in exchange for payment of our printing.

My wife Elissa had been with me since the start of my magazine career, and even though it had fallen apart around the same time as our wedding, she was incredibly supportive. She worked hard to earn money in the early days when I wasn't pulling my weight financially, and she was there for me emotionally, too.

She also knew I had it in me to be successful.

"You'll be okay, babe," she'd said, rubbing the back of my neck. "This magazine thing is just a blip on the radar. You'll go on to do bigger and better things."

And she was right about me moving on. In true entrepreneurial style, I turned to the next thing.

I'd always thought about being a real estate agent, and my mates in the industry said I was a natural.

I loved meeting the buyers and sellers, and I always had my clients front of mind.

"Look, I know you've got your heart set on $1,500,000, but as we've seen with the other offers and feedback from buyers, that price just isn't there at the moment," I'd say, being genuinely transparent with a seller. "You mentioned the property you want to buy could potentially be bought for $950,000, so if we accept the $1.44m we have, you're still out on top."

A conversation like that would be difficult for some agents, but when I knew what I was saying was true and was in the best interest of the client, it came naturally.

"Right now it feels like you're not getting what you want, but after you move into the new home, decorate it, have friends over and start building new memories, you'd have to agree the perceived loss will be insignificant?"

They'd accept the offer.

And so it went. I sold bigger and better homes and attracted clients from several of the upper-class areas.

Along with this, I also learned early in the game that a lot of real estate is about appearance.

"Mate, you can't drive that shit heap around," my colleague had said as we had both arrived for one of my first listing appointments.

"Get stuffed!" I said. "It gets me from A to B."

But he was serious. A real estate agent needs a great car, but I didn't have the money, so I got a loan for a shiny black BMW.

And a loan for a few other things it turned out I needed.

I felt like I needed the lifestyle to keep up with the image I'd created.

But I *was* a great agent. That part they were right about. I won an award as Residential Salesperson of the Year from the REIV (Real Estate Institute of Victoria) in 2007.

People are actually recognising my abilities.

It was a tremendous feeling. I had the support of a beautiful wife *and* the recognition of the industry.

I coasted along for years, on a high. Nothing and nobody could touch me.

This is what I was born to do.

But on the money front, I was overcommitting. My spending was out of control. I couldn't keep up repayments. I almost lost my beautiful car and the stress was beginning to show.

In 2011 I was officially declared bankrupt.

How could I tell my wife?

So I didn't.

I just acted like a stressed-out bastard instead.

I knew what a big deal this was. I imagined that if I told her what had happened, she'd end our marriage. Selfishly, I couldn't allow that to happen.

"Brett, can we discuss the money situation?" Elissa would complain.

"For fuck's sake, I've been doing my best. I've had to buy things for work... Just give me a break," I'd say.

I put her through hell.

"I think you need to see a psychologist," she said at the end of one particularly difficult day.

"I think you're right," I said, while not really believing it. Anything to keep the peace.

I just need to stop stressing about money and I'll be okay... I thought.

But it wasn't so simple.

Money wasn't the root cause of my issues, but I couldn't see it at the time.

I had my sessions with the psychologist, but I wasn't being honest enough with myself or her to get the help she could offer. "Oh yeah... I guess it's just the stress of work and not getting the results I want lately," I explained to the psych.

"Do you think if I gave you some exercises to do, it may help you with your ability to de-stress and work things out with your wife?" she questioned.

"Sure, yeah sure. I don't see why not," I said.

But I knew it wasn't going to help and had no real intention of doing them. It was just easier to tell her what I thought she wanted to hear.

She doesn't know what she's talking about.

Once Elissa and I have a baby, we'll focus on that, and things will get back to normal.

Although it seemed like even in that department, I was a failure.

I had lost interest in sex and was a terrible communicator.

"Come on, babe," she'd say. "We haven't been intimate in ages. I miss you." She'd wear nice lingerie and give me attention, but I was so out of touch, I couldn't show her the affection she deserved.

"Can you stop nagging me for sex?" I'd say. "I've got a lot on my mind right now."

I love her unconditionally, so what's the problem?

I was pushing her away, but I couldn't see it. So I focused on the things I thought were important.

I joined a business called Trainer HQ, where we helped personal trainers grow their business, and the money started rolling in.

Elissa and I moved to Noosa, and rented a stunning townhouse overlooking the Noosaville river. She was able to quit her job and we trained daily, went to the beach all the time, and had a much healthier diet.

Not long after, we discovered we were pregnant.

Finally, all the pieces were falling into place.

Or so I thought.

I had hoped her pregnancy would heal things between us, but I was wrong. Having a baby doesn't fix things; and it can certainly highlight the cracks in a crumbling marriage.

That's when I got the phone call about owing $50,000 to the business partners of Trainer HQ for incorrect invoicing. I was never great with numbers, so it was an honest mistake... but it was my mistake, and the debt still had to be paid.

And it was also time to pay the piper with my marriage.

We separated before our beautiful son, Orlando, was born.

It was time to get my life together.

Things had to change.

I had to change.

*

Over a decade earlier, my mate Hunter had shown me the film 'The Secret', which is about the law of attraction and manifesting the life you desire.

Bob Proctor was one of the experts in The Secret, and stood out to me as someone whose message I really liked. For 13 years I had been liking his social media posts and receiving his email newsletter... until one day I received an email which would ultimately change my life.

SUBJECT: Are you ready for a change? Have you been stuck?

It was an invitation to his world-famous Paradigm Shift event, live streamed from Los Angeles.

I sat down with a coffee to watch the event online. As soon as Bob walked on stage, I could feel the energy of those present at the live event.

"If you can see it in your mind, you can hold it in your hand."

"A paradigm is a multitude of habits stored in the subconscious mind," Bob proclaimed. "Once we change the Paradigms that are controlling the outcomes in life we don't desire, we can start attracting the life we truly do," he said.

I really can change, I thought.

I reached up to wipe away a tear which had sneakily dripped out of the corner of my eye. *Why on earth are you crying?*

As I watched Bob speak, lightning bolts of revelation kept hitting me.

You can do this.

Your old life doesn't define you.

Anything is possible.

Oh my God, you're going to be successful this time.

I felt around down the side of the lounge for a tissue box, as the tears started flowing. It was like my heart, my soul, my energy, my whole being had been broken down over time, until I didn't even know who I was anymore… and now I had finally been broken open.

I was ready.

I vowed that I was NEVER going to be this man again. I was going to change and make a big impact in the world.

I decided to write a book to help other men in a similar situation, to show them that it's possible to change and have the life you desire, even at an older age.

I repaid the debt to my bosses at Trainer HQ in less than a year and repaired the relationship to the point I was able to keep working with them. They have been an incredible support, and them backing me after what I put them through is a testament to their character.

Even though we divorced, I helped Elissa remain a stay-at-home-Mum for the first three years of our son's life, and still to this day I pay well above what most men pay their ex-partners for child support.

I worked full-time, studied at night to become a Personal Trainer, and continued working part time for Trainer HQ. I kept up a high level of fitness, competed in many runs and mountain challenges and most importantly, I made a decision to take 12 months off dating to spend time healing myself properly.

It's been quite a journey.

Along the way, I discovered exactly why I fucked up so many opportunities and wasn't achieving the life I knew was possible.

I soon came to accept that everything in this world which happens to us is totally our making. Some of these things we think are bad luck or out of our control have occurred when we have gotten ourselves into that situation in the first place.

When it comes to children and babies, the situations in their life are generally present due to the actions and decisions of the adults in their midst... but for everyone old enough to make decisions and choices, the results in our life are 100% our responsibility.

It took me sometime to really come to terms with this and understand the smallest decisions which I thought didn't mean much, actually, over time, meant a lot.

I changed the way I made decisions. I check in with my gut, and my intuition, and if it feels like I'm making a 'Yes' decision for the right purpose, not my own selfish reasons, then I keep moving. Even if I might fail.

Beyond that, I learned about the importance of making quick decisions. Why? Because often your first thought is the right one. Have you ever noticed the longer you take to decide, the more confusing it gets?

That's because if the program running in your subconscious mind doesn't agree with the thought or decision, it will try and talk you out of it. This makes it harder to distinguish intuition from experience, and a negative experience from the past can affect your decisions about the future, even when the outcome could have been very different.

This was backed by a study personally conducted by Napoleon Hill back in the 1920-1930s where he interviewed over 500 of the most successful people of that time. His interview subjects included Henry Ford, Thomas A. Edison and Andrew Carnegie, the richest man in the world at the time (and the person who hired Mr. Hill to create a modern philosophy about thinking and growing rich).

All of these people said the same thing – it was one of the common denominators of their success; speedy decisions. In fact, Mr. Carnegie later told Mr. Hill he was timing him for his decision to accept his proposal, and he certainly passed.

Bob Proctor reads *Think and Grow Rich* every single day, and it forms the foundations of his teachings.

Many of the people who have worked with Bob and followed his work, have become successful in a way which inspires me. They have prosperity and abundance way beyond the financial and material. They have effective relationships, good friendships, happiness, balance, and joy.

I wanted more of that, and over the last year, that's exactly what I've created in my life.

But I went further than what I learned with Bob, and have really thrown myself into changing my approach and living the life of my dreams.

I found a mentor/coach, invested in a program, invested in coaches to help where I don't have specialised knowledge, make speedy decisions and I keep these commitments, have patience and persistence on this journey of success… and I enjoy every single moment with gratitude.

I recognise the programs/beliefs/habits that were not serving me and changed them for more positive ones. I study, understand and apply the information learnt, without waiting until it's perfect.

My heart is full of gratitude.

Every morning and every night without fail, I make it a point to write, read, and say aloud the things I am grateful for. A grateful heart is paramount to your success.

"I'm so happy and grateful now that Orlando is my son, he loves me as I love him, and I'm the best Dad for him," I say daily. I also speak gratitude out loud for many things such as; I wake up healthy and well, able bodied, breathing fresh air, drinking clean water, have a great circle of friends and family, a super successful business, clients who achieve amazing results and are constantly attracting abundance.

It seemed strange at first, but I learned that the key to gratitude or positive things you might say you love about yourself, is that some things may already exist, but others may be aspects or things you were working on manifesting, like self-worth, millions of dollars (popular choice), certain skills, and new relationships. The list is endless.

I have also discovered joy in helping and inspiring others. My favourite practice is based on 'The Golden Rule', which is best summed up by my mentor Bob as the 'Impression of Increase'. Simply put, to convey the impression of increase, you must want the same for everybody that you want for yourself. It's about leaving others feeling better than before they met you.

In fact W. Clement Stone, who ended up working with Napoleon Hill, was reported the richest man in the world in the 1970s and he said one of the keys to his success was that every single day he ensured he found a way to help someone without them knowing he had done it.

My purpose in life is to help people in their late 30s and beyond, who feel as though time has pipped them at the post in regard to being successful.

I came so close to that decision. I started feeling like I should just be happy having mediocre success, being alive, and simply 'having a job'.

But deep down, that wasn't the life I wanted.

And luckily, it's not over until it's over, as they say… and even at 45, this beautiful life is far from over.

Today, I'm sitting on the beach, watching my son play. He's smiling and laughing over at me, kicking water at me. Before we came to the beach, we were playing, making jokes, listening to dance music and pretending to fart… Yes, pretending ;)

"Dad, can you carry me on your shoulders?" he says, lifting his arms up. I hoist him up and hear him laugh as he looks out to sea, sitting up so much higher on his dad's strong shoulders.

"I can see a dolphin!" he says, pointing out towards the horizon. I squint my eyes to see it too. I can't see anything, but I am sure it's out there somewhere.

Or maybe he is just seeing a life full of promise, where anything he dreams is possible.

I know I am.

CHAPTER 16

Healing autoimmune - naturally

Taking control of my health and debunking the 'no cure' myth

Marsha Schults

Sitting across my doctor's desk, with my heart in my throat, I couldn't believe what I was hearing... 'An MS Hug'.

"A what?"

I think I stopped breathing.

Did she just say 'MS'? Is this what I've been dealing with for the past 7 years??

My whole body started to tremble as I felt the familiar weakness of chronic fatigue I'd come to know so well, consume my whole body. My legs went numb. My heart started pounding. So much ran through my mind. I didn't know if I wanted to cry, scream or lunge at her across the desk. I was furious!! And relieved... *now I know for sure what I am dealing with, and I'm NOT going insane.*

"Do you have difficulty swallowing?"

"Yes, a little. Mostly tablets and I never used to have trouble."

"Has your handwriting been affected?"

"Yes, I have to write in capitals. I can't use running writing anymore."

I'd forgotten about that.

I wanted to cry from frustration. Finally, some answers. Barely able to walk, it took all my physical, emotional and mental energy just to stand and to get through each day while also suffering from severely debilitating systemic pain.

I dreaded going to my doctor with this latest episode of mysterious symptoms to add to my list. Was she going to believe me?

I'll never forget the last appointment, when she recommended that I see a psychiatrist. I was enraged! Of course, I didn't go... I knew there was nothing wrong with me mentally. I knew my own body and I most certainly did not want more drugs.

I clearly remember telling her five years before, "Something's wrong. I can feel it, I know it." I had always been intuitively connected to my own body.

I'd had every test you could think of and most came back clear. *I guess I can't blame her for thinking I'm nuts.* That's the problem with Autoimmune. It's an 'invisible' disease.

I always presented well, taking pride in my appearance. I never left the house on the days I looked unwell, even when I had to go to the doctor. I washed and blow dried my hair every morning into a stylish, short, concave bob and applied makeup. Only a small amount, but enough to hide the deep, dark circles around my eyes.

I loved wearing my shiny, white, pearl earrings or diamond studs. I always dressed in nice clothes and often wore my favourite, black patent shoes with a small fabric bow over the toes. Besides taking pride in my appearance, dressing nicely disguised how I really felt.

I didn't want to bring any attention to my ailing health or give 'it' any power over me. I wanted to stay in control. But, MS?

Thoughts were running through my head. I remembered years ago, our neighbour had MS and she was wheelchair-bound. She was dependent on her family and needed 24-hour care. I felt sick.

I'd always overcome any adversity in my life. I'd always climbed back on top. But for the first time, I felt defeated and it really scared me. Can I beat this, too? How? My mind whirled with all the natural therapies I'd already spent thousands of dollars on, not to mention the countless diets and supplements that only drained my bank account and made little impact on improving my health.

I had never heard of the 'MS Hug' and certainly did not expect this today. I struggled to explain the symptoms without feeling embarrassed.

"Three times this happened and I was home alone each time. I was SO scared!" *Actually, I thought I was going to collapse and die – but I didn't dare tell her that!* Tears started welling. "It was like a snake wrapped itself around me and squeezed all the air out of my lungs. I was gasping for air and I couldn't talk. It lasted about 20-30 seconds – but I didn't know that when it happened the first time…

"And the list of food intolerances is getting bigger, too. I can't eat out anymore." I had lost three kilos from my slim frame. "I'm scared of eating, because I don't know what's causing the anaphylaxis."

I showed her photos of my swollen face.

She didn't say anything.

It was obvious that she was having trouble keeping up with me as she tapped away at the keyboard. With my arms wrapped around my body and sitting on the edge of my seat, I demonstrated, "The sensation started here, under my ribs and went right up to my throat, like a tight band around my chest. Then the sensation reversed, from my throat down to my ribs and I was able to take a big breath again."

I was anxious, embarrassed and tears were now flowing. The stress of verbalizing the reality was far too much to bear. Telling the truth made it real. I was so embarrassed. *How did I get here? What would her reaction be?* I already felt like a hypochondriac every time I stepped foot into her office.

I knew I would be fatigued for several days, as my nervous system simply could not handle any type of stress. I had avoided crying for a long time so, internalising my emotions was the only way I could cope. This proved difficult when my mum passed away from Acute Myeloid Leukemia six months earlier, after a short, six-week battle. I had bottled it all up and with this news, I could feel the dis-ease building in my body…

Was this just emotion expressing itself? I dismissed the idea. I didn't have the mental strength to contemplate anything. I barely heard a word she said about what happens next. Something about a neurologist. I did hear that. "But I asked you about that two years ago and I'm still waiting for the appointment letter!" I felt justified feeling angry and raising my voice.

I had been passive for way too long and before I knew it, I was on prescription pain medication, sleep medication, antidepressants, Vitamin B12 shots, antihistamine, steroids, and anti-inflammatories.

How did this happen? I'd had a keen interest in natural health and supplementation for 17 years. I had researched, attended many talks and seminars, read books, and scoured the internet for information. How had I lost control of my health?

It was at this point that I decided to quit the practice where I didn't feel supported and find something new.

Making this decision empowered me, but that was short lived...

I was on my own.

As soon as I arrived home I looked up 'MS Hug' and there it was. Exactly what I had been experiencing...

> *'The MS hug is a multiple sclerosis symptom that feels like there is a tight band around the chest or torso. Like many MS symptoms, the MS hug feels different from person to person. Various people have described it as a feeling of pressure, an ache, a tickle, a pain, or a burning sensation.'*

I couldn't believe what I was reading. It made it so real. I started to panic.

The next few days went by in a haze. I was so scared. I didn't know what to do with myself. I didn't eat. I didn't sleep. The thought of 'surrendering' crossed my mind. *I can't do this anymore.* I had nothing left. I knew that if I decided to give up, I would fall to the floor and I wouldn't be able to get back up. I'd need the walker to support me.

*

Sitting in a sunny spot of a corner cafe only nine months earlier, with my head in my hands, I'd felt so nervous expressing my every-day struggle to Roslyn. Ros knew about the stressful events I had endured since we'd become friends in 2003.

We shared a common interest in health and nutrition and had attended many health seminars and personal development workshops together over the years.

I felt safe to open up and she recognised my struggle to speak fluently. Like a three-year-old learning to read, I missed words and lost my way mid-conversation.

I hadn't slept for months.

The pain in my head was difficult to describe. Swelling. *Was my brain swollen?* I felt like I was going crazy. For too long I had hidden my severe emotional, mental and physical suffering...

I expressed to Roslyn how bad things had become and reached for my tissues. My hay fever was out of control and antihistamines made me so tired. I was sick of myself. My doctor diagnosed me with major depressive disorder. I was SO embarrassed. I couldn't hold myself together and poured my heart out to Ros.

"I've even outsourced my accounts!" I told Ros. No, I wasn't running a business... I couldn't even manage my budget. It was costing me $45 a week and as a single parent barely managing to work part time, this added to my stress levels, but it was an absolute necessity, so I sacrificed in other areas.

Ros asked me how I was managing to work. I explained that working as a disability support worker was the perfect set up for me during this time and I was grateful for my job. I was able to disguise my suffering by working alone. My client was an intellectually disabled, non-verbal female in her early 30's, who liked to be left alone.

I was required to do basic household duties, personal care, and medication administration. After fulfilling my duties, my time was my own to lie on the floor and rest. Perfect.

I reminded Ros about how my ailing health had also cost me my job as a sign language interpreter in an early learning development centre, for deaf and hearing-impaired babies and children, aged one to five.

I had loved my job. It was very fulfilling. My daughter having a hearing impairment meant I could relate to mothers bringing their newborns in, with fear of what the future might hold for their child.

I had studied for 18 months. I noticed my memory wasn't as sharp as it used to be, and I struggled with learning. I left my job after two years, embarrassed that I wasn't improving like the others I had studied with.

"And remember the time I was diagnosed with PTSD when Taylor was hit by a car that went through a red light?"

"Oh Marsha, I remember. That was such a difficult time for you both."

*

It had happened the first day of our holiday on the Gold Coast. It was a spectacular sunny day. I felt happy. We were deep in conversation and feeling excited about her going into high school the following year. Making our way to the cinema, we were waiting patiently for the green walking signal.

We entered the intersection, but I didn't look before walking, which I would normally do.

Screeeeeeeech!

Adrenaline immediately hijacked my body as I looked right towards the car approaching us. We were directly in its path. I looked left at Taylor. Panic on her face. I took a step back, but Taylor decided to run to the traffic median.

"NOOOO!!!!" I yelled.

I pulled her back.

The car hit her left leg and she bounced onto the bonnet and then onto the road, with a hard thud. Her leg was twisted and broken in several places. The shock hit me instantly. I couldn't feel my body and I feared being hit by the cars going around us.

*

"No wonder you've been stressed," Ros said, remembering all that we'd been through after the accident. "I imagine it really compounded and added to your health issues." With everything we'd both been through over the years, we'd learned a lot about the effects of stress on the body...

I was becoming very uncomfortable sitting on the hard, wooden café chair. *This is why I don't go out.* My back was aching so badly.

I told Ros I was $10,000 in debt – and mortified to be standing in line to apply for government assistance, hoping no one saw me walk in. I didn't belong there. I wanted to work. I had goals and plans to travel and buy a house. I could even detect a look of confusion from the ladies behind the desk.

They're right to be confused. What am I doing here?

I stopped seeing family. The most embarrassing moment of my life was when I asked my stepmother how her mother was feeling – forgetting that she had passed away three months earlier.

Most days it took all my strength not to collapse into tears.

Listening to me speak, Ros had tears in her eyes and she clearly saw the desperation in mine. I trusted her, and she knew it was the right time to suggest a stem cell regeneration product she had been taking herself.

"It's only been available for 12 months in Australia and the stories I've been hearing are incredible. I even managed to convince my girls to take it, and now they're both off the drugs."

As long as I'd known Ros, three of her four adult children were deeply troubled by drugs and the lifestyle choices that come with addiction. They were always in and out of rehabs, prison, psychiatric wards, and one even had open heart surgery due to endocarditis from a dirty needle. I remember the day her cash was stolen and the police were called. It had been twenty years of pain, stress, and immense heartache in fear of losing her children.

"You know how hard it's been for me and I'm so glad they actually listened when I offered to pay for it. I would do anything to help them, and it's been absolutely amazing. They are really, truly off the drugs and thriving, and I'm even going to spend the weekend with them. This stem cell thing is the real deal, Marsha." Ros was positively glowing across the table and looked at me intently as she took both my hands in hers.

"This stuff changes brain chemistry. I even watched a video of a guy called Mike, who improved his MS. If there's a chance it would help, would you be keen?"

If this supplement could do all that, I'm in.

Ros handed me something when we said our goodbyes. I struggled to get up off my chair and almost fainted. My legs were heavy. The inflammation in my brain and the pain in my neck, back and shoulders was unbearable. I was so light-headed. This was something I had become used to and I refused to surrender to a walker. I was 45.

We said our goodbyes and left the café.

With anticipation, I inserted the testimonial CD into my car player. With my life depending on it, I listened to others talk about how they overcame their symptoms with this stem cell regeneration supplement.

My package arrived a week later, and I immediately doubled the recommended daily dose.

A week later, I felt a sense of lightness. Two weeks later, I felt I could talk a little better. My daughter had been finishing sentences for me, but I noticed this was not as frequent. Four weeks later, I realised I was sleeping.

Within eight weeks, I was back at full-time work.

I had so much energy, I didn't know what to do with myself. It felt like I had 'woken up' for the first time in 20 years. I was able to think of words! I could talk properly! My memory and cognitive functions were returning... I could remember people's names and noticed I was able to recall past events I'd forgotten about. I felt super excited and so optimistic.

I was sleeping like a baby. Every. Single. Night.

I started arranging to see friends. I was so happy. I hadn't been out for years. I even lost three friends in the previous seven years, due to cancelling outings multiple times. Having a shower or getting ready would take ALL my energy and I'd have nothing left.

The depth of my suffering flashed before me as I'd forgotten how much I had sacrificed. I had loved yoga on Saturday mornings – which had become impossible due to severe chronic fatigue, dizziness, nausea, and systemic pain, following my beginners' 'easy' class that I had been attending for 15 years.

I once loved riding my bicycle and going to the markets on a Sunday morning, but I couldn't walk for more than ten minutes or stand for that long.

I couldn't go shopping without holding onto a trolley, plus the lights and noise, was way too much stimulation. I really missed gardening and I hadn't walked my dogs in years. The sadness in their eyes made me feel so guilty... I couldn't manage even ten minutes without having to rest on the lounge for hours afterwards.

I was angry.

Angry about how long I'd been unwell and missing out on life. Seven years of suffering and searching for answers to my failing health, only to feel at least 50% better within weeks after using this product!

Angry about how I suffered financially as a result of lost income and due to seeing so many practitioners trying alternative, natural modalities without much success.

Angry that my beautiful daughter missed out on so many things, as I lay on the lounge day after day.

Angry at myself for giving my power away to the doctors who I trusted to help me. At my appointment, I remember her saying,

"Well, you did have a lot of stuff going on emotionally, so it was difficult to establish the true cause of all your problems."

I was furious!

Over the years, I had complained to her about everything from severe chronic fatigue, insomnia, bladder intolerance, IBS, asthma, tinnitus, photosensitivity, blurry vision, all-over body trembling, food intolerances, systemic pain, dizziness and this weird involuntary 'tick' in my neck... and she thought it was 'all in my head'.

I had sought help from physiotherapists, osteopaths, naturopaths, acupuncturists, massage therapy, chiropractors, EFT tapping, a musculoskeletal therapist and a homeopath.

I even saw a psychotherapist.

The one specialist that did help me was my counsellor, who came recommended by my kinesiologist. I always enjoyed seeing Margaret. She knew me well. After each session with her, I always walked out feeling stronger and in control, with an action plan. Thank God for Margaret. But this is something she couldn't help me with.

I turned to God.

Thank you for my healing. Thank you for my healing. Thank you for my healing... as I lay in bed that night tossing and turning... the MS diagnosis consuming me with fear and uncertainty.

The stem cell regeneration product had certainly helped to significantly improve many of my neurological symptoms, but addressing my severe food intolerances was my next focus.

I researched so much about intolerances, the symptoms and how they can suddenly appear. I'd had an intolerance to gluten and dairy for many years but never really considered looking for the reasons why. Then the effect of sulfates and lectins on the body really caught my attention and I created an elimination diet.

I was only able to eat four vegetables. All other vegetables contained lectins and sulfates. *Is this what was causing my anaphylactic reactions which then evolved into 'MS Hugs'??* The diet was so difficult, but the allergic reactions stopped within days. I was onto something...

The sound of my phone ringing interrupted my thoughts. It was Ros.

"Dr Curt is coming to Australia next week to talk about the stem cell product, wanna come?"

"Hell, yeah!"

It had been eight months since I started taking it.

I brought some friends with me to Ros' house that night. My stepmother came too. There must have been 30 people there. Only standing room for some… I shared my testimonial and ALL eyes were on me. My stepmother was shocked to hear of my struggles. To this point, she had NO idea I had suffered so much.

"All my cognitive function has returned, my memory is coming back, I don't have systemic pain anymore, the involuntary 'tick' in my neck has gone, my neck and shoulders have softened and I feel SOOO happy!"

I felt emotional. I wasn't used to talking about it. I never wanted to add energy to 'it' or admit my level of suffering, but hearing myself, made me feel happy. I was getting better. I had hope. This was no miracle pill, but it certainly worked a miracle. It had helped me significantly in so many ways.

Roslyn introduced me to Dr James* and suggested that he may be able to help with my recent diagnosis and food allergies. I remembered attending some of his talks in the past, but I had no idea he'd had success with healing autoimmune, using natural supplements. He gasped at the photos of my swollen face. I told him about my brain inflammation, food allergies and struggles to breathe and my recent 'MS hugs'.

Later that week, we chatted on the phone for four hours.

I told him about the elimination diet I created and that I was petrified of re-introducing the foods that cause me anaphylaxis and asthma-like symptoms. How will I know when I'm able to eat normal foods again? He sympathised with me and reassured me that I would get better. Within a few months!

"Have you ever taken any antibiotics in your life?"

"Many times. Hasn't everybody?"

"Antibiotics completely wipe out all the good bacteria in your gut, so you must always replenish them."

I remembered reading about the imbalance of bacteria and that it results in the gut becoming over-populated with parasites. *When parasites eat the lectins from the food we eat, they feel the effect of being 'killed off' too and as they fight for survival, they inject poison into the gut lining which adds to the toxicity in your blood.*

He wasn't surprised to hear that a few months earlier, after using a highly recommended parasite cleanse, I suffered severe stomach pain and cramping, nausea, dizziness, 'heavy legs' and near-immobility. After almost passing out one day, I had to stop.

I also told him that I had created my own elimination diet to avoid Thiol Sulfate foods, as I learned that they pull dormant heavy metals from the liver. It's this grand design of our food source nourishing us and also cleansing us. He agreed. I knew from my research into gut health that heavy metals are digested the normal 'natural' way which is great – but not if you have a leaky gut, as these heavy metals end up in the blood stream via the broken gut lining. Could this have been the cause of my severe trembling, cognitive/memory issues?

I had been my own 'guinea pig' testing different theories...

"Dr. James, how can I ever eat normal food again??"

I was convinced that the 'MS Hugs' were just an advanced form of anaphylactic symptoms.

He could sense the desperation in my voice. "This is NOT sustainable long term! I can't go out to eat at all". I had tried five different diets over the years, in vain, to heal myself.

Dr James shared his protocol with me, which to my surprise, included the same stem cell regeneration product. It included a scientifically formulated blend of synbiotics.

"What's synbiotics?"

"A combination of pre and probiotics. Prebiotics are the 'food' for probiotics. The one I recommend, delivers three trillion beneficial bacteria when you double-dose. Not the 30 billion you get from the chemist. It's not enough for you. You'll need to take this one for three months, minimum. Then you'll be able to eat what you want again".

Hang on, what? I've had this for YEARS. Why didn't my doctor tell me about this??

As soon as I hung up, I ordered everything online from various companies and continued researching everything Dr. Ross told me.

Suddenly it all made sense. It all pointed to one thing. Leaky, gut.

SEVERE leaky gut.

My doctor didn't verify this when I questioned it, or support my concerns. I'd had colonoscopies, abdominal ultrasounds, bladder function tests, and a myriad of blood tests, but you can't test for leaky gut. Many doctors don't even believe it exists!

I remembered that prescription drugs and over-the-counter medication create holes in the gut, especially anti-inflammatories – which I was taking daily – at the advice of my doctor.

I researched natural anti-inflammatory products and discovered that the same scientist who formulated the stem cell product, also created the world's most concentrated seaweed supplement.

I read: *This formulation is eight times stronger than any other seaweed supplement on the market today. So powerful, that it increases the immune system by 400% in TWELVE days. This product cuts off blood flow to tumours, kills fungal bacteria and is a powerful anti-inflammatory.* When it arrived, I was so excited. I accidentally drank the entire bottle within two weeks…

… and felt like there was NOTHING wrong with me for the first time in years!!

I researched a lot about fungus and mould toxins and how they grow on mucous in your gut. Mucous caused by dairy, read meat, gluten and especially sugar. These foods all cause an acidic environment and are a playground for mould, fungus, and parasites.

I learned that the immune system is created in the gut. But if the gut is leaky, inflamed, parasitic and full of sticky thick mucus and 'mucoid plaque', its function is severely compromised.

There was more… *The gut is responsible for creating and sending chemicals to the brain.* Information was coming thick and fast.

I was so excited I couldn't wait to come home every day and learn more.

Hormones are created in the gut. What? No one ever told me that! No wonder I suffered from depression, anxiety and panic attacks. How can my severely compromised, inflamed, leaky gut lining create an abundance of hormones? Now I understood the terminology 'gut brain'.

I was shocked to find so many articles about the connection to heart disease and the role hormones play in a healthy heart – and thyroid. My head was shaking. I was dumbfounded. I was angry. I was excited.

At this point, I realised I had given my power away to so many doctors and specialists. It was time to take back control of my health and share my story.

My research concluded that autoimmune starts when the immune system protects the cells from toxins. When the immune system detects a toxic 'invasion' in the bloodstream, it protects the cells with water – which is what we call inflammation. No wonder I didn't go to the toilet after drinking 1.5 litres of water, in the days I was severely inflamed. No wonder I had constipation... the immune system takes the water from the gut!

It was now that I understood how my allergies to so many foods were created. Undigested food particles would enter the bloodstream via the broken gut lining. The immune system then creates antibodies to those foods, rejecting them!

Gut bacteria, viruses, heavy metals, stomach acid and toxins (including those from personal care products and environmental toxins, like fumes and pesticides), also make their way into your blood steam via the leaky gut lining.

For this reason, doing a heavy metal detox is a very bad idea when you have a leaky gut, because they simply just end up back in the blood stream and contribute to neurological damage.

Many people with Autoimmune have liver and kidney problems, due because these organs are constantly attempting to filter the same toxins entering the blood via the leaky gut lining, over and over again.

At an Italian restaurant following an event three months after starting my protocol, I watched as everyone order garlic bread, pasta, and pizzas. I had snuck home on the way and had a healthy, pre-cooked snack. I was used to this.

I leant across the table and said "Hey Dr James, what do you think? Am I ready?"

"How long has it been, three months?"

"Yes, it has, almost exactly."

"Go for it. You'll be fine.

He could see the concern on my face, but with some reassurance from the others at our table who were aware of my situation, I decided it was time. I ate two pieces of pizza... and prayed.

I was in two minds that night. The old negative 'chronic illness' thought pattern wanted to resurface, but I stayed strong and didn't give in. I only allowed happy healthy thoughts that night, as I went to bed feeling confident.

I woke up.

I was fine.

No inflammation. No anaphylaxis. No headache, pain, fatigue, sweating or trembling.

I got up. I could stand. I could walk without holding onto walls.

I was healed. I laughed. I was overcome with gratitude.

I smiled from ear to ear. I did it!! I knew I had beaten the odds… Three months after sticking to a strict protocol, I was symptom free. I immediately called Dr James and told him how great I felt. I was so thrilled, I became emotional. "I have my life back Doc, thank you". My bright future flashed before me.

I must share my story…

I took to Facebook that night and created my page; 'Healing Autoimmune Naturally'.

Four months later, I had 500 followers. The reality of the Autoimmune epidemic was frightening. They'd suffered just like I did. The embarrassment, the financial strain, frustration, and confusion… it verified everything for me.

Receiving testimonials from those who followed my protocol, I felt grateful to have experienced the suffering and before I knew it, I had clients all over the world, wanting to take back control of their health too.

I have my life back, and I'm thriving!

* Not his real name.

CHAPTER 17

On the wings of grace, the Universe and I

Dr. Sherine Price

"You're pregnant," The nurse coldly announced.

Sheer panic engulfed me, "Ohhhh, my God. What am I gonna do?"

The Universe answered assuredly, *You're going to survive and thrive. This is your saving grace to help you put your life on track. Suck it up, Buttercup. Your life awaits.*

And so I did.

I was a 17-year-old high school senior on a turbulent path of self-destruction.

It began with the onset of adolescence and my strong will to fight for autonomy and personal power in the only way I knew how at the time: utter rebellion against a potent cocktail of years of rejection and abandonment, abuse and neglect, extreme loss and grief, bullies and enmeshment, painful shyness and obedient people-pleasing.

This tiny embryo, my first-born son Lance, saved me.

His father and I enthusiastically committed our lives to nurturing our family unit. We had our fairy-tale wedding and another baby boy soon thereafter.

We lived wonderful adventures together. We didn't have much money, but we had each other and lots of love. That was all we needed.

My sweet little tribe set me on a new and healthy path as a devoted mother, wife, and homemaker. In motherhood, I discovered my passion, bliss, and purpose. I found an identity, a mission, the motivation to take care of myself, and eager recipients of all of the love I have to give but didn't yet realize I had inside of me.

Lance was a talkative, candidly curious and inquisitive little angel with the sweetest little voice and an enormous heart. "Mommy, why is the sky blue? Mommy, who made the trees? Mommy, how did the rocks get here?"

"Great questions, sweetheart," I would say as I patiently answered every single question, and of course, without fail, he always replied again with, 'Why?'

Our youngest son was a quiet, deeply observant and contemplative little sage with a gentle and kind heart.

I relished in the sound of their delightful voices singing "Mommy", rambling on and on, and asking endless questions. It was music to my ears.

As I cherished the soulful innocence in their view of the world, they taught me so much.

Life was so sweet and never better than this.

I was quite sure my husband and two sons were my earth angels, and this was our heaven. I felt so much gratitude. *Thank you for saving me.*

Intuitively, we knew it was fleetingly impermanent though.

We knew the time would come when they would grow up and wouldn't need us so much anymore. We knew the day would come when we'd no longer be here for them, and they'd have to live on without us.

So we steadfastly prepared them for those days ahead and raised them to be resilient, self-actualized, and independent.

They grew up to be sovereign young men, and the day came when we found ourselves with an empty nest.

Parenting grown, adult offspring proved to be much more challenging than imagined. I mistakenly believed that raising small children to adulthood was the *difficult* part.

I expected that when they grew up and moved out things would be so much easier.

Wrong!

Oblivious to the terrors that lie ahead of me, I fantasized a dreamy vision of the empty nest's time freedom, romantic weddings, beloved grandchildren, intimate family gatherings, love and respect, deep and lasting relationships, and long full lives together with my husband and I as the highly respected elders of the tribe we created.

Yada, yada, yada... Can you hear the Universe laughing hysterically?

As Woody Allen wisely said many years ago, "If you want to make God laugh, tell him about your plans."

"She's pregnant," Lance announced cautiously after inviting us to meet for dinner at his favorite restaurant. He had a giant grin on his face and was beaming with pride and trepidation.

"I'm gonna be a Grandma!" I said with excitement tinged with a little apprehension.

My heart leaped out of my chest, and my head swirled with questions.

Who is this pregnant woman we've never heard about before?

Will they get married and stay together?

Is she healthy?

Will everything work out well for all of us?

"It's gonna be great, Mom. Don't worry," Lance promised.

And I knew it would be.

In my mind I was already shopping for frilly pink dresses, dainty shoes, and lacy hair bows.

This is it! My vision is unfolding!

Naiive elation set in and lasted for quite some time as the embryo evolved into a beautiful baby girl who was born on a splendid Monday afternoon and is absolutely the most precious angel the world has ever seen. I'm quite certain of that.

I helped them buy and remodel their first home for the princess' arrival. I helped them with the purchase of a car that could safely transport the precious VIP. I was passionately devoted and elated to be a Grandma.

For the first year, being a grandmother was everything I'd hoped it would be and more. I was blessed to be her caregiver while her parents worked, and we formed an unbreakable bond.

Raising two sons was wonderful, but I'd always wanted a daughter too. I'd been unable to conceive again after years of futile, extremely stressful attempts. We came very close to adopting a daughter multiple times, but it never worked out. Now I had two daughters: my angelic granddaughter and her beautiful mommy!

I felt so blessed; *Thank you for these blessings.*

Thud.

"We're moving to Texas," Lance announced reluctantly but surely with his signature smirk which is so adorable and endearing.

"Oh..." My heart sank, and I couldn't find words to express the crushing feeling.

"It'll be difficult, but I can't turn down this job opportunity. We'll stay in touch and visit you often. We'll move back within five years. It'll be okay, Mom."

He gave me a big hug, and I felt the love in his heart. He knew my heart was breaking, and he showed me that he deeply cared about my feelings.

"Maybe you'll move to Texas too, Mom! Hint. Hint," he jokingly persuaded.

I helped them stage and sell their adorable nest, then pack and move hundreds of miles and five long hours away from me.

Anxiety and grief overwhelmed me, but I focused on tenacious efforts to keep the relationships connected regardless of the distance, time, costs, and challenges involved.

Then Lance's little family gained another tremendous blessing with the birth of our handsome grandson and all of the joy a baby boy brings. Everything was going to be just fine in our little tribe.

Please help me keep these relationships strong in spite of the distance.

Whack!

Another proverbial shoe dropped. My husband's health, career, and our financial future became suspect, and we were forced to move out of state for his job.

I can't do this!

*

We lamented being so far away from our loved ones, so we scrambled precisely and moved back home within six short months. We mistakenly assumed that in moving back we'd be welcomed with open arms of excitement, enthusiasm and love.

Instead, we were met with betrayal we will never understand.

We could only guess.

In fact, guessing would become one of our few coping mechanisms in the nightmare which was unfolding before us.

Our cherished family unit and our hearts were slowly ripped apart by covert manipulations and disrespect by others, not the actions of my husband, myself, nor our sons.

We were given the occasional scraps of hope to string us along, while the manipulations left us blamed and bewildered.

Help me, please!

We were devastated, but life dragged us onward as it does.

Our tribe was growing again and shining with hope as our youngest son got married and became a father. Another beautiful daughter-in-law, handsome step-grandson, and later another handsome grandson joined our little tribe.

We were oblivious to the concept that things could get any worse. But then they did.

"Hey, Lance!" I joyfully answered my iphone as it rang with his name on the caller ID. I felt excited and relieved to hear from him as it had been a while since we'd spoken.

Just a few minutes prior, I had sent him a motherly text message with smiley-heart emojis saying, 'Hi. Are you okay?' It was as if my intuition had known something was wrong.

The quivering voice on the other end of the phone line reported "I've got some bad news… Lance has been in a car accident… and it's pretty bad." My heart sank and panicked into oblivion as I entered into every parent's worst nightmare.

With harrowing pangs of terror in every cell of my body, I screamed "Is he okay?! What happened?! Where is he?! Oh my God! No!"

A tsunami of salty tears engulfed me while my body trembled uncontrollably and my mind spiraled.

No! No! No!

Lance fervently fought for his life for five long days in the surgical intensive care unit while we prayed incessantly and endured horrors no one should ever have to endure.

And then he was gone.

He had saved my life all those years ago when he chose me to be his mommy, but I couldn't save him now.

How could this happen? You took my son.

The Universe answered profoundly, *He was never yours.*

Bam.

Based on how things had been going, my husband and I knew intuitively what was likely coming next but didn't dare to speak it nor think it.

We both silently begged, *Please, help us.*

Looking back, we have come to realize how strong Lance was and how he was advocating for us through all of the nonsense of the previous five years. My husband and I both felt that without our beloved peacemaker, it could be the beginning of the end of our connection to his children. And it was.

As Lance would often say, "It's not going to end well." He knew all too well what we were dealing with from our tormentors.

We lost our beloved son... and two precious grandchildren that day... and a beautiful dream we'd been nurturing for many, many years.

The overwhelming terror visited me often with the internal scream *'No! No! No!'* followed by *'He's gone. He's gone,'* and then again, *'No! No! No!'* in the never-ending cycle of terror, denial, anger, short-lived acceptance, and the deepest grief I've ever felt.

In the wake of this tragedy, surely it couldn't get any worse.

Smack!

Life continued to blindside us with unbelievable horrors.

Holidays and birthdays passed us by most of the time with no call, no card, no gift, no invitation. Our little family was having gatherings, and we were excluded and alienated.

Our phone calls and text messages were ignored. We were blocked on social media. We were not given a current address for Lance's children, so we couldn't send them cards and gifts like we always had.

Our grandchildren were being emotionally and psychologically injured with false stories and estrangement from their loving grandparents.

They were being robbed of their relationships with us and all of the love we have to give them. There are so many opportunities missed and memories that will never be made.

Looking back over my life, I had lost so much. It was inconceivable and unbearable.

Will my heart ever accept these losses and feel joy again?

The Universe wrapped me up in a warm, comforting hug and whispered, *You ARE joy, peace and love without ANY conditions required. You're stronger and more powerful than you can imagine. Stand in your power.*

But I've lost so much.

I was reminded, *They were never yours to lose. That is the lesson my beloved Buttercup.*

No! I don't want that lesson! It felt like a long, beautiful, yet harrowing journey in which I had approached the edge of a cliff overlooking a dark abyss. I couldn't turn back, but oh, I wanted to so intensely.

As I fell into the chasm, I grasped for edges to cling to.

Letting go and free-falling into oblivion, I hoped these wings would take flight, and perhaps my angel, Lance, would help me from wherever he is now.

*

In the years since Lance's passing, I've muddled through the stages of grief and all that comes along with them.

I prayed daily for the strength to survive it somehow, although I had no concept of how I would do so. Sometimes faith was all that I could grasp onto as it carried me to my destiny on gentle wings of grace.

Sometimes I had to decline the whispered invitation to end my life. The proverbial demon on my shoulder persuaded me, "This is too much. You can't handle this anymore. Just end it now."

Instead, I avowed every day that *I will carry on.*

To the proverbial angel on my other shoulder I affirmed... *I won't give up on life. I won't let anyone or anything define me or my worth. I've got projects to finish, dreams to fulfill, and services to provide to humanity. Life is a precious gift.*

The grief rollercoaster ride of shock and denial, pain and guilt, anger and bargaining, depression and loneliness, and elusive acceptance is a torturous ride that never ends. It never stops. It just keeps going up, down, around, and around.

It wails, How could this happen to me? Why is this happening?

There are no answers to those questions.

I wanted to wave a magic wand, say a few 'magic' words, and watch my son reappear. *I just want my son back. Now. Right now.*

I tried bargaining, *Take my life instead, and give him his life back!*

But he's gone.

No! I want him back!

Thoughts, internal dialogues, and images replayed over and over.

Just breathe. Just feel. Just let it pass. The Universe lovingly whispered in my ear. *You'll get through this.*

The pangs of guilt came and went like knives twisting in my gut. *If only... What if... I wish I had... I should've... I shouldn't have... I failed him...*

Breathe. Feel. Let it pass. I was gently reminded.

The anger was so intense, it was frightening.

Breathe. Feel. Let it pass. Angelic comfort was always right there with me like a best friend.

I want a rewind button. I petitioned. *Please, just put things back the way they were, and I'll do whatever you want me to do.*

Can't do that, Buttercup. Breathe. Feel. Let it pass.

Shock, denial, guilt, bargaining, and anger would sometimes fade into the numbness of depression. It was a welcome retreat. But it was dark, bland and dangerous in there.

A soft voice called. *Turn on the light. Find something, anything to feel happy about.* In the dark vacuum of depression, it was almost impossible to hear that voice and even more difficult to let myself feel happiness.

Happiness bred painful guilt which dangled pleasure just out of reach. *How can I possibly feel happiness after everything that has happened?!*

Grief stole a good chunk of my capacity to think, process, remember, and keep up with everything that was coming at me on a daily basis. I struggled to keep my life, my home, and my businesses functional. I just couldn't think and manage things the way I could before.

Divine grace assured me, *You're doing just fine, my beloved.*

I attempted to escape the nightmare by working incessantly. Beer, wine, and cocktails tried to become my new best friends for a while. Pharmaceuticals and M.D.'s have never been my thing. I've insisted on surviving without them as they are also highly overrated and deadly.

There was a mass exodus of everyone I've ever known. Yes, at the time when I needed support more than ever, everyone quietly disappeared... after they politely but briefly paid their condolences, sent flowers and cards, and offered their support.

Then they gave me the 'last look', or sometimes it was just the 'radio silence', which actually meant, 'Good luck... but you'll probably never see me again... I am eliminating you and your dark cloud from my reality. Sorry.'

I suppose they couldn't handle the concept of the pain I'm living with, didn't know what to say to me or what to do for me, and were afraid they'd say or do something that would upset me.

Maybe they didn't want this reality in *their* reality, to be forced to acknowledge that it could happen to them, too, and afraid they'd catch whatever horrible, possibly contagious 'curse' or 'disease' I've acquired.

It was all a very large, jagged pill to swallow, but I eventually began to learn to live with it.

What choice did I have? The world kept spinning while I couldn't fathom how or why.

Everyone else's lives moved forward while mine seemed to be over, or at best, spiraling out of control. Loss and grief had left my life in ruins.

However... the grief was the evidence of the immense love I have for my family and for life.

And love is all we need, right? *I'll be okay. I've got this.*

The tragedies that have scarred me are not the interesting or important parts of the story. The story worth telling is how I survived, transformed myself, and thrived in the face of inconceivable horrors.

My grief process continues in waves. It never ends. It just gets easier as I become a stronger and better surfer and as I shift my perspective into higher realms.

Through all that I've survived in my life, I've always known there had to be more to life than suffering and loss.

Since I was a small child, I've always felt that shimmer of hope that there *can* be happiness in spite of the suffering.

Each year, I made my wish before blowing out the candles on my birthday cake. *I wish to be happy.* I didn't wish for bicycles, puppies or barbie dolls, I just wanted to feel happy.

Decades later I'm finally learning how to create happiness for myself while in the midst of devastation.

I'm a perpetually proactive 'work in progress' with a ravenous obsession for all things self-help, spiritual and mystical. I've learned from awesome therapists, energy healers, hypnotists, intuitives, thought leaders, books, videos, workshops, and various practices and modalities.

Essential oils, crystals, kundalini yoga, meditations, affirmations, massage, Reiki, EFT, astrology, numerology, divination tools, hiking, hobbies, poetry, music, journaling, self-care, service to others, a newsfeed full of inspiring quotes, unplugging from negative media have been some of my tools used to pull my big-girl panties up and carry on.

My husband has been my loving and loyal, brave and strong Superman through it all. He has suffered immensely too, but is flying right along beside me.

We've built successful businesses, travel in our RV and abroad, and enjoy our life to the fullest.

I've earned my PhD along with several other degrees and certifications and devoted myself to applying my knowledge, experience, and gifts to serve others and leave the world a lot better than I found it.

I'm earnestly creating a new tribe of loving 'family of choice'. My heart and door are always open to family and friends who have wandered off or have been misled away.

Thanks to the losses, I've learned so much about life and love, personal power, and resilience, and the importance of faith, gratitude, and acceptance.

In mastering the high road with healthier boundaries and higher perspectives, I love everyone unconditionally and with compassion and forgiveness.

I'm creating happiness and peace from within, in spite of what's occurring around me.

Gracefully, I soar and surf through the many phases and stages, blessings and curses, lessons and losses, triumphs and tragedies that life serves up.

The longer I live, the more of them I collect along the way, and it just keeps on going, yet never letting me in on the dreaded secret of when and how the adventure will end.

That cryptic, lurking thing called death is coming for me someday. It teaches me to enjoy and make the most of every moment. My son's transition taught me that quite distinctly.

Sometimes, as I get older, I do wish it would just go ahead and get it over with already. *I'm tired. I've lived long enough!* I facetiously proclaim.

But reality sets in. I'm still here, and I must keep going.

Fly or splat, I'll adjust and reinvent myself again and trudge forward into the next phase of my life.

Life just keeps pulling me upward like a lotus flower blossoming from the depths of the mud towards the light. It calls to me daily. It tests and teaches to learn or ignore, try or quit, rise or fall, forgive or blame, heal or hurt, love or fear.

My choices in how I respond are always mine and ultimately the only things that matter. They're the only things I'll be able to take with me when I transition. They are my proverbial heaven... or hell. I'm choosing heaven.

Although I've always been a spiritual seeker and student, since Lance's transition I've found solace in a zealous quest for an ever-deepening understanding of the meaning of life and the nature of reality.

Where is Lance now? What is it 'like' there?

Is he okay? What is he doing?

Can I communicate with him? How?

Will I see him again?

Do we choose our life, our family, and our death before we are born?

What am I supposed to learn from these experiences?

What happens when our body dies?

What is the meaning of life?

With the ravenous hunger for answers and the courage to be curious, I step outside the comfort zone to be enlightened and bloodied.

Devoted to being fully awake, aware, and alive, I daringly seek happiness in adversity and create heaven on earth while surrounded by a fantastic hell.

I show up courageously every day, determined to keep going, growing, and daring to be unstoppable and invincible.

In choosing unconditional love, forgiveness, and compassion for those who have hurt me, I'm becoming the stronger person their actions invited me to be. I reverently honor, thank, and bless them for those gifts.

Just as Dorothy did in Oz, I've come to realize I had the power all along, and I just had to discover it for myself.

Knowing that my power and worth are inherent, I acknowledge that never again will I be defined or devalued by anyone or anything outside of me.

I reclaim my power from those whom I've given it away to when I've believed their assessments of me, craved their approval or attention, blamed them, complained, felt victimized, or pitied myself.

I have empathy for everyone, especially those who have hurt me. I recognize that there are a lot of things I'm not aware of which have contributed to their behaviors and actions. There are misunderstandings that inevitably occur. Each of us perceives life circumstances through our own unique 'filter' skewed by the pain and beliefs we carry.

For these reasons and more, I wish everyone would just be kind, and love each other. Give each other the benefit of the doubt. Forgive, and let things go. Have compassion for each other, and be curious in lieu of judgment.

Recognize that we all have troubles and losses, and we all make mistakes. We're all unique, yet we're all the same. We're all in this together. Commit to love without conditions.

Slow down and make time for loved ones. Connect, and celebrate life together.

When someone is being alienated, bullied, or mistreated, be their advocate. Your apathy or silence is participation in the cruelty.

Life's too short and precious to muck it up with nonsense and shenanigans. Instead, we can create heaven on earth in each heart and in each life.

Our children are watching us. What are we teaching them?

When my beloveds want the truth and answers to their questions, I am right here for them. I trust they will reject the untruths that have misled them. I hope they'll open their heart and mind to love, to me, and to my side of the story.

They are forever loved, missed, cherished, and welcomed deep within my heart. I love them immeasurably, and that has been my greatest honor in this lifetime.

Missing them profoundly, I channel that energy into thoughts, prayers and blessings for them daily, and I do various things in honor of them on a regular basis. I know they can feel it in their heart.

They will have a slew of cards, gifts, photos, videos, journals, and letters to peruse. I keep them carefully stored away in fervent hope they'll receive them someday.

In spirit, I know we're eternally together and nothing can ever separate us. I have heartfelt conversations with my loved ones regularly, in my dreams and in my heart. That's where they truly are and always will be. I know they can feel and hear me in their dreams and heart. We're connected there forever in love.

The memories are now my saving grace. I have so many treasured memories of my sweet little boys and grandchildren who have touched my heart in so many ways. In spite of the tragedies, my life is filled with these beautiful blessings, and I am eternally grateful.

It's truly amazing what we can endure in this life.

We rise like a Phoenix from the ashes.

Bring it on! Give me all you've got!

I'll reinvent myself and my life again and again and again, I declare. I will fly!

CHAPTER 18

Finding me again
Juliette Mullen

I feel the heat fill my body – my palms sweating. I'm clenching as hard as I can.

I feel my tummy squirm. Spasms. I'm doubled over – a shooting pain across my stomach.

Then it happens.

I feel the warm, wet area in my pants.

The smell.

I gulp. My mouth is dry – I have no saliva.

I'm blinded by the lights and the space closes in on me.

There are people everywhere. A mum walking with her toddler, casually doing her shopping. Two women chatting and laughing. I can hear them at the end of the tunnel.

It's hazy, then I hear his voice in my head, the memory paralysing me.

"Why would you go to the toilet just as we're going to bed? That's disgusting! I need to go in there to brush my teeth, to get washed. You knew I was going to bed, why the fuck would you use the toilet?" I hear him say.

My chest tightens.

My feet are glued to the floor. My legs locked.

I can't stay here. The heat is rising like a wave from my feet.

I grip the cold bars of the trolley even tighter, urging my legs to move with all my strength.

I feel my pants squish as I walk to the escalator.

I move in small steps, weaving through all the people, praying they can't see the wet patch now forming in my trousers.

My face is hot with sweat and humiliation.

I feel my energy draining, being sucked into the floor as I walk. I want to go home and curl into my bed.

My head is spinning, chest tightening, I can't breathe. It's hard to concentrate. How much farther?

I just need to make it ten more steps. The room spins

I go into the disabled toilet – I've made it. I survived.

I need a wine.

*

I live in Scotland – so much clean fresh air to breathe, so much nature and beauty everywhere. It is exactly as serene as it sounds. My home is in the countryside with horses in the fields, and life is a little more relaxed, but it's not too far from the city and the hustle and bustle of daily life.

Sometime later, in the early hours, I tumble into a taxi with my best friend laughing, the supermarket panic anxiety incident faded from my mind. We collapse in the back seat, the taxi metre a blur.

How did I get home so fast?

A second ago, we were laughing in the taxi and now I'm standing at my front door, alone.

Where are my keys? I search the bottomless bag.

Blackness. Again.

I wake up in my car. It's cold and the condensation from my breath covers the windows. It's 5am. My handbag is emptied on the seat – money, lipstick, mascara.

I'm in front of my house, but I don't have a key. Now that I live alone again, I can't simply knock on the door to be let in. Not that it would have been taken very well anyway, to turn up drunk in the wee hours. It was probably better I was alone. Still, I'll have to call my mum and explain how clumsy and hilarious I am, and hope she doesn't notice the slur on my tongue from the Jager bombs.

I exchange some pleasantries with mum to prove I'm not too drunk.

"Hi Mum, I was out, and my keys must've fallen out my bag," I say.

"Jules, I am in my bed. It's only 5 o'clock."

"I can't get in, I only have my car key."

"Ok I will come up with your spare key."

I'm proud of how steady my voice actually sounds. I don't want her thinking I've done it again.

Sometimes the anxiety and panic will come out of the blue. And then the blackness. A curtain comes down, leaving me in the dark abyss of nothingness. The problem is that I don't know it's coming.

*

Apart from me, no one knew how badly I felt. My problems were my secret. I had gone through my childhood, teens and twenties, pretty much unscathed. I had a feeling that somehow I just didn't fit in, that no-one understood me.

Looking back, I realise I've struggled with anxiety for pretty much my whole life.

It didn't just start when both my marriages fell apart or when my dad died.

I can still see her – that wee girl – every night before sleeping, nervously, cuddled into my teddy and praying, bargaining with God. "Please let me do okay and keep my mum and dad and brother safe." The black and white portable tv always on, down low enough not to disturb my sleep but loud enough I couldn't hear the arguing of my parents.

I felt powerless but also responsible, somehow. How could I help? What could I do?

I learned to bury my feelings, deep inside.

And there I hid. For two decades.

*

The day after my night out, I am in my house lying on the sofa. I hear laughter outside as the kids are playing in the street. It's a beautiful summer day and it seems like everyone is out enjoying it, except me. I can hear one neighbour cutting his grass with the loud lawnmower; I can smell the freshly cut grass coming in the open window and the sunlight is warm on my face.

I curl into the blanket.

I suddenly think about my garden, a complete mess, and I feel the anxiety rise from the pit of my stomach to my chest and I can't breathe.

It was pretty when I moved into this house, full of beautiful rose bushes, plants, and little trees. Now, it is overgrown and unloved. I had the lawnmower and all the tools, still shiny and new, sitting in my garage.

I don't know where to start.

The TV is on but I am not following the story. I don't even know what the programme is. Paralysed by my thoughts as they rage around in my head, I struggle to breathe. My chest is tight, and my head feels like it's going to explode. The weight on my chest is always there. I can hardly lift my head from the pillow.

How can everyone else cope except me?

My heart races and feels like it's going to burst out of my chest. I close my eyes and try to tell myself it will be okay. Tears fall from the corners of my eyes as I try not to think about the pain.

The air is so thin.

I feel like such a burden, a waste of space, like a shell of a person. So small and worthless... and then I slide into the darkness.

A few hours later, my stomach rumbles and I remember that I haven't eaten today, I look at my phone, it's already 19:00. Where did the time go?

I stumble into the kitchen and look in the fridge, there are lots of things to cook.

I feel dizzy and weak; my head is so heavy. I can't face cooking, but I know I need to eat something today.

I call a takeaway, again, and change the channel on the TV. I try not to think about my life but it doesn't work.

I think about how I couldn't save him.

I picture my dad, standing there in the hospice, a skeleton compared to how he normally was, full of life with his friends. In his well-turned-out pyjamas with a handkerchief nearly tucked into his pyjama pocket, pleading with my brother and I to take him home, begging us not to leave him there, to die.

The doctors said we couldn't take him home; this was it. He spent five brave years fighting for his life, before he died at age 57 from cancer.

That week in the hospice was one of the worst times in my life, watching him slip away. Watching him and my family suffer and there was nothing I could do.

I let him down. I felt that I let everyone down.

I think of my mum crying and screaming in disbelief when he passed. Completely lost without him, the love of her life.

I feel helpless again.

The food arrives and my I feel completely exhausted and nauseous. I don't feel like eating. I leave the food in the kitchen and go to bed. Exhausted, I fall asleep.

*

Boom, boom, boom!

I wake up, startled – a thudding noise loud in my ears.

Terrified – tears falling from my eyes; the pillow wet.

My heart is racing, my mouth dry. I am soaked in sweat. A knot of fear erupts in my stomach – it flips, and I feel sick. I feel the loud thud of my heart in my ears.

I can't breathe.

The air is thin.

Where am I?

I lie still – at home, in bed. I am dripping in sweat, my hair and the covers wet. It's 3am.

This feeling is not new. It happened almost every night since I have been alone. I wasn't sure what hurt more – the heartbreak of losing my dad, the collapse of my family unit, the raw ache that my marriage was over, two marriages over – or the despair and anger I felt because I had allowed all this to happen.

I never intended this – to be here, alone.

I deliberately chose what I thought was a quiet, supportive guy to marry and be my partner, for life. I tried to do things right. I had been married and in relationships for more than two decades with Tom, and then John, and now I am alone.

Sadly, I realise that I lost my voice and myself in the process.

The anxiety worsened. Terrifying nightmares that I'm being chased, or my family and friends are killed. So vivid.

My head feels like it might explode.

I feel like if I move, I will die, like I'm paralysed, stuck to the bed. The same feeling I used to get as a child listening to the arguments of my parents.

Beep, beep, beep, beep... 6am. My alarm.

I feel hungover, with exhaustion. My head like concrete.

"Mum!" my daughter shouts, interrupting my anxiety.

I drag myself up to get ready for the day ahead. I need to get to work. I look at her and my heart feels like it might break in two. She is just a toddler but already has her father's eyes, sparkling blue like the ocean.

And I feel filled with shame and failure.

*

When I'd met John seven years earlier, I had so much hope for our future.

"Just leave him," he'd say. "Come and live here, with me. Move in, I'll look after you."

"I can't," I'd respond.

I had never felt like that before; he awakened something deep inside me that I didn't recognise. For the first time, I had felt free and passionate. Free to be me. I feel excited about the future and the life we could lead. I felt hope when we were together.

But how could I leave Tom, who was lovely and who I'd been with for so long? Crippled with guilt and shame. How could I shatter his world? I knew I couldn't go on like that.

Torn.

It's no surprise really that I had married Tom, the first guy that showed me any real attention. To some, the "ideal guy". You know the one, blonde hair, blue eyes, popular, the school captain, footballer. The one everyone loved.

And I was none of those.

We met when we were teenagers and married a few years later, I had dreams to travel and be someone I was proud of, that my parents could be proud of. Someone who made a difference in the world. I went to university and cancelled my year abroad studying instead to work, and save. On the outside, we had the house, the job, the car.

We had big plans, but none of them came true.

Throwing myself into work and studying, being who I thought I was supposed to be, time passed. And I still felt a failure. It was engrained in me. I didn't know what to do. My mind whirled fast and thick with all the worries, I felt completely lost and out of control.

Everyone looking in probably thought we had the perfect life. Together for over a decade. I felt like such a fraud. I could see everyone else progress in their lives and we were stuck.

He knew about John, you see. It's not as though I hadn't told him. But he said he couldn't cope if I left. How could I do that to him?

I had expected so much of that marriage. But the truth was we were tens of thousands of pounds in debt and going nowhere. Still in the same flat, loan after loan, credit card after credit card.

I couldn't breathe. There was no way out. I didn't even know where to start.

Maybe I will get better if I try harder. If I am a better person. Maybe I'm meant to be successful in my career and I'm just not good at relationships.

"Why on earth would you leave him? He adores you. You're on a pedestal," my friends used to tell me. They always thought Tom was a catch and wondered what he was doing with me.

I think that was the problem; I couldn't live up to those expectations. I was suffocating and drowning. I wanted to be me, but I had no idea who that was.

I felt guilty all the time, lost, stuck and wondering if I was going crazy, losing my mind. I begin losing control.

"I forgive you. We can get past this," Tom would tell me. "Let's just have a baby. That will bring us closer together," he says. My heart sank.

How can that happen when we don't even have sex? You deserve better than me. I am such a failure! I would scream inside.

Why did this happen to me?

In the end, we divorced and remained friends for the first year or so, but the pain was too much to bear.

The loss. The constant reminder of my failure. I threw myself into work.

*

The clock in the corner of my screen flashes 18:38 and I scan the office. I frantically tap my keyboard, working as fast as I can to meet my deadline. I know there will be trouble.

"See you tomorrow," I whisper as I dash out the door.

I know half the team are going to be sat there for another few hours, probably eating chocolate at their desks for dinner. And where am I going? Home, to my three-year-old.

I'm wracked with guilt, not for my daughter, which is terrible, but I know she is happy with her dad. She adores him. I am filled with guilt for my colleagues left sitting at their desks, working. I'm never scared to put the hours in and work hard, I know that comes with the territory to be successful in life. In fact, I was used to being the last person in the office. Before my daughter was born, I travelled all around the country working in different offices. And now what was I doing? Abandoning them. I can't shake off the feeling as I do the long commute home.

Late home. Again.

"Where the fuck have you been?" John asks.

"Work."

"What are you playing at, Julie? We've been waiting on you! You've missed dinner and bath time. You're a fucking disgrace of a mother. Why can't you just behave and be normal?" his chin stern and face hard and I just know from the look.

I try to swallow.

I have no saliva.

"I got away as quickly as I could. I had meetings and things to do. My team are still there," I attempt to justify, feeling the cloudiness washing over my body and the energy drain from my feet. I can't even think.

*

I had spent years trying to make it work when we were together, for those few years we were married. I'd leave the house before 7am and send emails from the car, head to the office to a day packed with relentless conference calls and meetings, run – often late – for nursery, or home, then pick up my phone and carry on, sending emails at 3am, 6am, whatever it took.

More guilt.

Looking back, my life, my relationship, my job, were completely out of balance. I can see that I was in my masculine energy, trying to prove to the world that I was coping, that I was good enough. Good enough as a mum, as a partner, as a daughter, an employee. I was putting in all the hours I could.

I accepted it. Guilty at work, guilty at home, and completely worn out.

After all, I had debts to pay and that was like a weight chained to my ankle. I couldn't work any harder. I couldn't do anymore.

Physically, it was showing. I had illness after illness and I just couldn't shake the feeling of not being enough. The relationship suffered. Constant arguments, sometimes physical. Toxic.

The dreams, the excitement, and the passion we once felt, long gone.

I lost myself. And him.

Our parting was not pretty. I wish we could have found a better way to do it, but we were both stubborn, in need of the control, and I was feeling broken.

Dreams broken. Physically, mentally, and emotionally broken.

I didn't even know who I was. Had I ever?

I didn't feel like I had a problem. He was always telling me that I wasn't 'normal' and reminding me of all the things I didn't do or do to his standards.

I worked constantly, as hard as I could. Thinking that's what people did. I studied, I learned, I tried to be a better person.

I was doing the best I could. The most I could. It wasn't enough. It would never be enough.

Life got so stressful; I was just trying to cope. To get through the day and do all the things I had to do. There was just never enough time.

I wanted to be in all places at all times. I felt split. Never really present with anyone, I was always thinking of ever-growing list of things to be done. Knowing that it was just never good enough.

When I went out with my friends, who I only saw a couple of times a year as I was so busy with work and family life, we often drank cocktails and partied.

Hard.

I didn't see the connection between the anxiety I suffered and binge drinking and blackouts.

My first blackout happened when I was 15. I was the typical, quiet, anxious, co-dependent teenager, nervous and not in the popular crowd. All my friends appeared so confident and I drank to fit in.

When I felt anxious, sad, and alone, I would boost myself up having alcohol with my friends... but it was never just one drink and I would end up in the blackness.

Afterwards I'd come crashing down with shame and guilt.

Anxiety. Drink. Crash. Anxiety. Drink. Crash.

I had to face it when I went out one night with my friend and suffered another blackout and the unthinkable happened; I was sexually assaulted on the way home.

Up until then, I had tried to convince myself it wasn't a problem, and didn't acknowledge the pain I was feeling.

But even then, I knew. She knew. That small voice – the wee girl inside me – always knew.

*

I saw a doctor. She told me I had anxiety and Post Traumatic Stress Disorder and prescribed beta blockers and anti-depressants, saying it would stop my heart from racing, symptoms of anxiety, and help me sleep.

My stomach churned as I felt the rawness in my body, like I was literally seeping shame from every cell and if I got too close to people, they would be able to see it. I'd seen many doctors and counsellors; about the breakup, about that night, the gynaecological issues that followed, and checked into a rehabilitation hospital for anxiety – and still nothing helped.

As the months went on, I became increasingly hopeless. I no longer wanted to die, like I had all those years ago when I'd taken hundreds of pills. I just couldn't see any other way to escape how I felt – weak and exhausted.

And a complete failure. I knew something had to change or I'd lose myself forever. And I had my beautiful daughter that I had to fight for. I had tried for years to have her before she arrived in our lives, my rainbow baby who I loved so much.

*

I put everything into my life with my daughter. I had to show her another way. I was seeing a counsellor, trying to make sense of things, and learned about attachment and boundaries and learned why my previous relationships didn't work. The truth is that the relationship we have with ourselves set the tone for every other relationship we have, and I had never really worked on me before. I was so busy with all the external things, validation in academic achievements, in relationships and judging myself, critically.

I read about the benefits of meditation and thought, *How hard can it be?* It was incredibly popular, famous people were doing it, even kids were learning it at school. But I struggled to stop my thoughts and felt completely overwhelmed, at first.

Another thing I failed at.

But I heard that it took time and practice, so I just kept going, determined to heal. My mind jumped around so much at first, into the past failures, into the future, filled with worry and fear.

My NLP Coach was in her eighties. She'd had so many different careers and experiences in her life and I found her youthfulness and view on life fascinating. She told me that the anxiety I felt is pretty normal; that it was my body's way of communicating with me about the pain I had felt. We spent the long days learning and practicing the techniques. I began to sleep better.

After training for a couple of weeks, I was hooked.

I became a self-development junkie, reading every book I could find. I had spent years studying academically. It hadn't occurred to me to learn about emotional resilience and wellbeing. Isn't that funny?

I threw myself into learning as many healing modalities as I could to understand the connection between the mind and body, cause and effect, thoughts, and how the brain works. Most importantly, I learned about the power of the subconscious mind and how to let go of the past.

I was able to breathe.

Properly.

And it changed everything.

On a course one rainy day in Glasgow, "What if there is nothing wrong with you?" my coach at that time asked me.

My mind raced as I searched all the files of my brain. This had never occurred to me before! I had literally spent the last thirty years believing that somehow there was something fundamentally wrong with me – that I was a failure.

It might seem odd after how much pain there had been, how much suffering, but in that moment, I learned that just because we think something, it doesn't mean it's true and that was a major turning point in my life.

I decided to train as Clinical Hypnotherapist, NLP Practitioner, and Energy Healer to learn everything there was to know about healing so that I could help others heal, too.

I realised that somehow, I had developed limiting beliefs about myself in childhood that I was a failure and they had shaped my life, my relationships, and how I felt about myself. I had felt it in my core.

I was able to reframe these thoughts and beliefs. I was able to finally acknowledge and release the pain.

I was able to deal with the deep grief, shame, and anxiety I felt. To go on a journey – back to me.

I was finally able to forgive my parents, my partners, and myself, as I realised we were all just doing the best we could. I had struggled internally for years and no one knew – I realised that I had been trying to numb the pain. The pain I felt from not being good enough, from not being perfect.

That wee girl had still been inside. Terrified.

It was time to let myself be free. Finally.

Out of the bubble where I kept people at a distance through fear that they would see who I really was inside.

The truth is that we are all doing our best with what we know at the time. I realised that by numbing the pain, I was also numbing the joy. Now, there was no need to hide.

I spent years studying and applying changes, I focused on myself and my daughter. I built new connections and new healthy relationships.

A few years later when I had my second daughter, these skills were life changing as my womb and bladder burst in labour. I had months of surgeries and procedures and I feel very lucky that I was able to apply this wellbeing knowledge to my life in order to recover.

I left my high-powered, corporate role and I'm now a Resilience Coach, empowering women to love themselves, to reclaim their sense of calm and wellbeing so that they can show up with power and cope with confidence in all area of their life, love, and business.

When you see me now, you probably won't know I've had anxiety or these struggles. When I tell people my story, they always remark how strong and resilient I am.

Life doesn't have to be a struggle. We can all learn confidence and resilience. We can learn how to love ourselves. If I can do it, I believe that anyone can.

It's like going to the gym; you can't go once and expect a six pack. It's about showing up for yourself every day. Going on a journey of self-discovery back to love and peace.

Choosing love, every day. Creating healthy relationships with healthy boundaries and following your passion and mission in life. Life is about loving every moment and living in alignment with who you really are and who you want to become.

I look back at the hardest moments of my life and I am filled with love and forgiveness. Without self-love and confidence to be ourselves, we are empty, neurotic and out of control, looking for our sense of self-worth in all the wrong places. Numbing and self-sabotaging, just to get by. We are constantly comparing ourselves to others, and that's the most negative energy on the planet.

When we accept ourselves – the good and the bad – we find peace and contentment with life, and compassion for ourselves and others.

I now have a career I love helping women to reconnect – to themselves and two beautiful daughters. I live in alignment with myself and nourish my mind, body and spirit, having reached a place of acceptance about my past, but most importantly, acceptance of who I am. Inside and out.

And that that is enough – it was always enough.

I certainly haven't mastered life, but have learned some challenging lessons along the way and the biggest thing I have realised is that our past doesn't define us.

The future is wide open.

CHAPTER 19

A journey to rise

Jo Jacobs 

"You're shitting me, right?" I say, leaning forward.

"No, I assure you that I am not shitting you," replies the nurse.

How the hell is this possible?

I have been on the contraceptive pill for years, and have always been pretty precise with taking them, so this news doesn't make sense. The nurse asks if I had any symptoms, but I haven't, really. I've had a few weird cravings and sensitivities to smells, but I've even had recent bloodwork which didn't show anything.

Being pregnant just doesn't seem feasible.

But the real question is a nagging voice at the back of my mind.

Who is the father?

*

Five months later, I am most definitely having a baby… and after 24 hours in labor, my mind is so blurry due to sheer exhaustion, I can't tell who is all in the delivery room.

After three or four bags of liquids and the epidural shot that has still not kicked in, a yellow oxygen mask is thrust upon my face, while a passing nurse states, "She's going to possibly need a C-section or the baby and her won't survive."

Under no circumstances am I going to have a C-section.

229

I feel my breathing speed up and go shallow, the normal signs that a panic attack is looming. The threat of life for both my son and I is more than I can bear.

But then he is there. A full set of hair and the start of his forehead becomes visible. I feel myself exhale with relief.

Nearly breaking the nurse's hand, enduring a little more pain, the bloody delivery is finally done. The nurse then thrusts this slimy alien looking lifeform semi gently onto my chest, and shoves his face into my breast.

The nurse blabs on and on about the connection of mother and child and how the hospitals policy is to have the nurses push mothers to breastfeed.

Seriously, leave me alone!

I feel mentally and physically incapable of anything at this point due to exhaustion, and the medication has finally kicks in.

Damn it, let me sleep.

But sleep isn't going to happen. It seems like all the nurses take turns coming up to my bedside to take my blood pressure, refill my water cup, monitor my baby's heart rate, double check my identity, check the IV and whatever else their obligated duties are.

"Uggggghhhh!" I can't contain all the pent-up energy of my emotions.

Sore all over from being pricked and prodded with stabbing of needles, emotionally aggravated by the obnoxious beep, beep, beeping of monitors, and more attempts at forced breastfeeding by the nurses upon my raw cracked, and bleeding nipples, I am at my wit's end.

I just want some fucking sleep, nothing more. Leave me the fuck alone!

Tired and overwhelmed, all the comments and demands begin drowning in my ears. Rather than a blessing, having a delivery and recovery hospital room right next to the nurses' station is quite burdensome. Squeaky wheels of beds, the hustle of feet roaming by, and the occasional hollering of another mom-to-be in a nearby delivery room doesn't drown out the crushing blows that come from the nurses' reception area.

"Yea, the unwed girl in delivery room..." one nurse says.

"She is so young," another nurse says, followed with a rough tone, "... and unmarried."

"Sign these hospital legal forms, right here, Ms."

I can barely focus, let alone answer any of them before I have additional questions or comments thrown at me by yet another nurse.

Over and over the latest doctor on call arrives. "Ma'am, you aren't married?" each quizzingly echoes.

"Who is the father?" another hospital worker whose position I didn't know has the audacity to ask.

Another nurse comes in and asks similar veins of questions. "What is the name of the child to be on the birth certificate? What about placing the father's name on it?"

Squeaking like that of a tiny mouse caught in a trap. My mouth is all dry and I have the added anxiety of admitting I have no knowledge of exactly who the father is.

In that moment, as the eyes of hospital employees peer into the room, I believe they think I am nothing more than scum, laying there in a hospital bed. It seems that whoever comes into my room, leaves as quickly as they enter.

As a nurse walks by my recovery room, I hear her mumble, "Here's another unfit mother who doesn't know who the father is."

Paranoia creeps in. I am trying to see the hospital name badges of anyone coming into my room to make sure they work here, for I fear for my son's life and my own life. After everything I have gone through up to this point in my life, it is no surprise I am on edge.

I trust no one.

*

Bringing my son at two months old to get his mouth swabbed to find the legit birth father is extremely difficult.

Sitting in the waiting room, my nerves are so shot that my right leg begins to twitch uncontrollably up and down, and I'm biting my fingernails. I'm constantly surveying the room due to the amount of people there that day.

The only thing I have been told is that once I am called, I will go inside and get my mouth swabbed. My son will also get his mouth swabbed, and then we will be able to leave, and the results will be mailed to me.

Suddenly time stops. While in the waiting room, I see an all too familiar face at the doorway and my body goes cold.

Why did they let him come here at the same time as me?

Staring profusely at the nearest emergency exit. Run! Leaping up, I run. Blood dripping down the insides of my legs, sweat plastered upon my uncleaned body. Alarm blaring. Don't look back. Run!

The walls start closing in on me. My rapist has just strutted into the room.

After everything that had happened in the past, and the trauma I have been through because of his actions against me, I have been trying to live my life in the present, and have not yet figured out how to deal with the trauma.

I've been looking toward the future the best I can, focusing on the birth of my beautiful son.

But as soon as I see that monster walk nonchalantly into that waiting room, my mind spirals backwards with haunted whispers of the past.

I shake uncontrollably and my nails dig into my palms as I ball my hands into tight fists. I feel the burn of acid bile in my throat.

I can't breathe.

I just need to escape, to run away from my life. I want to die right there.

Why is this happening?

As I struggle to regain composure, someone comes to my aid. It turns out while the courthouse receptionist is new, she has also failed to read my chart in a timely manner. After she finally reads my chart, she realizes the vile asshole who has just entered the waiting room is the rapist whose DNA is being tested as the prospective father.

"I am so unbelievably sorry for the screw up. I never meant to cause you more pain," the receptionist apologizes repeatedly as she rushes my son and I out of the room where my rapist is now waiting to be tested.

How the hell am I supposed to get out of living here in this metaphorical bubble of existence?

I no longer exist as I once did – I no longer know who I am.

People who once knew me, are now strangers. For those who don't know, this is what happens when you're forced to endure the poisons of trauma from the filthy hands of another.

In the instant I see him, my world once again shatters right before my eyes. He has seen my innocent little boy. We both know that depending on the test results he might have the right to claim custody.

Please, don't let him be the father.

Will nothing ever come easy for me?

Growing up in foster care I was forced to eat dog food from a bowl on the floor any time my foster parents didn't get their paycheck from the state. Later, I came to know that horrors only prevail. My adopted family, a family who had taught me to tie my shoes, taught me etiquette, the principles of life and religion, but beyond the public face hid the terrors of child molestation.

When I met and worked with the *rapist*, I was in a relationship. Gashing furious pain stole what I thought was my happiness. Aching and nauseated all the time.

Wanting to scream, wanting to cry, hating all, and wanting nothing more than to die. I want to stop this constant hurt, to stop the voices inside my throbbing head. All the inner scars, and my mind filled with scorn. Silhouetted ghosts spontaneously appear. Those demons never stop, instead, they dance atop my never-ending thoughts.

I wait for what seems like years, in reality, the results take only a couple of weeks. When the white envelope with the courthouse emblem finally arrives, I rip it open, and watch as shreds fall to the floor.

Speed reading through the paperwork, my hand suddenly clasps over my mouth. My heart begins thumping so loud I can hear it in my ears.

It's not him! He's NOT the father.

Relief washes over me. The father of my child is not the co-worker who had raped me.

But... now I have to tell the real father, and that isn't going to be easy, either. Thanks to the words of both his sister and a friend, my now ex-fiancé believes I cheated on him, and does not believe the fact that I've been raped.

Based on his judgement, he rejects the notion that the child is his son. He leaves for California to visit his sister.

This can't get any worse.

Oh, but they do. Things soon get much worse.

I've been under contract at my one job... the same job where my non-convicted, rapist co-worker still works. And I am forced to return to that same job. The same job with the same bosses I told a year ago that I had been raped. The same bunch of degenerates who had initially laughed and replied with lines like, "If you weren't so pretty, he wouldn't have wanted to sleep with you," or "What were you wearing at the time?"

This was NOT my fault! Why can't they understand that?

Thankfully it isn't long before I receive documents stating I am being transferred, not just out of my position, but out of state. I breath a short-lived sigh of relief.

Then, changes once more within the organization end up sending me back to the same place from where I was transferred from.

With all the back and forth, along with being a new mom, it gets to a point where I am so overwhelmed with frustration, agony and hatred, it seems unbearable. To top it off, no form of punishment or reprimanding has even occurred against the co-worker who had raped me.

I want to be able to say, "Life gets better and there's a light at the end of the tunnel." But my world isn't making that kind of sense.

I don't have those responses or the best answers. I have been living in the deep abyss far too long. Simply 'getting over' what happened isn't my reality.

I have to find another way to thrive. Here and there, there are some people who try to help. "Change your perspective," they say. "Think about how to turn everything positive."

I try to change my perspective, but it isn't as easy as I'd hoped. Old habits and mindsets keep showing their ugly faces, trying to sabotage my world.

Nobody knows by looking at the surface, the depths of human pain which lies beneath. My hope is worn down by the world, where nothing in it can refresh my mind from the constant bustling buzzing.

I am tired.

"I can't take this shit anymore!" I scream, after many more months of sleepless nights and tear-stained pillows.

It is then that something clicks.

I realize the importance of asking the right question in order to arrive at the correct answer.

Each night I ask myself, *Why was I the one chosen to live in this hell? Why was I chosen to endure child sexual violence? Why was I chosen to be raped? Why did I live while others die? Why me?*

And each night, a terrible voice says, "Why not you?"

Gradually though, I realize that yes, very terrible things happened, but they were not of my doing and none of them were my fault. My demons come from circumstances of being at the hands of others; foster parents and adopted parents, who neglected their responsibilities... and later, a vile sexual predator using whatever thoughtless reasoning he felt justified his disgusting actions.

But I had survived, despite what was done to me!

I am someone with a fighting spirit – a warrior – a survivor!

It is then that I realise I need to do something new to draw my attention, to focus on something positive.

One afternoon, a sparkling crown icon with red roses appears online, and catches my attention. *Pageantry? No. No way!*

And yet, as I hear some fretful doubts dancing in my head, I know I already have my answer.

Seriously, you're really applying? Not like you haven't done a bit of modeling before. This tomboy cannot be stopped. I'll do it just for fun.

To my absolute surprise, I win. I am Ms. American Rose, City Queen!

As I get to know the director Lynanne White better, I learn much more about the pageant community. It isn't long before I am representing as Pennsylvania State Queen, and then the reigning international title holder as Ms. World Rose.

As exciting and wonderful as this is, the anger still hasn't dissipated. I still feel irritable, restless, resentful. My moods impact the others around me, because my unsettled anger penetrates my every being.

Will it ever go away? What can I do?

It feels that there is no way to be whole again.

Eventually this living on the verge results in a complete meltdown. My withdraw from reality and sense of overwhelming sadness and anger forces me to take a leave of absence in every aspect of life.

I have to free myself to live and learn from the experience, to grow and progress in life.

Outspoken, direct, and vigilant I begin to open my can of worms to reveal the horrors of trauma to everyone I meet.

During the process, I learn that if someone has suffered (or currently suffers) too much, some damage cannot be repaired. But despite that damage, each of us still has our own character, and self-worth.

It is through true and loyal advocates: a few family members, a select set of amazing friends, and a very outspoken, tolerant therapist, who restore some hope of humanity within my universe. This creates the next era of questioning...

What is the world preparing me for now? What am I meant to accomplish?

*

Late one evening, I leave my laptop atop the desk, wide open, and I come back to see my little man banging on the keyboard. I dash over to help him off the desk chair, but in the short time he was banging on the keyboard, he has clicked on multiple links which somehow sends a request to someone on an online dating site I have never heard of.

A couple weeks go by and of course I completely forget about it.

Another month flies by, when I receive an email in my spam folder from some random person, who just so happens to be the same person my little man had sent a request to. I don't know what to really expect to read if I open the email. I contemplate deleting it, but I choose to open it to see what it contains.

Back and forth fly the emails, the anticipation is like in the movie, *You've Got Mail*, minus the waiting on AOL. We have numerous late-night phone calls, and I feel a bit like a little schoolgirl giggling on the phone for hours. A few months pass and we agree to meet at a halfway point planned out to each of our locations in a public area, for safety purposes.

"Hi, you're really pretty," he says.

Not being a techy I couldn't upload a photo online, I'd told him in an email, "I know it's hard to believe, but the only picture I have is on my bio on a pageant website."

"You look just as cute in person, as you do in the photo I found of you, online," he says, stretching out his hand awkwardly.

Clearly unsure whether to shake my hand or kiss my cheek, he grabs my suitcase instead and closes up the trunk. Then without a thought I give him a hug.

Ohhhh, he's so warm.

One date turns into a whole weekend, full of deep conversation, flirting, and fun. I have already revealed myself and all the dark secrets of my past in our hundreds of emails and phone calls, and he has always held a space for me to truly be myself.

In person he is the same... no, he is better.

Life is full of surprises, and I know I have finally found my person.

We get engaged that very weekend.

*

He moved over 6,000 miles to be with us. In the beginning it was three of us living together in a small apartment. Four short years, and two children later, life continued to be full of surprises, and they were good ones.

We took the long drive from Pennsylvania back to his home state of Kansas and within weeks of arrival, discovered I was pregnant with another munchkin to add into our crazy mix of life.

I continued to enter into and won not just local titles, but National and International pageant titles. Pageants and my husband were the start of my guiding light on the road to recovery.

Numerous people tell me I should say my life changed once I became a mother. Yes, it did, but honestly it was my husband with his support, along with pageantry, which truly changed allowed me to bloom into the woman I am today.

Similar to a rebirth, after bearing three children with my husband, and watching him being the true fatherly figure to my first and oldest son, I realized that he has always been by my side through everything. His support has never wavered, and he always lends me an ear as I ramble on about various topics. Especially with me going on about the injustice of child abuse, child molesters, rapists, and even the topic of religion (a topic where we are on opposite ends of the belief spectrum).

Throughout our marriage, his patience and love for me has helped me learn the art of being calmer. I still feel the pull to impatiently zoom onward through life, conversations, and projects, but he has been encouraging me to grow my patience.

"I missed that line during the life creation center. Bypassed it entirely for the chatterbox lane instead," I constantly explain to him.

"You don't say," he smirks with a hint of a chuckle. Then he moves in for a kiss and I playfully pretend to shove him.

"No way! You aren't getting these soft lips after that comment."

Instead I wrap him up with my arms around his neck, standing on tiptoes, and kiss him anyway.

"You always show patience with me. I know that there has been a lot of times that I make it difficult with my recovery, even still to this day."

He just gives me a hug and says, "I love you."

He remains my mountain standing along, by my side.

If someone were to ask if you know your self-value, what would you say? Do others know and understand that the price of life is non-negotiable?

There is only one of each of us and we cannot be replaced. None of us are for sale or rent, and we need to stop letting our thoughts be the price of what our self-worth is. The self-worth price of myself is my character, my being, and what makes me, me.

Hello, world. I am flawed in many ways, but I know that I am loved and must remain true to myself. No one knows how you truly feel unless you choose to share. Everyone has gone through something, and if you got to this point, it is worth acknowledging. Some will listen and make judgment, while others will listen with a heart of compassion. They may offer advice either with or without fully understanding, but it's your decision to choose what advice you will listen to.

For those not in the pageantry world, it's not all glitz, glam, and evening gowns. Each pageant had many contestants who were either going through or overcoming life situations of their very own, and it opened my eyes wider to the broader perspective.

Beauty, Brains & Heart™ Team Queens, founded and directed by Jackie Russo, taught me the love of volunteering and that pageant queens are more than just a pretty face. To this day, Mrs. Jackie embodies the art of kindness and displays grace with a love of humanity which initially inspired me to build connections in community life.

After competing in her pageant, I entered into more pageants. With each pageant I continued to make great friends along the way. Many of them have their own online or onstage pageant systems which I have entered into, won, and even received the honor of being a judge. Pageantry allows me the opportunity to become the feminine voice for others, that I had always wanted to hear.

It's the collaboration, compassion, consistency, caring, kindness, comfort, companionship, willingness to help and celebrate with others. It's in the creativeness, cheerfulness, communication, contribution, confidence in yourself and others around you. It's challenging yourself to do and to be better. The ability to embrace change, to get clarity, and have concentration, contentment and consciousness. All of these are found in pageantry, and all are also found in self-love.

*

The heat of the multi-colored lights protrude upon me. The shimmer of another contestant's shoes keeps me at bay from swaying back and forth. Is that a loose stone on her gown?

Startled by the mouth near my ear. Breathing, "Go."

The white spotlight strobes upon me, making my evening gown sparkle ever more elegant. The only question, which the contestant before me answered, I cannot recall. My brain has zoned out minutes ago as I stand frozen in my spot.

"Whaaa...?"

"Go!" and a grab of my hand brings me back into focus. "They are calling your name!"

"I am unique. You are unique. There is only one version of me, and only one version of you. We are special and amazing. Nobody else in the entire world is like me, nor like you. I have scars, that others could not bear."

Oh, hell, what is flying prevalently out of my mouth?

"I totally accept that I am not responsible for anyone else's beliefs or perspectives, even if they pertain to me. Those are entirely their own choice."

Where am I headed with this? Blah, blah, blah.

Are people staring? What on earth am I saying? I am not prepared for this.

Just keep talking, you've got just three minutes!

"Once you find yourself a survivor of traumatic experiences, and you choose life over death, that is when the light shines from within you. Then you can enter the shadows that the others around, cast upon you and the world. It is time to S.T.O.P the A.S.H.E.S. Start Thriving On Process, take a stand and speak out about Abuse, Sexual Violence, Harassment, Excuses, and Silence."

Squinting, hues of people sitting in upright theatre chairs, with the occasional wailing of a young child. *Hello, anyone out there? You going to shut me up any time now?*

"Do not just preach to each other. Show them that there is something worth standing for even in the darkness, by letting them know they are not alone."

Did everyone leave? Am I boring? Why...is everyone...so...silent?

"Consider ways in which you might be able to pass on the same to someone you encounter, even to a stranger, knowing that this act of kindness may help them in ways you can never again. You might just find that your heart wants to expand."

"30 seconds!" squeaks the microphone with the host announcer holding it.

"Take some action and make something beautiful happen in your life."

Because of pageantry, the love of a great man, and finally my belief in myself, I have been able to discover my self-worth and my voice. I have found the beauty in life, through helping others. Fulfillment.

This is why I continue to be the light for others, their outer voice, in one way or another.

So they too, will thrive on the journey they call LIFE.

CHAPTER 20

I once had cancer for two weeks

Taryn Claire

The wind barrels in, bullish and charging, in contrast to the delicate nature of our conversation. When my champagne flute goes flying in the gale, shards of glass spray across the floor, witnessed but barely heard between the howling gusts. The crazy weather matches the crazy upheaval we have found ourselves in since this morning. Yet still we sit, determined to nut out all possibilities for moving forward, our tone casual and cavalier, in contrast to the deathly subject at hand.

We both consciously choose words between pregnant pauses and audible inhales. Huddled on the front veranda under the streetlight, facing the churning sea, away from the laughter and childish teasing indoors. Anchored to our seats in unified focus and growing awareness for what feels like hours.

My ears pound in pulsating booms, each bit of new information received echoes ominously inside my head. I desperately try to recalibrate. Attempt to adjust to this new world through a disoriented bifocal which constantly shifts and distorts my perceptions.

The night is dark, yet the topic of discussion darker. The contrast of mood from the evening before palpably different. This morning's unexpected discovery looms thick in the air despite attempts to engage in other possibilities.

How life can simply shift gears in an instant has been demonstrably clear today. The family holiday has altered course sharply from rambunctious, gregarious freedom to an eerie abrupt slamming into a metaphorical wall.

"It's quite possibly OLUBS," Baci, my Beloved, chimes in, head tilted enough for me to catch the softest twinkle in his eye.

"OLUBS?" I enquire.

"Old Lady Ugly Breast Syndrome." And we laugh in unison while I wipe my salty wet cheeks.

We are both acutely aware of his strategy. My husband is a GP and after two decades together I easily recognise what he is gallantly attempting to do. Weaving in additional possibilities of what it may be, he is trying to make it sound as though there is hope, unaware that this morning his ashen face gave it all away.

Unlike our hometown, where it is so hot that you drip dry from shower to dressing room, the cooler climate on this holiday meant that this morning I had to bend over to dry my legs.

I discovered an anomaly in my left breast, which disappears like vanishing ink when I stand back up. A mountain-peaked right breast looms in contrast to the stomped-on hillock of the left. It instantly shifts the atmosphere, like a low-pressure storm cell arriving on a hot sultry day.

Temporarily caught in the thicket of a frown, I lean in closer, raising my eyebrows with wide-eyed disbelief. It fails to bring clarity to what I am seeing. My eyes struggle to refocus with their rapid pulsed blinking in confusion while mentally processing the failed physical attempt to see things more clearly.

My husband whispers softly and slowly, "It's a retracted nipple."

Our gaze locks, there's a momentary falter, before the tortured suspended tension is sliced by the familial arguing of testosterone-fuelled teens in the next room.

Two reality checks rolled into one payday, have knocked the wind from me. I crumple to my knees as I gasp, the impact like a punch to the paunch. I'm precariously navigating a tightrope, an overfilled rucksack on my back stuffed with a lifetime of precious breakables, teetering now... the balancing pole in my damp slippery hands. Overwhelmingly overburdened. Skidding into the recognition that I lack the very skills or equipment to walk these dizzying and dangerous heights.

"Shit. What about the kids?"

Grade 12 starts in seven weeks for the middle-born and this is hardly the start a mother plans for such an important year.

"FUCK. What about all my *issues*?"

I feel myself mentally back pedalling. The comfortable tandem cycling through life, switching to precarious unicycling in a split moment.

This will be, ultimately, a solo journey forward... as no-one can physically share my vehicle to negotiate the corrugations that lie ahead. A lifetime of fears jams up in quick succession, knocking the chain off my cogs of life and tripping me up. I know this landing is going to hurt. I am no longer in control to stop this.

So many buried and ignored fears to face. My doctor and needle phobias ensure the journey ahead will be bumpy. No suspension or metaphorical bike seat to rest upon. Both fitness and endurance put to a test that I didn't know I'd signed up for – yet here I am lined up with my assigned number in the race of my life. WTF. What the fuck has just happened?

Frozen with wide-eyed awareness and cold realisation. What lies ahead is expansively filled with unknowns. It requires epic personal stretching, resilience, and flexibility.

Even if I don't feel up to the job there is no easy exit clause.

The days which follow morph into forced acting, fake smiles, chipper tones, and suspiciously upbeat conversations burdening my already overwhelmed state. Pretence is at the forefront of every interaction.

Managing the unaware and oblivious state is certainly a challenging chore to maintain. Keeping an even keel, with the holiday charade momentum ongoing, is excruciatingly exhausting.

Mentally fatigued with repeatedly playing out potential scenarios in my head, keeps me distracted from being entirely in the moment in those final days as the holiday draws to a close. I wade through waking hours both inside myself and outside myself. My head contains an inner dialogue of constant mind whirrings and churnings.

Inside, is an entire jungle-like ecosystem, with choking vines and violent storms that bucket rain in lashings and electrical flashes of lightning set light to kindling fears. From my own dissociate outside view I see a person who is contained, in control, temperate and introspective. Cool, calm, and collected. The contrasting state beckons belief.

The flight home is spent blissfully suspended above the cloudy landscape in a random staying pattern of disconnect, the brief reprieve a welcomed state. Upon landing, the pressure descends once again, piercing me with relentless awareness, reminding me that all is not well in my world.

*

SPLAT.

The gel is squirted on my right breast and the cool steel glides effortlessly, bouncing frequency waves in search of abnormalities. The quiet conversation sparse while I fixate my eyes on the ceiling, feigning calm, catching wayward breaths and tethering them inward to steady the rising internal jitters.

Baci had arranged this appointment on my behalf. This morning I had panicked at the possibility that a male sonographer could be performing the examination of an intimate area of mine. I called ahead, ready to cancel the appointment if it was with a male, but felt a warm rush of relief to hear that only females are assigned to this sensitive task.

The cascading challenges of phobias hit me in quick succession. The room tempo alters when the sonographer moves to the left breast, instant animation bursting the bubble of reserve. Her waterfalling words gush into the space, filling the air, as a fine mist of unease sprays over me. Her eyes dart sharply between screen and keyboard. I suspect she is measuring something she has found. She excuses herself to seek further clarification.

Less than two minutes later, the sonographer returns, joined by a pleasant, smiling, friendly, younger man. "It's the C word. We don't have a lot of time. I would like to perform a biopsy right now if that's ok. What we need to do next is…"

The walls of the room cave in, my chest crumples, the air is vacuumed out. I am goldfish staring at the radiologist, through choking thick air as his words swim slowly, stretched and distorted in my direction.

My head is bobbing in a conditioned agreeable state, the strain of a polite smile pasted incongruously on my face. Disconnected from self, I overhear my voice controlled and composed. "Thank you, yes of course, I understand…" But I don't.

I wonder if this is how fast it usually happens for others. I've seen it in the movies but I question if this is the way other people find out in real life. I shove my phobias back down, squish them and pack them tight before stomping on them and squeezing them into the tight space of a cramped, crumpled heart. External stoic indifference contrasting the internal machinations and scramblings.

All three phobias arrive in unison, digging up and revealing the stench of buried childhood issues. Body exposure issues. Male medico issues. Needle phobias. These constant companions have lurked in the shadows of avoidance for years. I have hit the trifecta today. I have cracked the dreaded code for messy unravelling and feel like I am going to spill my guts all over the floor in a giant anxiety-fuelled spew.

The radiologist states the tumour appears to be around 14mm. But it is the sharp biopsy needle that's called into action to confirm exact diagnosis with extracted cellular pathology that truly grabs my attention. I must now expose my left breast to a male doctor and have it stabbed in three different spots with a long clawing needle.

*

We take the clunking lift up to the third floor. It's after hours and the building is quiet except for the echo of a singular set of heels clicking confidently up the corridor. Smiles and small talk are exchanged under a heavy bellied cloud, looming and large like the ever-described elephant in the room. The surgeon's office is surprisingly warm and inviting with personal photos on display and artwork that distractedly catches my eye.

I am caught unaware when a spire of emotion rises rapidly up through my body, it rings and reverberates through each and every cell before spilling out of my eyes. Precariously perched on the edge of my seat, leaning into the conversation, my laboured effort to slow my breath and get more air into my lungs filters into my awareness. The room is caving in on me, imploding all my senses into a psychedelic mess.

My deliberate unwavering focus homes in on the specialist as her measured words spell things out. I take stock. I am still physically present despite the desire to run, to scream or to tap out of this wrangled wrestling.

What a morbid mishmash lies before me.

She paints a dismal picture of chemo to shrink the tumour, surgery, more chemo, hormone therapy and radiation too.

The biopsy histology has confirmed that it is indeed a 20mm tumour. I feel foolish when I realise I hadn't been mentally prepared for the number to change. The report reveals my type of breast cancer is one women in their late 60s get after a dalliance with Hormone Replacement Therapy. I am 41 and haven't been on hormones for over a decade.

Invasive Lobular Carcinoma is rare for my age group and yet here I am.

The surgeon, with more experience in these matters than me, is considerably grave about where things are at due to my young age for this type. Before we wrap up the appointment she lightly plays it off the heavy mood with offerings of a new 'rack' at the end – when it's all done. Brand new fake ones, FOOBS to be exact. It feels like a tv shop-direct show with "and here's your bonus: but wait there's more... more needles!"

*

I lie face down, breasts freefalling into the two holes designed specifically for breast cancer diagnostics and listen to what sounds like sports shoes in a tumble dryer, thumping so loudly it drowns out the CD I brought with me. I hum the drowned-out beats in the music inside my head. I play a little mind game with myself to see if I can match the tempo when it is silenced by the MRI's cacophony of bullets and bangs.

Quietly reflecting, today has been a huge day of diagnostic testing. CT scan and MRI at two different physical locations has added to the exhaustion. Cannulation for radioactive dye has taken my frayed nerves up to the next level but I talk myself off the ledge knowing they need this to get more details of where it may have metastasised. Inserting the needle was predictably traumatic. I observe that people without needle phobias have little compassion or patience for my histrionics. I am awash with tiredness from having to 'adult' all day. I am grateful to be lying down once again, especially as the dye flooding my veins has left me somewhat woozy despite assurances that there are no side effects to be felt.

This past week I have been forced to dig deep. I have dipped into my reserves. It's been a crazy time being thrown head-on into this unsettling world of my phobias. An anxiety vomit posset rises up my throat, biting and burning before seeping back down in a reflexive swallow. This cancer carousel revisits the same carnival of horror each day with dizzying demands.

Stop. Dammit. I want to get off. Now.

Baci brings home a printed copy of the MRI results for me... the convenient joys of having a medico in the house. Lowering my eyes to read the lines, they jumble and swim around the 35mm measurement of the tumour and claim it has 'friends' too. Cold shockwaves radiate through me. I feel ill equipped to transition to the ever-shifting border of where the edge of the tumour actually sits. MRI with contrast is considered in some countries to be the gold standard for diagnosing women with breast cancer and I am starting to see why. I cannot quite process the jump from 14mm to 35mm. With the constant shifting of the size of the tumour I feel unsettled, unsure, and unsafe.

*

It's exactly two weeks and two days since my discovery. The room is dark except for the fairy lights my girlfriends have hung in the room. The two hourly OBS roll around all too quickly and I am woken once again with a blood pressure cuff around my right arm while a nurse takes my temperature and pulse.

The worn threads of the hospital gown are soft against my skin. Where it gapes open reveals a strip of flat, white, spongy tape where my DD's once were. I am expecting to be awash with rogue waves of realisation as the gravity of my new way of being seeps in, yet I am quietly relieved instead. Whew, it's over. This chapter anyway. The emotion of relief is sweet and syrupy. I am more than okay with being flat.

It's been a crazy turbulent head spin this past fortnight. Each and every day filled with more testing, further waiting on results and an endless string of people touching, prodding, poking, and sitting themselves plum in my personal space. It feels so good for this chapter to close.

*

The final histology report comes in. The tumour measured 55mm with 'friends' and had spread to lymph nodes. I steady myself momentarily. I transition effortlessly this time with a wave of gratitude.

In this moment I am grateful that I fought to have a bilateral mastectomy when the advice was originally purely to have a lumpectomy.

In this moment I am grateful I have a strong sense of self and enough confidence to stand up for what I want and go against the new way in favour of as much breast preservation as possible.

In this moment I celebrate that no matter the journey that still lays before me, I've faced cancer and my fears too and can proudly say out loud...

I once had cancer for two weeks.

Authors

Annette Densham
Writer, Storyteller, and Author

With a gypsy as a mother, I sought refuge in stories while we were moving. By the time I was 17 I had lived in 96 houses. The books in the library became my best friends and I immersed myself in tales of courageous heroes, incredible adventures, and seeking knowledge about the world.

It was no surprise when I chose to go into journalism, the perfect career for my inquisitive and curious mind. After decades of writing, from major print publications and online magazines on topics from business and computers to seniors' issues and forklifts, I moved into corporate comms. Here I honed my storytelling skills, weaving words that moved people to tears so they would give generously to worthy causes, and to educate, empower and inspire.

Faced with the loss of my cushy corporate role in a 'financial restructure', I ventured out into entrepreneur land, eager to use my 30 plus years in media to help people in small business. Working in public relations, I found a passion helping equip, educate and encourage businesses to use their stories to promote what they do across multiple channels... and I won a few awards along the way for the impact I have had.

E: annette@theaudacsiouagency.com
L: www.linkedin.com/annettedensham
W: www.theaudaciousagency.com

Bisi Osundeko

Entrepreneur, Public speaker, Property Investor, Life Coach and Politician

I have a passion for raising the next generation of business leaders from parents/carers of disabled children. Having navigated my entrepreneurial journey for over a decade as a parent to two little ones who were born with complex disabilities, I have a first-hand experience of the sort of challenges that this section of our entrepreneurial community face.

Outside business, special needs parenting can be very isolating, so I have set up a closed Facebook group (Joy and Joe SEN parenting support group) where parents of children with special needs can be empowered to start their own business whilst we also support each other emotionally. I look forward to welcoming you into our community.

In 2012, I won the prestigious mumsclub award as one of the top 100 business mums in the UK. In 2015, my business won the prestigious venture further award by the University of Manchester business school. In 2017, I won the Talk of Manchester Business Award and Best Female Entrepreneur in 2017. I'm also currently a Councillor in St. Helens.

A graduate of the University of Nottingham and scholar. I am the recipient of the prestigious DFID/Commonwealth scholarship for postgraduate studies. An OFSTED registered Early years expert and governor in two special needs primary schools in the United Kingdom.

E: bisi@joyandjoebaby.co.uk
W: www.bisiosundeko.co.uk
F: @BisiOsundeko
I: @joyandjoefamily

Bonnie Jo Guidry

Entrepreneur/Multiple Small Business Owner

Growing up in an unstable environment, I had a tendency to escape into my own little inner world. Genetics certainly had its claim to my introverted nature and anxiety-prone mind. This predisposition, inundated with influences of dysfunction, left me limping into adulthood. Depression, anxiety and Obsessive Compulsive Disorder, foes which showed no mercy, held me captive by chains of emotional and mental torment, giving rise to self-hate and sabotaging behaviors.

Armed with pure determination and a desire to help others, I set out on an expedition of self-discovery and healing. Acquiring a master's degree in Counseling served as a gateway to the study of everything I could get my hands on regarding my own diagnoses. Learning of the plasticity of the brain and the power of thought was the key to my emotional freedom.

An entrepreneur at heart, I've owned and operated multiple successful small businesses for nearly twenty years. This book comes on the brink of transition for me as I embark on new business ventures which will allow me to step into my authentic self and walk in my purpose.

My mission is to help others find wellness in body, mind and soul.

E: bonniejoguidry@gmail.com

Brett D. Scott
Freedom Coaching

I look after those people who feel like perhaps they've missed the boat. They think their failures have defined them, or maybe that their personality just isn't going to allow them to have the breakthroughs they hoped they would. Whether it's finding purpose, getting in touch with yourself, or achieving financial freedom, I've got the help you need.

I help men (and women) who get to their late 30s and above, who feel and believe they are failures or simply have hit the imaginary ceiling of success, just as I did at 43. I help them open up and embrace the changes to be able to live their very best life.

My background is customer service, sales and coaching via hotels, real estate and fitness and they've all played a part in helping me become the best at what I now do; as a Success Coach in guiding people towards transforming their lives, forever.

E: info@brettdscott.com
F: @freedomcoachingbybds
I: @freedom_coaching_by_bds

Camilla Constance
Sex and Intimacy Coach

I currently live in Hampshire, England with my partner Simon, three children, two cats, a dog and a guinea pig. I am a mother, a teacher, a dreamer, a rebel. I am a Sex and Intimacy coach with a passion to preach the power and importance of female sexual pleasure.

It is my mission to guide women to liberate and heal their sexuality. Sexuality is our birthright. We have been conditioned out of it. We have been told our sexuality is our weakness and our vulnerability when it is actually our strength and our power.

Studying Anthropology at university and NLP as a young mother, I have long understood that we are all conditioned into social models. Sometimes those models serve us and sometimes they don't. The crucial thing is that we can decide to choose our models.

In my search for new models of human sexuality I discovered the world of Conscious Sexuality or Tantra. I learned pleasure and embodiment practices which are now at the core of my coaching.

No one is broken. Time after time I have guided women to reconnect with their sexual pleasure; to release and heal significant trauma, establish nourishing relationships and yes, become the bedrock of happy families.

Don't wait. Don't settle. Connect with your pleasure now and see how your life transforms!

And PS, It's never too late to work with me. Women in their 80s are discovering their sexual selves!

E: camillaconstance.coaching@gmail.com
W: www.camillaconstance.com
F: @Camilla Constance

Charlene Kay Fouts
Speaker, Founder of Healing Acres Never Again and Author

The storms we experience in life either build or break us. They ultimately forge our character, build our inner strength, and create our foundation in life, as well as our faith in God.

I grew up in an abusive environment that carried over into my adult life, experiencing brutal violence in relationships and marriage. I was a Flight Attendant for many years, but now I am pursuing a Psychology degree from the University of South Florida (USF) and am in the process of publishing another book called "Never Again, Finding the Silver Linings". This entails my lifelong journey and healing process of removing layers of pain and shame from my life.

My non-profit organization, Healing Acres Never Again, Inc. was created as a part of healing from my own tragedy and injustices, to walk alongside others experiencing the same traumas that God helped me walk out of. Healing is a journey, and as we grow, we discover different layers to remove. It's a lifelong process, but one that is meant to free us and allow us to fly!

HANA focuses on recovery for people who have experienced trauma from incest, domestic violence, sexual abuse, rape, and abortion. These traumas are often left unchecked and lie dormant until a circumstance in life draws them out, usually in the form of nightmares, addictions, or unhealthy patterns and cycles in life. This mostly goes unnoticed by the victim of these kinds of traumas and abuses, until the pain of the event can no longer be contained.

If you have unhealed trauma in your life, or if you would like to support HANA, please contact:

W: www.healingacresneveragain.org
E: info@healingacresneveragain.org
Ph: 813-577-2747

Charleen Sitiene

Early Childhood Educator and Author

Growing up I had a massive passion for reading and writing fictional stories.

I remember being asked in high school what career path I wanted to venture into. Two things came to mind, one of them being a Children's Author and the other an Early Childhood Teacher. I studied and qualified as the latter.

I worked in Early Childhood Education for eight years back home in New Zealand and Australia in various Childcare Centres.

I loved working in that industry. I got to see so many children grow and develop into the happiest little human beings, and it made me feel that I did a job well done as their teacher.

These days I am a mother of five children. My great joy is watching them grow and develop into beautiful humans. They bring so much love and joy into my life with their different personalities.

I also love helping other women who have been in similar situations to mine and letting them know that time does heal all wounds and that are never ever alone.

When my children are older, I plan to return to study and achieve my Diploma of Counselling.

Gabrielle Conescu
Artist, Speaker, Coach, Mentor and Author

From Brisbane, Australia, I finished high school believing I had no special talent. Office work sustained me while I worked out what I really wanted to do. My artistic nature seemed inconsequential in the real world and I set aside my creative desires to fulfil the roles society laid out for me.

My sons Troy and Blair make me proud. They have both grown to be very capable young men.

My workplace experience was the catalyst for taking my own desires seriously. My soul was calling me back to my artistic self.

In search for truth, I studied Leadership, Coaching and Mentoring and set about discovering the real me. In my brave new world, there was no room for believing I had no talent.

Art fired up my capacity to function wholly giving me new life. Nurturing my creativity became vitally important. I discarded the old habit of measuring myself against others.

Now I am Gabrielle the Artist, fully aware of art's power to heal. I exhibit paintings locally and to international audiences at the Mental Health Services Conference, Brisbane Entertainment Centre and the Global Wave Conference, Gold Coast. I love speaking to inspire others and shared my transformation story on radio.

When we focus on beauty and joy, our lives return to balance. We transform. I'm on a mission to help others awaken their soul's creative spirit through my workshops and retreats.

W: www.fifthdimensionart.com.au
F: @fifthdimensionart
I: @fifthdimensionart

Ivan Brewer

Restaurant Profitability Expert and Chronic Pain Advocate

I grew up the son of an inventor and wordsmith, in a world barely known today; full of rough and tumble, scrapes and scratches, full of sport and activity. Since a child I have held tightly to a book every day, and every night. I fell madly in love with words and their promise of bright new adventures and wonderful escape. I have longed to write myself, but it took losing almost everything I had known to find my voice.

The great Industry of Hospitality has been my calling; I have found a new way to be profitable and continue on my path to improve the profitability of SME's throughout the world.

And then I became disabled.

My life finds itself split into three: Hospitality consulting and research, Chronic Pain management, and my wife and two kids.

I am driven daily to better understand how to live the best version of life I have available to me. I promise myself that, despite everything that has happened, I am determined my disability will become the best thing that ever happened.

Chronic Pain is an epidemic, yet the knowledge of it and how to manage it is so nascent.

I have learned so much, and gone so far beyond what experts thought possible, that I hope to inspire and incite sufferers to live their fullest life, as I am.

For if even one person makes a change that keeps them here in this world, it will make my journey worthwhile.

E: ivan@ivanbrewer.com.au
L: linkedin.com/in/ivanbrewer
Tw: @ivantudorbrewer

Jo Jacobs

Author, Mom, Military Spouse and Veteran, Mrs. United States, Founder of- Just BEing Me Creations, LLC and S.T.O.P the A.S.H.E.S

Spells of rage, and forging anger. Surviving sexual trauma takes a lifetime of pressing through your own battlefield in your mind to find your own personal self-worth, self-confidence, self-empowerment.

Pregnancy through the birth of my oldest son, to falling into the world of pageantry, began to take on a whole new meaning of life and learning not to just be a "survivor" but that there was more to life.

At first I denounced wanting to speak openly about sexual violence and abuse. After much time had passed and I continued to find my own self stuck, in what I consider to be the "pits of hell on Earth", in places I wouldn't cast upon any other human being.

However, it was a complete breakdown in 2015 that landed me into therapy.

Through these sessions, and working to coordinate new classes for military personnel, the need grew even stronger. My platform: S.T.O.P the A.S.H.E.S, was born.

From writing this co-authored book "I Fly", I have become even more inspired on how much more my personal platform is needed.

Juliette Mullen

Resilience Coach, Clinical Hypnotherapist, Change Catalyst and Author

I grew up on a council estate in Scotland and was an anxious child who didn't find her voice. I decided early on that I wanted to do things differently from those around me and despite meeting my first husband at the age of 17 and getting married at 22, we had no children and divorced 7 years later.

By this time, I had successfully completed my Masters in Human Resources and was a professional in my field. As I was going through the separation, I suffered from anxiety which got out of control. In tens of thousands of pounds of debt, I took an overdose. After recovering, I continued to climb the career ladder and within two years of meeting my next partner, I was married and had my first child but my anxiety levels soared. It wasn't long before my second marriage ended and my father passed away. I was also made redundant from my job and I looked in all the wrong places for healing.

Undeterred, I became determined to re-write my story and help others do the same and studied to become a certified Life Coach and Clinical Hypnotherapist and set up my own Wellbeing business.

Although I have faced some tough life challenges, I am happier than I have ever been as the mum to two amazing girls and I know I had to go on this difficult journey in order to help others navigate theirs.

E: juliette@juliettemullen.co.uk
L: linkedin.com/in/juliette-mullen/
W: www.juliettemullen.co.uk/

Kenneth Nathan

Professional Trainer, Author and Keynote Speaker

After RAGE won the award, I saw the need to start my own organization and called it Interventions Plus. It's an organisation I've been running for 10 years now, which is committed to breaking the cycle of violence by offering courses, workshops, seminars and counselling to young people, parents and carers, and professionals.

Uncontrollable anger, violence and anti-social behaviour are huge problems in our communities. Signs of out of uncontrollable anger abound all over the place. There's road rage, domestic and family violence, violence in sport, youth crime, violent outbursts in the classroom, extremist ideologies, bullying and the list goes on.

Whether it's in the home or media, young people's minds are becoming increasingly desensitised to violence through TV shows, movies, music, peers, computer games, and even sports heroes who are supposed to be role models! The cycle is then handed down to the next generation and so forth. There is no doubt about it that we are living in an age of rage and this cycle needs to be broken right now.

I'm glad that I found my purpose and passion in life and started Interventions Plus. I will continue to do my part in stopping the violence in the world.

Mahatma Gandhi once said, "Be the change you want to see in the world." It all has to begin with me first.

E: Kenneth@interventionsplus.com.au
W: www.interventionsplus.com.au

Lisa Jane Boorer
Business and Personal Consultant

I have spent my whole life being a student of the Universe and sharing my experiences and insights with others. My focus as a Businessperson has been in strategy, business practices, compliance, and staff training, I prefer to have a hands-on approach to work.

Through my work and my children, I been involved with many people and inevitably I become their go to person their sounding board. I share openly and honestly from my personal experiences and the experiences of those who have guided me at different times of my life.

I have been able to identify how each of the betrayals in my life have turned into benefits for me and for my children. I have been able to do this by identifying the fear, hurt or trauma that is usually behind the persons actions.

As the mother of 3 amazing people, my 2 sons who are in their 30s and my baby girl who is just 18, I continue to marvel at the lessons they bring me and the opportunities to connect with varying age groups through them.

I am focusing the next part of my life on assisting others with personal growth through online courses and public speaking.

E: lisaboorer@icloud.com
L: linkedin.com/in/lisaboorer

Marsha Schults

Health Coach, Chief-Hope-Giver, Keynote Speaker, Researcher

My mission for anyone suffering from autoimmune symptoms, is for people to regain control of their health by questioning the medical model and believing that 'your body can heal itself', with the right nutritional support and emotional sobriety.

Having lived through the pain and chronic symptoms of several Autoimmune conditions for 7 years and then healing myself in a matter of months – with the guidance of some of the world's leading scientists, clinical nutritionists, microbiologists and counsellors, I have a powerful message that shows your health is in your hands.

Emotional trauma and physical stress are in fact the biggest contributors to the development of autoimmune symptoms. Sexual abuse, migrating to another country at the age of 10, being bullied at school, feeling abandoned as a child, being in foster care for 3 years, domestic violence, sexual abuse (again), bankruptcy, a cheating husband, divorce, a very sick daughter, no family support and severe financial stress led to my 'dis-ease'.

My healing journey not only eliminated my pain and suffering. I found strength and courage and confidence. I healed emotionally. I am strong. My purpose came from my pain. I now help others heal and rebuild their lives with the knowledge I have gained from 17 years of research into health, supplementation and being my own 'guinea pig'.

My mission is to educate you to understand HOW your condition came about and WHY you need the protocol I recommend, so that you can take control of your health and live pain free.

W: www.marshaschults.com
E: marsha@marshaschults.com
F: @naturalautoimmunerecovery
M: 0413 704 061
L: linkedin.com/in/marsha-schults-21590919a

Marta Madeira-Mulungo
Entrepreneur, Results Coach, Human Capital Consultant and Speaker

The first twenty years of my life were a true revelation of who I am as a person and what my strengths are. When I look back, I see that I emerged from extreme poverty to now what I feel is great success, and I am just getting started.

Inspire by my humble beginnings, I learned to believe in people, probably because I believed in myself. I knew that my mission would come to pass as it did, and it's still doing. I slowly developed a passion for inspiring to develop confidence in themselves and today this is my life passion. I help people whose doubts and fears keep them away from the life and the success they desire. When they work with me, I help them dissolve the doubts and fears holding them back and create quantum leaps in their career and business.

My life path and experience are a true proof that if you know what you want, you can get it. I have a unique talent to strengthen the confidence of people and help them step into their power. When I Coach or Mentor my clients around the world, I help them see the true potential within themselves and get to the root cause of their doubts and fears and lack of focus. My clients are typically professionals and business owners who aspire for more out of life.

I hold a Master's degree in Human Resources Management and Development from the University of Manchester, a Bachelor degree in Organizational Psychology. I am Certified a Results Coach through the Proctor Gallagher Institute, USA, a Humanistic Coach through MORE Institute, Germany and as an International Coach through International Coaching Community

W: www.mmcoachingeng.com
F: @mmcoachingeng

Mary Wong

International Speaker, Trainer, Coach and Mentor

I live in Brisbane, Australia and have been speaking internationally for 15 years.

We all have big stories, yet often don't realise the power of our story because we lived it, and it is so familiar to us. I have a belief that your lived journey holds the key to your life mission.

My mission is to help people into a space of collective magic that many don't realise is possible; help them connect and co-create; discover their inner brilliance; and find their voice to make a difference – working with people to bring out their inner superstar speaker really lights me up!

I know what is possible, because I have lived it, and because I have seen my clients live it too.

When I didn't speak out about my story, it overpowered me with pain and guilt. I made many poor choices based on my low opinion of myself.

Once I started to talk about what happened, the realisation that it wasn't my fault helped me to look at myself differently. I was able to identify the gifts that were held within. In doing so, I rediscovered myself and my voice and now my purpose and vision is to help others do the same.

Speaking out is not about being a victim. Speaking out is about being a victor – about taking back your power, whilst you share the wisdom you gained to help lift others to the victory podium.

Everyone deserves to fly.

Optimal Life Solutions

W: www.optimalcoaching.com.au

Peta Cashion

Wellbeing and Resilience Coach & Author

The greatest teacher of all has been my life experiences.

This has taken flight in my own healing journey.

Whilst making a conscious choice to grow through the pain of emotional, physical and sexual abuse, finding the privilege to re-evaluate my own self-worth has empowered me with the courage and vulnerability to share my story.

I started to accept I do deserve a full, abundant, joyful life, full of fun, happiness, love and success, discovering my own truth and authenticity.

My greatest hope is for people to know that they are not alone. It is often through suffering that we grow and reach out to connect with others as well as ourselves.

I am passionate about inspiring and empowering others in healing their own inner child to reveal their greatest strengths, higher self-esteem and confidence already within them.

May living in the present empower us to break through the darkness of shame and into the light of forgiveness.

E: PetaCashion@yahoo.com

Roslyn Donaldson

Empowerment and Wellness Coach &Author

My story is about surviving and thriving from Domestic Violence.

My father would beat us down, but I always got up and never gave up, believing there must be a better life for me one day.

I did survive and thrive to become a successful corporate businesswoman and Coach.

I own an investment property, which is a refuge house for Women and children sheltering from Domestic Violence, called "Carrie's Place".

I am an ambassador for "White Ribbon", an organisation helping to end violence against women and girls, and an advocate for the Red Heart campaign.

I have been happily married for 35 years to a kind and loving man who can't understand why men do this to the women and families they love.

We have two grown up children, Karla and Blake.

As an Empowerment and Wellness Coach, I am passionate about helping women build their resilience and their courage to know their own uniqueness is enough.

We are enough.

We can achieve our dreams.

E: roslyn239.donaldson@yahoo.com.au

Dr. Sherine Ajai Price
Holistic Life Coach, Photographer, Traveller, Lover of Life

Please join me on the Peace Path of Empowerment and the Celebration of life in spite of its challenges, Uniting the world to live in peace, love and joy.

I specialize in empowering those who are grieving and surviving extreme losses including estrangement from and/or the death of loved ones, abuse, neglect, and bullying.

My career began as a wife, mother, and homemaker. Later I was a social worker and child abuse treatment and prevention therapist, a real estate agent, and owner/operator of our inspection company.

I currently support others by utilizing a potent combination of empowering practices including coaching, ceremony, Reiki, kundalini yoga and meditations, breath work, essential oils, crystals, journaling, divination tools, and more.

When I'm not writing, researching, and conducting workshops, I'm spending time with my beloveds, traveling, hiking, taking photographs, and celebrating life in spite of the challenging experiences I've survived.

Ph.D. Holistic Life Coach/Metaphysics, Family/Child Studies, Guidance/Counseling
Reiki Master, Kundalini Yoga Teacher
doTerra Wellness Advocate
JVP Certified Spiritual Healer
Infinite Possibilities Certified Trainer

E: sherine@peacepathproject.com
F: @peacepathproject
I: @peacepathproject
W: www.PeacePathProject.com

Taryn Claire Le Nu
Spiritual Mentor and Practitioner of Hypnotherapy

As a Breast Cancer Thriver and Survivor I advocate, support, empower and educate those traversing the tricky terrain of Cancerland.

I used blogging during my cancer journey as a form of therapy to help me process and transition, which culminated in me writing my first book To Cancer with Love. This book has helped me reach many more women who have been tainted by the Breast Cancer Brush.

Alongside this support to those women, my mission in life is to take people on a journey from spiritual newbies to spiritual know-it-all's. I am passionate about helping people stand in their own power and unlock their true potential. It is incredibly rewarding to be part of this transformative process.

I am an Author and Speaker, a Breast Cancer Survivor and Thriver, I live life with Lymphoedema, I am a Gratitude Junkie, a Rawfood Chef, an Urban Farmer, Beekeeper, Hypnotherapist and Spiritual Mentor.

Starting life doing a Bachelor of Business I gradually expanded into other deliciously diverse areas of interest like Raw Food Chef qualifications, Reiki Master, Extended Disc Profiling, Forensic Healing, Hypnotherapy, Timeline Therapy and Neurolinguistic Programming.

JOIN my groups on Facebook: Women Raising Vibration and Le Nu Tribe ... I'd love to connect with you there!

E: connect@tarynclairelenu.com
W: www.tarynclairelenu.com; www.diaryofadoctorswife.com
F: @lenuhealing
I: @taryncairelenu

WRITE YOUR OWN BOOK

Have you thought about writing a book?

Do you want to raise your profile, get professional speaking engagements, or charge more for your coaching or consulting?

But you're overwhelmed with where to start…?

Maybe you're worried that you're not a good enough writer or concerned what others will think?

You can write a beautiful book, with the right guidance.

Our aim with book coaching is to provide you with all the guidance and support you need to:

- Get clarity on the exact book idea which will position you as an authority and raise your profile so you can attract high calibre clients and/or opportunities.

- Have a clear map of which steps to take each week through the entire writing and publishing process so you never get overwhelmed wondering what to do next.

- Keep accountable to your writing goals so you can set a launch date and stick to it without feeling like this book is taking over your whole life.

- Get feedback to improve your writing each week so you don't have to worry if your book is any good and just know that you're delivering a high quality product.

- Create a strategy for promoting your book so you can be seen in all the right places by the right people, and ultimately, earn more money.

- Have my team take care of editing, formatting and publishing so that you can just focus on writing your book and doing what you do best!

Please visit www.changeempire.com and schedule a free initial chat about your book idea.

I can't wait to hear from you.

Cathryn Mora

Founder, Head Coach and Publishing Director
Change Empire Books

I: @change.empire.book.coaching
L: linkedin.com/in/cathryn-mora/
E: hello@changeempire.com

Made in the USA
Coppell, TX
03 May 2020

22798636R00157